The End of the Church?

Conversations with the Work of David Jasper

— EDITED BY —

BRIDGET NICHOLS

NICHOLAS TAYLOR

Sacristy
Press

Sacristy Press
PO Box 612, Durham, DH1 9HT

www.sacristy.co.uk

First published in 2022 by Sacristy Press, Durham

Sacristy Limited, registered in England & Wales, number 7565667

British Library Cataloguing-in-Publication Data
A catalogue record for the book is available from the British Library

ISBN 978-1-78959-252-8

Contents

List of Illustrations

Figure 1: Edouard Manet, *Olympia*, 1863 (public domain)

Figure 2: El Greco, *The Burial of the Count of Orgaz*, 1586 (public domain)

Figure 3: Robert Motherwell (1915–1991). *Elegy to the Spanish Republic XXXIV*, 1953–1954. Oil on canvas, 80 × 100 inches (203.2 × 254 cm). Collection Albright-Knox Art Gallery, Buffalo, New York; Gift of Seymour H. Knox, Jr., 1957 (K1957:6). © Dedalus Foundation, Inc. / Licensed by VAGA at Artists Rights Society (ARS), NY. Photo: Tom Loonan and Brenda Bieger for Albright-Knox Art Gallery. © *The Robert Motherwell Estate, Dedalus Foundation, Inc. ARS NY/IVARO Dublin, 2022*

Figure 4: Anselm Kiefer *La Résurrection* (photograph by Jean-Philippe Simard, 2019). Reproduced by kind permission of Fr Marc Chaveau of the Dominican Priory of Sainte Marie de La Tourette, Éveux, France.

Acknowledgements

Our thanks are due, first, to the fourteen authors who so generously accepted the invitation to write for this collection. Alison Jasper has advised strategically and tactfully from the moment the idea of a set of essays was born and has been a valuable consultant as the project has progressed.

Fr Marc Chaveau of the Dominican Priory of Sainte Marie de La Tourette in Éveux generously gave permission for the use of an image of Anselm Kiefer's *Résurrection*, exhibited at La Tourette as part of a larger exhibition of Kiefer's work between 24 September and 22 December 2019. We thank him and the photographer, Jean-Philippe Simard, for their support of this project.

We also acknowledge the help and interest of the Albright-Knox Gallery, Buffalo, New York, who have granted permission for use of their digital image of Robert Motherwell's *Elegy to the Spanish Republic XXXIV 1953–1954*.

The excellent and knowledgeable professional support of Natalie Watson, our editor at Sacristy Press and one-time fellow student in Durham, as well as her personal encouragement, have made the production of this collection a great pleasure. Jon Idle's meticulous copy-editing has ensured a level of presentation that honours the quality of the essays. A generous grant from the Drummond Trust has made their publication possible.

Finally, we thank David, who has been mentor, inspiration, colleague, fellow researcher, priest and friend to all who have been part of this venture.

Foreword

This fine collection provides a fitting tribute to the extraordinary achievements of David Jasper. In surveying the various contributions gathered here, one is immediately struck by David's range and energy. An internationally acknowledged expert on religion and literature, he has become a leading figure in an area of growing significance. Much of the impetus in the field today derives from his own writings, his academic leadership in Glasgow, his founding of *Literature and Theology*, and the many graduates whom he has mentored. Providing institutional leadership in the academy, he has maintained momentum in his own scholarly work while diligently attending to the needs of his students and engaging collaboratively with colleagues across the world. This has demanded industry, skill and generosity over many years, qualities that David has displayed in abundance.

What is also apparent, particularly in the productive years that have followed his retirement from full-time teaching, is David's commitment to the Church. In the imaginative leadership of the Doctrine Commission of the Scottish Episcopal Church and through his dedication to pastoral care and the leading of worship in more local contexts, he has been assiduous in his calling as a priest. Though critical of the institution and often displaying a radical theological scepticism, David has remained within the household of faith. His blending of intellectual interrogation and spiritual intensity is attested not only in his writings but by example. With its enthusiasm for new beginnings and fresh possibilities, his work has a hopeful dimension. Though labels are always hazardous and of limited use, I would judge David to represent a Christian humanism that is much needed today. In this, he points us towards the end of the Church.

The admiration and affection that David commands is evident in this rich set of essays from colleagues, friends, and former students. A particular debt of gratitude is owed the editors for their patience and skill in assembling the collection.

David Fergusson
University of Cambridge

Preface

When conversations towards honouring David Jasper's enormous and formative contribution to the interdisciplinary study of literature, theology and the arts began, it was with one firm resolution: whatever shape the eventual volume might take, it was not a festschrift. The editors could not imagine David in the passive role of recipient, or object of commemoration. His work has been characterized by lively engagement, conversation and the testing of boundaries, and it has not stopped in any way which could be definitively summed up in a series of thematically or chronologically ordered essays. Our ambition has been to capture some of that energy, not in tributes, but in contributions that pay David's work the compliment of continuing development and exploration.

"The End of the Church?" was the question we suggested to contributors at the outset—a title provoked by the ambiguity and creative tension that have characterized David's own relationship with the Church he has served as priest and theologian. That tension has been made more complex by virtue of a career that has found him within the structures of two distinct expressions of the Anglican world: the established Church of England into which he was born and in which he was ordained, and the accidentally but resolutely disestablished Scottish Episcopal Church, which has been his home for nearly half his life.

Not all critical friends of the Church work out this relationship within its structures. Perhaps unusually for a priest holding a succession of academic positions, David has chosen to be actively committed to the liturgical and pastoral life of the congregations to which he belongs. He continues to preside at the Eucharist and to preach regularly and is conscientious in visiting the sick and ministering to the dying, whatever the inconvenience. It is as a pastorally minded priest that he has served on Church committees responsible for matters of liturgy and doctrine and continues to reflect theologically on liturgy as the work of the Church.

He has frequently expressed despair at the institutional myopia of the Church and its leaders, on both sides of the border (Elisabeth Jay's assessment of the Church of England's response to the Covid-19 pandemic is instructive in this light), but he has also shown a loving determination, despite or because of this, to exercise the prophetic voice of the theologian in the hope that it might still express something of the beauty, truth and mystery of God, and contribute to the transformation of an increasingly unjust society into something approaching the love and justice of God.

This is reflected in his own writings over several decades, and it comes as no surprise that truth, and the Church's public responsibility to speak the truth, have continued to be prominent motifs. One example of this was his conceiving and editing, while Convenor of the Doctrine Committee of the Scottish Episcopal Church, of *Truth and the Church in a Secular Age*, as responsible people of all persuasions responded with horror to the outcome of the 2016 presidential election in the United States, but also as the Church resorted increasingly to gimmicks born of the advertising industry, and to a managerialism inseparable from the capitalist will to dominate and exploit people and the resources of the earth for profit, precisely the forces which precipitated and have continued to aggravate the environmental and climate crisis we now face.

The quest for language with truth-bearing capacity begins much earlier in David's career as both priest and scholar. It is worth recalling that the foundation of the journal, *Literature and Theology*, was in large part a response to the question of truthful speaking after the Holocaust, an issue to which he was powerfully exposed through a long-term family friendship with Ulrich Simon, whose thirty-five years at King's College, London, saw him move from University Lecturer to Dean. A convert from Judaism, Simon was ordained in the Church of England in 1939. He had lost a brother in the Moscow Trials in 1937, and his father would die in Auschwitz in 1944. He was part of the first Literature and Theology Conference organized by David in Durham in 1982, a gathering that confronted theology's failure to address the atrocities of the twentieth century, yet refused to abandon language itself, even language that had been put to evil and tyrannical purposes.

Much later, David would reflect that "it was in the dark abysses of such language that we sought recovery—in the capacity of language itself to find new birth and possibilities in the spaces of literature.... If theology was immobilized and forgiveness—atonement—impossible, words still called to us to be spoken and written".[1] Heather Walton writes of the demanding nature of the journal, which in her case was life-changing: "The atrocities of the age were named there and their implications for faith acknowledged." In literature, and also in film, theatre and the visual arts, David has found imaginative approaches to the great theological themes of sacrifice, salvation, sin, atonement, redemption and glory. Showing how they could be pursued without being made mere proxies has been one of many contributions to what is now a well-established field, which, thanks to his gift for intercultural friendship, thrives not only in England, Scotland and the United States, but also in Scandinavia, Eastern Europe and China.

Several of the voices in this collection found an intellectual direction and commitment by discovering *Literature and Theology* and through participation in the Centre for Literature and Theology in Durham. With Heather Walton, Margaret Masson records her choice of Durham as an academic home precisely because of the work that David was developing. Lori Kanitz and Tibor Fabiny experienced its vibrancy as research student and visiting fellow respectively. Ann Loades actively supported the Centre and the journal and accompanied David through the Durham doctoral work on Coleridge that would become his first book.[2] Hannah Altorf, Michael Fuller, Trevor Hart, Alison Jack, Vassiliki Kolocotroni, Ann Loades, Donald Orr and Heather Walton have shared the enterprise in Scotland. Elisabeth Jay, a lifelong friend, co-edited *The Oxford Handbook of English Literature and Theology* (2009) with David and another former doctoral student, Andrew Hass.

---

[1]   David Jasper, "Retrieving a Theological Sense of Being Human", *Literature & Theology* 29/2 (2015), pp. 125–37, here at p. 129.

[2]   David Jasper, *Coleridge as Poet and Religious Thinker: Inspiration and Revelation* (London: Macmillan, 1985; Allison Park, PA: Pickwick Publications, 1985).

Two contributors have arrived by other routes. John Davies has
served with David at an exciting time in the life of the Scottish Episcopal
Church's Liturgical Committee, as it considers the revision of the
Church's 1982 liturgy and looks to its current and future needs. Jeremy
Smith has become a partner in writing and research. The innovative and
multilayered study of the late medieval guide for worshippers, *The Lay
Folks' Mass Book*, in which he and David have collaborated, was nearing
completion as this introduction was being written.

That is to describe only some of the intersecting communities
represented in this collection. All of the contributors belong to the
community of friends which has gathered around David in the course
of a long career, and the editors are delighted to count themselves in this
number. Bridget Nichols was one of David's Durham doctoral students,
who found a direction in the study of Anglican liturgy under his guidance
and continues to benefit from his writing, conversation, intellectual
energy and support in research. Nicholas Taylor was a doctoral student
in New Testament Studies in Durham in the years immediately before
David's move to Glasgow. Somewhat later, he found himself a fellow priest
in the Scottish Episcopal Church, a colleague on various Church bodies
responsible for doctrine and liturgy, and geographically a near neighbour.
What they share, theologically, pastorally and spiritually, is beautifully
illustrated in a jointly authored piece in the special issue of the *Scottish
Episcopal Institute Journal* reflecting on the pandemic. Here, they guide
readers through proclaiming the gospel in Holy Week under lockdown
in a mode which is part assistance for preachers, part meditation and
part theological poetics.[3]

The order we have imposed on the fourteen essays is not arbitrary, but
neither is it static or final. They have found their own places in the thematic
areas of The Church and the Arts, Literature and Theology, Institutions
(Church, Academy and Society), David Jasper in Scotland (Theology,
Imagination and the Arts), Theology, Writing and Memory. Our efforts at
a tidy arrangement continue to be subverted by the conversations which

---

[3]   David Jasper and Nicholas Taylor, "Proclaiming the Gospel of Holy Week
and Easter Under Lockdown", *Scottish Episcopal Institute Journal* 4/2 (2020),
pp. 99–111.

individual contributions have begun with one another, and if that is at times frustrating, it is always a source of joy. These are conversations that David himself would find invigorating, and in many ways, the first three essays propose their subject matter. Michael Fuller's account of the commissioning of a new musical composition for St Matthew's, Northampton, both captures the relationship that grew between the Rector, Walter Hussey (later Dean of Chichester), and Benjamin Britten, and sheds light on the boundaries between theology, the Church and the arts. Donald Orr turns to the visual arts as he confronts the responsibility of the arts to address the darkness and brutality of life and history. He takes us on a paradoxical journey "beyond black", which discovers light by venturing into darkness. Heather Walton explores the space that opens for art and literature to speak when theology is silent. She brings the work of Anselm Kiefer alongside David's own preoccupations, showing how, in the bleakest times, art might yet claw redemption out of ruins.

Three close and luminous readings of literary works suggest new perspectives on subjects often treated theologically. Readers will encounter steadfast faith maintained at personal cost in Tibor Fabiny's study of Abdiel, one of Milton's less noticed angels. Vassiliki Kolocotroni finds sacrament and transformation emerging as themes from Muriel Spark's reflection on Proust and extends this into acute readings of Spark's novels that invite us back to the texts themselves. Alison Jack sets David beside Seamus Heaney as she considers the kind of vocation that may embody two or more callings at once—priest and theologian in one case, poet and teacher, but in a way also priest, in the other.

David's creatively critical relationship with institutions has been mentioned more than once. Three essays suggest that they too may be read under the rubrics of beauty, transformation and steadfastness. Elisabeth Jay addresses the Church of England (especially as it has been judged during the Covid-19 pandemic) and distinguishes prophetically between its structural shortcomings and failures, and its resilience as a place which might, in Philip Larkin's words, still be "proper to grow wise in". Margaret Masson offers an almost meditative review of the life of St Chad's College, Durham, where David was principal from 1989 to 1991 and where she now occupies that role. While no longer explicitly invoking its Anglican foundation, St Chad's is still finding a vocation which she sees as closely bound up in greater attention to beauty in its many expressions. Lori Kanitz writes of the choices of Protestant communities in the polarized political landscape of the United States in the light of her own Durham research project. She is honest but not despairing, finding hope in her own continuing reflection on Salman Rushdie's *The Satanic Verses* for cultural "translation" of human beings as a transformation.

Institutions are also importantly located in places. Ann Loades evokes this in a piece which in many ways gives the volume a centre and among other things, provides a biographical portrait. To be strictly accurate, it is a triptych, which sets David Jasper beside two other priest-scholars who have had substantial careers in England and in Scotland—David Brown and George Pattison. It is also a magisterial overview of theology's encounters with the visual arts, literature and European philosophy, and with its rich bibliographical additions it represents an essential source of reference. A fourth priest-theologian speaks in his own right alongside this essay. Trevor Hart played a significant role in the Institute for Theology, Imagination and the Arts at St Andrews before returning to parish ministry. He honours David's long-term engagement with nineteenth-century theology in his study of transcendence and immanence, the simultaneous distance and proximity of creature and creator, and the relationship between the divine and human imaginations. His own attentiveness to context, place and creativity in theology and literature in the career of the Scottish poet, theologian and Congregational minister, George MacDonald, is a subtle and powerful tribute to David.

The three final essays explore writing, memory and liturgy. They return us to the quest for truth-bearing language and communication, for missing and suppressed voices, and for a proper relationship with memory. Hannah Altorf provides a sermon delivered by one of the daughters of Moses, recounting his ascent and descent of the mountain. She invokes David's own experience of living alone in desert conditions in her description of disorientation and uncertainty about the passage of time and the order of events.[4] Allowing such uncertainty is an audacious

---

[4]   David Jasper, *The Sacred Desert: Religion, Literature, Art, and Culture* (Oxford: Blackwell, 2004).

challenge to the notion of canon itself as a body of writing which records events in a way that is taken to be authoritative, yet which can only sustain this claim by suppressing other voices. Jeremy Smith describes two further intriguing instances of writing in the history of English language and literature—the runic quotation from the great Anglo-Saxon poem, *The Dream of the Rood*, inscribed on the monumental eighth-century Ruthwell Cross in Dumfriesshire, and a sixteenth-century printer's scrupulous edition of an Anglo-Saxon text, rendered anachronistic by being too technically accurate. Writing systems, he shows, require decoding, but decoding itself does not entitle later audiences to an understanding of the societies that produced them. Such reserve in reading, even in approaching the materiality of the "text", is something David would affirm.

The last word, at least provisionally, belongs to John Davies. We have placed his essay here not only for its profound insights on memory, its dangers, and its indispensable necessity, but also because it moves into territory which David has been reluctant to occupy—the liturgy of the Church. Despite his protestations that he is not a liturgist, David has for much of his life inhabited a world in which the forms of service of the Churches of the Anglican communion and particularly the Church of England have been examined and revised. This is not simply because these things could not be avoided by practising Anglicans in the later twentieth century. His father was a distinguished liturgical scholar, for many years Chair of the Church of England's Liturgical Commission, and the figure most associated with the publication of the *Alternative Service Book* in 1980. Liturgical revisers seldom receive compliments and the ASB still awaits proper appreciation of what it did achieve. For David, that has perhaps produced its own tensions—admiration of the enterprise that sought a liturgical style for its own times using the best scholarship then available, together with a conviction that the language of the Prayer Book of 1549 had an integrity and a directness that has not been surpassed in any contemporary idiom.[5]

---

5   See David Jasper, *The Language of the Liturgy: A Ritual Poetics* (London: SCM Press, 2018).

Davies explores memory and the dangerous consequences of awakening it through a reading of the almost fabular plot of Kazuo Ishiguro's novel, *The Buried Giant*. This leads to a wider meditation on communities of memory, in which churches have become more prominent as they have confronted their own pasts. How proper remembering can become the beginning of healing and reconciliation, and how such renewal might seek its ultimate destination in the already given promise of the eucharist are questions which confirm in the very best sense "the end of the church".

A list of David's formidable body of published writing is to be found at the end of this collection. It has been a source of fascination to see how different contributors have found their way to works in this library that have spoken distinctively to them. If he were asked which of his books most accurately represented the matters he has most cared about, and the scholarly encounters that have been most life-giving, he might name the trilogy, *The Sacred Desert*, *The Sacred Body*, and *The Sacred Community*.[6] If these books have occasionally puzzled and frustrated critics, that is because they themselves cross boundaries which still exist in the study of literature and theology. The personal is allowed into the academic task; the body is admitted as part of what some might prefer to be an investigation of spirituality; and finally, the community gathered with saints and angels round the eucharistic table becomes part of the theological treatment of art and literature. We have been extraordinarily fortunate to work with fourteen members of this community and enriched by the arrival of each new manuscript. There are inevitably missing voices and though it is dangerous to single out individuals, we mention three. Merete Thomassen was prevented by illness from offering an essay. Premature death robbed us of Pamela Sue Anderson and Dorota Filipczak. *Requiescant in pace.*

Bridget Nichols and Nicholas Taylor

---

6   David Jasper, *Sacred Desert*; *The Sacred Body: Asceticism in Religion, Literature, Art, and Culture* (Waco, TX: Baylor University Press, 2009); *The Sacred Community: Art, Sacrament, and the People of God* (Waco, TX: Baylor University Press, 2012).

Contributors

Hannah Marije Altorf was, until autumn 2020, Reader in Philosophy at St Mary's University, Strawberry Hill. She has written on the philosophical and literary works of Iris Murdoch and on different forms of philosophical dialogue. She is the author of *Iris Murdoch and the Art of Imagining* (Continuum, 2008) and together with Mariëtte Willemsen she translated Iris Murdoch's *The Sovereignty of Good* into Dutch (Boom, 2003). Currently, she is a student rabbi at Leo Baeck College and writing a book on public philosophy, tentatively called *Thinking in Public*.

John Reuben Davies is Research Fellow in the School of Humanities, University of Glasgow, where he is Associate Director of Arts Lab. His scholarly output has ranged from the history of the early medieval Britons to contemporary issues in liturgy. He has been a member of the Liturgy Committee of the Scottish Episcopal Church since 2009 (as Convenor 2015 to 2020) and is also actively involved in the work of the International Anglican Liturgical Consultation.

Tibor Fabiny is Professor of Literature and Hermeneutics and former Head of the Institute for English and American Studies and currently the director of the Center for Hermeneutical Research and the Jonathan Edwards Center-Hungary at the Károli Gáspár University of the Reformed Church in Hungary. His publications include *The Lion and the Lamb: Figuralism and Fulfilment in the Bible, Art and Literature* (Macmillan, 1992; enlarged edition: *Figura and Fulfillment in the Bible, Art and Literature* (Wipf and Stock, 2016)) and numerous articles in English and Hungarian related to Shakespeare and iconography and literature, hermeneutics and theology. His most recent book in Hungarian is *Isten maszkjai: Luther olvasása közben* (The Masks of God: On Reading Luther), published by L'Harmattan in 2021. He was the recipient of HUSSE's László Országh Award in 2014 and the Hungarian Government's Károli Gáspár Award in 2018.

Michael Fuller is Senior Teaching Fellow at New College, University of Edinburgh, where he lectures in the field of science and religion. He has published widely in this field, and has also written on themes in theology and literature, and theology and music. He is Vice-President for Publications of the European Society for the Study of Science and Theology, a Fellow of the International Society for Science and Religion, and a past Chair of the Science and Religion Forum. He sits on the Doctrine Committee of the Scottish Episcopal Church, and is an Honorary Canon of St Mary's Cathedral, Edinburgh.

Trevor Hart was formerly Professor of Divinity and Director of the Institute for Theology, Imagination and the Arts in the University of St Andrews. He is currently Rector of St Andrew's Episcopal Church in St Andrews and Canon Theologian of St Ninian's Cathedral, Perth. Among his recent publications are *In Him Was Life: The Person and Work of Christ* (Baylor, 2019), *Faith Thinking: The Dynamics of Christian Theology* (Wipf and Stock, 2020) and *Confessing and Believing: The Apostles' Creed as Script for the Christian Life* (Fortress, 2022).

Alison Jack is Professor of Bible and Literature at the School of Divinity, University of Edinburgh. She is Principal of New College and a minister of the Church of Scotland. Her research interests lie in the interaction between biblical narratives and literature from the Victorian to the current era. Her recent publications include *The Prodigal Son in English and American Literature: Five Hundred Years of Literary Homecomings* (Oxford University Press, 2019). She is currently working on biblical imagery in twentieth-century Scottish and Irish poetry.

Elisabeth Jay is Professor Emerita of English at Oxford Brookes University where she was Director of the Institute for Historical and Cultural Research. Her research interests lie predominantly in the nineteenth and early twentieth centuries, and she has published widely on the fiction, prose and poetry of this period. Her other major interest lies in the interdisciplinary area of literature and theology where she has frequently collaborated with David Jasper: they were co-editors, along with Andrew Hass, of *The Oxford Handbook of English Literature and Theology* (2009).

Lori A. Kanitz earned a BA in English with Highest Honours from the University of Oklahoma; an MA in literature and theology from Durham University, in Durham, England; and a PhD in literature and theology from the University of St Andrews, St Andrews, Scotland. She currently serves at Baylor University as the Project Director, Federal Grants with the Baylor Collaborative on Hunger and Poverty. Prior to her current role, she served for four years as the Assistant Director of Baylor's Institute for Faith and Learning.

Dr Kanitz came to Baylor in 2016 from Oral Roberts University in Tulsa, Oklahoma, where she served as Associate Professor of English and chair of the English and Modern Languages Department. There she also held administrative roles overseeing the development and evaluation of university-wide projects, including Writing Across the Curriculum and General Education. She earned multiple teaching and service awards, including Outstanding Faculty Member of the College of Arts and Cultural Studies (2014) and Outstanding Service Award for the College of Arts and Cultural Studies (2016).

Her research interests centre on the intersections between theology, literature and culture, including biblical perspectives on metaphorical language, ecology and social innovation with regard to hunger and poverty. Her work has been published in *Christian Higher Education*, *The Encyclopedia of Christian Literature* and *Last Things: Essays on Ends and Endings* (Peter Lang, 2015). Dr Kanitz is also the author of *A Literary Shema: Annie Dillard's Judeo-Christian Vision and Voice* (Pickwick/Wipf and Stock, 2020).

Vassiliki Kolocotroni is Senior Lecturer in English Literature at the University of Glasgow. She works in the areas of international modernism and the avant-garde, theory, classical reception, travel and film. She is the co-editor of *Modernism: An Anthology of Sources and Documents*; *The Edinburgh Dictionary of Modernism*; *In the Country of the Moon: British*

Women Travelers to Greece, 1718–1932; *Women Writing Greece: Essays on Hellenism, Orientalism and Travel*, two books on the Surrealist theorist and poet Nicolas Calas, and many journal essays and book chapters on modernist writing and literary and cultural theory. In 2018, Vassiliki also co-edited a Special Issue of *Textual Practice*, titled *The Prime of Muriel Spark: A Centenary Retrospect*. Among her current projects are a study of modernist Hellenism and a collection of essays on *Hotel Modernisms*.

Ann Loades CBE is Professor Emerita of Divinity University of Durham and Honorary Professor in the School of Divinity, University of St Andrews. She is currently preparing a book of essays—including some previously unpublished (selected and edited by Stephen Burns). Her most recent publication is *Grace is not Faceless: Reflections on Mary*, edited by Stephen Burns, and published in 2021 by Darton, Longman and Todd.

Margaret Masson is the Principal of St Chad's College in Durham. A Scot born and brought up in Zambia who lectured in English in the USA for a number of years, her teaching and research has focused on D. H. Lawrence, Postcolonial Literature, and Literature and Theology.

Bridget Nichols lectures in liturgy and Anglicanism at the Church of Ireland Theological Institute in Dublin. She is the author of *Liturgical Hermeneutics* (Peter Lang GmbH, 1996), editor of *The Collect of the Churches of the Reformation* (SCM Press, 2010) and co-editor of *Lively Oracles of God: Perspectives on the Bible and Liturgy* (Liturgical Press, 2022).

Donald Orr is a retired priest in the Scottish Episcopal Church and academic who specializes in Fine Art and Theology. He has lectured on the subject and contributed to various texts dealing with the analysis and relationship of image to text in religion.

His interest in mountaineering sees his articles on mountains and paintings as regular contributions to the Scottish Mountaineering Club Journal and the Alpine Club Journal.

Jeremy J. Smith is Professor of English Philology in the University of Glasgow, and a Fellow of the Royal Society of Edinburgh. He has written on a wide range of philological topics, from the history of sound-change in English to the language of Robert Burns. His most recent monograph is *Transforming Early English: the reinvention of Early English and Older Scots* (Cambridge University Press, 2020), which shows how historical pragmatics offers a powerful explanatory framework for the changes texts undergo as they are transmitted over time and space. With David Jasper, he is currently engaged on a project on the afterlives of the Middle English *Lay Folks' Mass Book.*

Nicholas Taylor is Rector of St Aidan's, Clarkston, an Honorary Fellow of New College, Edinburgh, and Convenor of the Liturgy Committee of the Scottish Episcopal Church; recent publications include *Paul on Baptism* (SCM Press, 2016), *Lay Presidency at the Eucharist?* (Continuum, 2009), and several articles on liturgical renewal in the *Scottish Episcopal Institute Journal.*

Heather Walton is Professor of Theology and Creative Practice (Theology and Religious Studies) in the School of Critical Studies of the University of Glasgow and Director of the Centre for Literature, Theology and the Arts. Her research interests include Practical Theology, Methodologies for Research and Reflective Practice, Theopoetics, Life Writing and Spirituality, and Gender and Sexuality, reflected in a wide range of publications. Her recent books include *Writing Methods in Theological Reflection* (SCM Press, 2014), *Not Eden: Spiritual Life Writing for This World* (SCM Press, 2015), and a co-edited volume, *Christian Pilgrimage, Landscape, and Heritage: Journeying to the Sacred* (Routledge, 2014).

1

Boundaries and Creativity: The Church and Art

Michael Fuller

Introduction

From its earliest days, the Christian Church has been a sponsor of art. Church buildings themselves, and the decoration and furnishings they contain, have offered opportunities for Christians to reflect on their faith and to be drawn deeper into it, both through liturgical participation and through private devotion. David Jasper's ministry has been rich and multi-faceted, and an important part of it has been devoted to an exploration of the role which the arts can play in enriching the resources available to the Church, both in terms of deepening the theological reflections of those within it and in terms of speaking the Christian message afresh to those outside it. His engagement with the journal *Literature and Theology* from its foundation, and with the Arts Chaplaincy project in Durham (which brought the name of video artist Bill Viola to the attention of many in the UK, leading ultimately to the permanent installations of his work which may now be seen in London's St Paul's Cathedral) may serve as instances of this Janus-faced aspect of the arts—looking both inwards, to the Church, and outwards, to the world around it—which Jasper's work exemplifies.

This observation serves also to alert us to the fact that any institution, including the Church, necessarily creates an "in group" and an "out group". On the one hand, some people identify themselves as "members" of a Church: in ministering to them, the Church seeks to offer means of deepening their faith and responding directly to any pastoral needs which this "in group" may have. On the other, the majority of people in the UK today would not identify themselves in this way, and therefore *ipso facto* constitute an "out group"; yet the Church seeks also to minister to them, perhaps through planting, nurturing or awakening the seeds of faith within them, perhaps through offering assistance to meet their physical needs (for example, through the provision of facilities for homeless people, or through food banks), perhaps simply by offering a space for contemplation. The idea of an "in group" and an "out group" *ipso facto* creates also the idea of a boundary between the two.

Boundaries

From many perspectives, the idea of a boundary is a fascinating one. A liminal position involving regimes of any sort encourages reflection on both, which needs not necessarily entail a merging of the two, but rather places them in a mutually questioning and stimulating relationship. Within the natural sciences, some systems are referred to as "chaotic": although they may be described by deterministic equations, their unfolding through time may happen in a rich variety of ways depending on the initial conditions of the system. (The celebrated "butterfly effect" is an expression of the way in which weather systems are subject to alteration by minute perturbations.) It has been noted that it is at the boundary between ordered and chaotic systems that a spontaneous self-ordering of molecular species can occur—what one commentator has referred to as "order for free".[1] Now, the terms "order" and "chaos" are being used here in a very specific kind of way; but the idea of systems which are unpredictable—which may produce unexpected results, in a non-reproducible way—and the idea that it is the boundary between regimes that can be a locus for the production of something fresh and spontaneous, are both highly suggestive.

In a Christian perspective, theology has historically been an enterprise carried out within the Church: it involves ratiocination about God and

---

[1]   Stuart Kauffmann, *At Home in the Universe: The Search for Laws of Complexity* (London: Penguin, 1996), pp. 71 ff.

is predicated on shared assumptions about God. Sometimes, theology may attempt to speak "across the boundary", to address those outside the Church—through apologetic writings for example. These inevitably tend to have embedded within them perspectives that reflect their origins. Similarly, writings addressed to the Church from outside its boundary—analyses or critiques of religious behaviour, for example—will tend to have embedded within them views which may or may not be recognizable to those within. But what about theology undertaken *at* the boundary, rather than on one or the other side of it? Might it be that it is at the boundary between the two, which itself will be imprecise, fluid and contested, where a dynamic and genuinely mutual engagement and enrichment can take place?

This in turn raises the question of the most suitable means through which such engagement can take place. I suggest that it is the arts, rather than straightforward verbal dialogue, which constitute the most appropriate media to employ in this liminal space. In the right conditions, such boundary-originating art might (by analogy with chaos and complexity theory) give rise to spontaneous, emergent expressions of the human spirit which are confined neither by ecclesiastical orthodoxy nor by secular presuppositions. (A corollary of this is that such art will originate at particular times and within particular contexts, which will shape its expression within a particular historical, cultural and geographical envelope, and these conditions are non-reproducible; but it is a property of great art from all ages to speak meaningfully to those who contemplate it outwith its original context.)

Church art need not come from such a boundary, of course. The engagement of artists, musicians and theologians in collaborative undertakings—such as those which took place under the auspices of the "Theology through the Arts" project based at the Universities of Cambridge and St Andrews—have produced some remarkable work, but the nature of such projects sets particular parameters around possible outcomes.[2] For example, when planning a new sculpture for Ely cathedral, "the starting-point was to search for an artist who . . . would

---

[2] Jeremy Begbie (ed.), *Sounding the Depths: Theology through the Arts* (London: SCM Press, 2002), pp. 3 ff.

enjoy the collaborative aspect of the commission . . . had an interest in Christian theology . . . would be excited by pioneering new models by which theology can be explored by visual art".[3] There was clearly an expectation that the artwork produced would be specifically informed by an "in group" outlook. Now theologically informed art may, of course, be both powerful in its expression and thought-provoking in its content; but might works of art originating at the boundary between the Church and broader society speak in a different kind of way? Might its use of unusual materials and theologically heterodox approaches generate fresh and valid insights for those within the Church—and might such materials and approaches lead to a capacity for its appreciation by those on both sides of the boundary?

With this preamble in place, the remainder of this essay considers one particular creative locus, which arose in a very specific context—the mid-twentieth-century Church of England. As we have noted, it would be foolish to attempt to see in it a template for artistic creation outwith that context; small perturbations in the initial conditions for the production of such work might have produced huge differences in the outcome at the time, and would certainly do so were any attempt to be made to reproduce that locus at any other geographical or temporal point. Nevertheless, it may be that it is possible to draw interesting conclusions from a consideration of it. The example is that of the Anglican clergyman Canon Walter Hussey. After setting his work in the context of his life, we will consider in more detail one specific work which he commissioned— Benjamin Britten's cantata, *Rejoice in the Lamb*.

Walter Hussey (and Benjamin Britten)

In his roles as Vicar of St Matthew's, Northampton, and subsequently as Dean of Chichester, Walter Hussey commissioned a wide range of major artists to produce work for the Church. The results include a statue of the Madonna and Child by Henry Moore; a Crucifixion by Graham

---

[3]   Alistair McFadyen and John Inge, "Art in a Cathedral", in Begbie, *Sounding the Depths*, pp. 119–58.

Sutherland; the festival cantata *Rejoice in the Lamb* by Benjamin Britten for St Matthew's; tapestries by John Piper; an altarpiece by Sutherland; a stained-glass window by Marc Chagall; and the *Chichester Psalms* by Leonard Bernstein for Chichester. Before considering the Britten cantata as a specific case study of a "boundary" engagement of Church and artist, let us briefly explore the background to this commission, which offers a fascinating perspective on how "boundary" art may, or may not, arise. As we shall see, certain generalizable aspects of such art are illustrated by it.

Hussey was by all accounts a quiet and reserved man. This is borne out by his autobiography, *Patron of Art*, in which the emphasis is very much on the Art rather than the Patron.[4] Hussey's book relates some of the conversations he had with the artists whom he commissioned, and it contains some fascinating excerpts from his correspondence with those artists. However, it is strikingly reticent when it comes to speaking of Hussey himself, offering the briefest of details concerning his life and few insights into his friendships with the artists he cultivated. Thus we learn little more of Hussey's relationship with John Piper, for example, than that "he was a friend of long standing and most approachable";[5] and his motivation is summed up, with a simplicity that approaches naivety, in the following passage:

> How sad it was, I felt, that the arts had become largely divorced from the Church: sad because artists think and meditate a lot and are in the broadest sense of the word religious. They create fine expressions of the human spirit which can symbolize and express worship, as well as conveying the truths of God to mankind in a vivid and memorable way.[6]

Peter Webster, a recent biographer of Hussey, has commented that "*Patron of Art* in many ways obscures as much as it reveals. In it, Hussey eschewed almost entirely the question of his motives for pursuing the task

---

[4]   Walter Hussey, *Patron of Art: The Revival of a Great Tradition Among Modern Artists* (London: Weidenfeld and Nicolson, 1985).

[5]   Hussey, *Patron of Art*, p. 121.

[6]   Hussey, *Patron of Art*, p. 3.

with such tenacity. Absent also . . . is any sustained theological reflection on the relationship of the arts and the church, or of truth and beauty".[7] Webster supplies many of the lacunae in Hussey's own account of his early life, noting his education at Marlborough and Keble College, Oxford, his training for ministry at Cuddesdon College, his ordination in 1932 and his curacies in London (where he developed his interests in art and music), before his appointment to St Matthew's, Northampton in 1937.[8] Here he succeeded his father, who had been vicar since the foundation of the parish (Hussey notes, almost apologetically, "Perhaps my succeeding him may suggest nepotism, but I don't think it was. I was not anxious to go there . . . I was from a very early age attracted to London. But my various authorities advised me that it was right that I should go").[9] After eighteen years in Northampton, Hussey was appointed Dean of Chichester in 1955, remaining there until his retirement in 1977. *Patron of Art* was published just months before Hussey's death, in July 1985.

In contrast to Hussey, Britten's life is well documented through the publication of his letters, and through numerous biographical studies which began to appear during his lifetime.[10] His work encompasses a wide range of musical forms: he is renowned in particular for his operatic output, but he also wrote many songs, choral works, symphonic works and chamber pieces. A significant amount of his work was intended for Church performance: in addition to liturgical settings, he composed a number of dramatic works for ecclesiastical locations (for example, *Noye's Fludde* (1957) and the three Church Parables (1964–8)). Theological

---

[7]   Peter Webster, *Church and Patronage in 20th Century Britain: Walter Hussey and the Arts* (London: Palgrave Macmillan, 2017), p. 6.

[8]   Webster, *Church and Patronage*, pp. 17–24.

[9]   Hussey, *Patron of Art*, p. 4.

[10]   See, for example, Imogen Holst, *Britten* (London: Faber and Faber, 1966); Michael Kennedy, *Britten* (London: J. M. Dent & Sons, 1981); Eric Walter White, *Benjamin Britten: His Life and Operas* (London: Faber and Faber, 1983); Humphrey Carpenter, *Benjamin Britten: A Biography* (New York: Charles Scribner's Sons, 1992); Neil Powell, *Benjamin Britten: A Life for Music* (London: Windmill Books, 2014); Paul Kildea, *Benjamin Britten: A Life in the Twentieth Century* (London: Penguin, 2014).

themes may be discerned in many of his works, not least in his operatic output.[11] Indeed, it has been asserted that Britten's works "were motivated by a deep spiritual consciousness and . . . this same spiritual dimension spread far beyond the ostensibly 'religious' works".[12]

Hussey himself clearly also believed this to be the case. Preaching at Britten's memorial service in Westminster Abbey in 1977, he quoted Britten as saying that "I am coming to feel more and more that all my music must be written to the glory of God", adding: "Perhaps partly because of firmly held ethical views, Ben did not feel able to describe himself as an orthodox churchman; but he was a person of deeply thoughtful moral character and believed wholeheartedly in a power greater than the universe."[13] It is Hussey's recognition in Britten of someone who was not "an orthodox churchman" which suggests that the relationship between the two men might be located within the "boundary space" identified above as having particular creative potential.

Art at the boundary: *Rejoice in the Lamb*

Let us now consider the artistic relationship of Hussey and Britten in more depth, beginning with the specific event which brought them together: Hussey's commissioning of a new work from the composer. This was the first major project which Hussey recounts in *Patron of Art*, and it was timed to coincide with the fiftieth anniversary of the founding of St Matthew's, in 1943. Of his choice of Britten, Hussey writes: "I was anxious to get a younger composer who had not yet established a great reputation to write something for us, partly because there was little money available and partly because, if it was to reflect the spirit of the time, it

---

[11] See, for example, Michael Fuller, "Living on the Edge: Renewal in Britten's *The Rape of Lucretia*", *Musical Times* 141 (2000), pp. 45–9; Michael Fuller, "The Far-Shining Sail: A Glimpse of Salvation in Britten's *Billy Budd*", *Musical Times* 147 (2006), pp. 17–24; Graham Elliott, *Benjamin Britten: The Spiritual Dimension* (Oxford: Oxford University Press, 2006).

[12] Elliott, *Benjamin Britten*, p. 158.

[13] Hussey, *Patron of Art*, p. 150.

seemed desirable to find someone who had not yet written much church music." After first approaching William Walton, "at that time the leader of the younger composers", who turned him down, Hussey describes being deeply impressed by a radio broadcast of Britten's *Sinfonia da Requiem* and by a radio programme playing music which Britten had selected.[14] Britten's comments on this music clearly suggested to Hussey that he might be a kindred spirit, so he wrote to the composer, care of the BBC, saying that he "hoped he would forgive [his] writing to him but [he] had a bee in [his] bonnet about a closer connection between the Church and the arts".[15] The letter was forwarded to Britten, who replied: "As I also have a 'bee' about closer connection between the arts & the Church, I am sure that I shall have an idea before next September for an anthem for your jubilee." He went on to ask practical questions about the choral forces for which he would be writing.[16]

It should be noted that at this point Britten and his partner, the tenor Peter Pears, had recently returned to Britain from the United States, whence they had moved in 1939, and registered as conscientious objectors. This led to a feeling of estrangement, and of "outsider" status. Michael Kennedy quotes Britten's comment in an interview in 1945, "As conscientious objectors we were out of it", adding, "Is it to be seriously doubted that 'and homosexuals' were unspoken but implied words in that statement?"[17] It is quite conceivable that a commission for the established Church would have been attractive to the composer, in deflecting some of the mistrust that could be drawn by "outsiders" such as himself and his partner. Webster suggests that it was a brave move on Hussey's part to approach a "conchie" in this way at that time.[18]

The choice of words was left to Britten, who selected sections from the lengthy poem *Rejoice in the Lamb* by the eighteenth-century poet

---

[14] Hussey, *Patron of Art*, p. 4.

[15] Hussey, *Patron of Art*, p. 5.

[16] Hussey, *Patron of Art*, p. 5. The author quotes from Donald Mitchell and Philip Reed (eds), *Letters from a Life: The Selected Letters of Benjamin Britten, vol. 2, 1939–1945* (London: Faber and Faber, 1991), p. 1142.

[17] Kennedy, *Britten*, pp. 123–4.

[18] Webster, *Church and Patronage*, p. 64.

Christopher Smart, written whilst its author was confined in an asylum. The manuscript of this poem had been published as recently as 1939, and Britten had been directed towards it shortly afterwards by his friend W. H. Auden.[19] Britten told Hussey that he found Smart "a great inspiration",[20] whilst Hussey writes of the poem:

> With hindsight it is not surprising that the tragic story of Christopher Smart should have appealed to Britten and that, with his keen interest in poetry and sensitive ear, he should have discovered these moving lines in a poem that was at that time practically unknown. I felt that it is important that a composer should have a text to set which stirs him and so I readily agreed.[21]

This approach seems to have been typical of Hussey. Webster observes, "Hussey gave space and support to individual artists so that they might respond to Christian themes, some of which he suggested or helped the artist to choose. Their responses, however, were each according to their own faculties and temperaments; Hussey's direct influence on the finished work was necessarily very limited."[22] This is borne out in the case of *Rejoice in the Lamb*: it appears that Hussey expressed doubt about part of the text used by Britten, since the composer wrote to tell him, "I am afraid I have gone ahead, and used abit [sic] about the cat Jeffrey [sic], but I don't see how it could hurt anyone—he is such a nice cat."[23] This provision of space—and with it, a lack of control—might be considered an important aspect of "boundary art".

In a leaflet published for the first performance of *Rejoice in the Lamb* (the text of which Britten approved), Hussey wrote that the poem "is chaotic in form but contains many flashes of genius. It is a few of the finest passages that Mr Britten has chosen to set to music. The main theme of

---

[19]   Mitchell and Reed, *Letters from a Life*, vol. 2, p. 1157.

[20]   Mitchell and Reed, *Letters from a Life*, vol. 2, p. 1157.

[21]   Hussey, *Patron of Art*, p. 6.

[22]   Webster, *Church and Patronage*, p. 14.

[23]   A sentiment with which I am sure the dedicatee of the present volume will concur! Mitchell and Reed, *Letters from a Life*, vol. 2, p. 1157.

the poem, and of the cantata, is the worship of God, by all created beings and things, each in its own way".[24] The poet Peter Porter has given a valuable insight into why Britten may have been inspired by this poem:

> Smart captures in his poem an innocence known perhaps only to children and the benignly insane, and in so doing shows the rest of us, labouring under the full weight of our super-egos, that heaven does indeed lie about us. Britten's lines from Smart are more than well-chosen; they amount to a biopsy of the poem. ... It is inspiring to find an artist in another discipline showing the way to literary taste.[25]

The composer David Matthews, who knew Britten, has also commented on "Smart's childlike innocence" as something which "ensured his appeal to Britten".[26] *Rejoice in the Lamb* received its premiere at St Matthew's, Northampton, at its patronal festival on 21 September 1943. Britten subsequently told Hussey he had found this "a very beautiful and moving occasion".[27]

Another remark by Porter is of particular interest: "I can think of no other composer who would have perceived the musical potential of the poem, nor of anyone else undaunted by its oddity, its departure from canons of sense and taste".[28] We may also note Peter Evans' citation of *Rejoice in the Lamb* as one of Britten's "inspired commentaries on unconventional texts" through which he has "enriched the music of Christianity".[29] Here, perhaps, we see some further characteristics of art from a boundary. Sense, taste and convention might be expected to play a significant role in shaping art from what I have called an "insider"

---

[24]   Hussey, *Patron of Art*, p. 8.

[25]   Peter Porter, "Composer and Poet", in Christopher Palmer (ed.), *The Britten Companion* (London: Faber and Faber, 1984), pp. 271–85, here at pp. 276–7.

[26]   David Matthews, *Britten* (London: Haus Publishing, 2003), p. 74.

[27]   Mitchell and Reed, *Letters from a Life*, vol. 2, p. 1161.

[28]   Porter, "Composer and Poet", p. 276.

[29]   Peter Evans, *The Music of Benjamin Britten* (Oxford: Oxford University Press, 1996), p. 68.

perspective: departing from them still leads to a cantata of which it has been said "the music matches the thrilling visionary quality of the words",[30] and which has been described as "luminously radiant in spirit"[31] and "captivating".[32] Yet it is noteworthy that appreciation of the work was in no way confined to an elite. Webster notes that "the critical and lay reaction to the piece was, in general, very positive . . . letters of congratulation came [to Hussey] from members of the public".[33] Britten's work, however unconventional, was—and is—still capable of offering profound experiences to the listener on either side of the boundary at which it was produced.

Beyond *Rejoice in the Lamb*

Hussey and Britten remained in regular contact. Britten and Pears gave a number of recitals at St Matthew's,[34] and Britten sometimes suggested younger composers whom Hussey might commission.[35] A suggestion that Britten might set to music an anthem written for St Matthew's in 1946 by W. H. Auden came to nothing,[36] although Britten's organ solo *Prelude and Fugue on a theme of Vittoria* was first performed in Northampton for the patronal festival in that year.[37] From Britten's correspondence it is clear

---

[30] White, *Benjamin Britten*, p. 45.

[31] Kennedy, *Britten*, p. 165.

[32] Kildea, *Benjamin Britten*, p. 224.

[33] Webster, *Church and Patronage*, p. 67.

[34] See Mitchell and Reed, *Letters from a Life*, vol. 2, pp. 1220 ff. and Philip Reed, Mervyn Cooke and Donald Mitchell (eds), *Letters from a Life: The Selected Letters of Benjamin Britten, vol. 4: 1952–1957* (Woodbridge: The Boydell Press, 2008), p. 89.

[35] See Hussey, *Patron of Art*, pp. 14, 94, 96, and Donald Mitchell, Philip Reed and Mervyn Cooke (eds), *Letters from a Life: The Selected Letters of Benjamin Britten, vol. 3: 1946–1951* (London: Faber and Faber, 2004), pp. 411–12 and 595–7.

[36] Hussey, *Patron of Art*, p. 83.

[37] Reed, Cooke and Mitchell, *Letters from a Life*, vol. 4, p. 165.

that Hussey continued to hope that he would produce further liturgical music: a Mass setting is mentioned in letters of 1948 and 1950,[38] and is raised again in correspondence of 1966–7 and 1970–1 in connection with a commission for the Southern Cathedrals Festival,[39] but no setting materialized. Britten clearly felt an ongoing sense of gratitude to Hussey, writing to a correspondent in 1953 that "if ever there was a case of one person being responsible for an idea [*Rejoice in the Lamb*] this is it".[40] Hussey contributed a letter to a Tribute which was published in honour of Peter Pears' seventy-fifth birthday, in which he recalled "the unforgettable experience of the first night of *Peter Grimes*".[41]

Britten's letters to Hussey are warm in tone, and in a letter to Pears in 1959 the composer wrote, "It was lovely to see Walter, who was very sweet."[42] The strength of the friendship between Britten and Hussey is illustrated in a paradoxical way by an incident in 1953, when Hussey was lunching with Britten and others after preaching a sermon in Aldeburgh, prior to a concert to be given by the composer. Hussey recalled an outburst in which the distraught composer (who was famously prone to stage fright) said, "There are times when I feel I have no talents—no talents at all!"

> Then I leaned forward and said, 'You know, Ben, when you're in this mood we love you best of all.' And he simply gave a great shout, 'I hate you, Walter!' From that moment, he was entirely all right! It was very strange: a tremendous tension built up, but then

[38]   Reed, Cooke and Mitchell, *Letters from a Life*, vol. 4, pp. 388 ff. & 595.

[39]   Philip Reed and Mervyn Cooke (eds), *Letters from a Life: The Selected Letters of Benjamin Britten, vol. 6: 1966–1976* (Woodbridge: The Boydell Press, 2012), pp. 166 ff. & 405.

[40]   Reed, Cooke and Mitchell, *Letters from a Life*, vol. 4, p. 196.

[41]   Marion Thorpe (ed.), *Peter Pears: A Tribute on his 75th Birthday* (London: Faber Music, 1985), p. 48.

[42]   Philip Reed and Mervyn Cooke (eds), *Letters from a Life: Selected Letters of Benjamin Britten, vol. 5: 1958–1965* (Woodbridge: The Boydell Press, 2010), p. 157.

it was like lancing a boil. After that he chatted and was friendly
and went off and gave a marvellous concert.[43]

It is also noteworthy that Hussey was apparently close enough to
Britten and Pears to be aware of their sexual practices, which one of
them presumably confided to him in the knowledge that he would be
a sympathetic ear.[44] Concerning Hussey himself, Webster notes that
"Hussey's own homosexuality presents the historian with a difficulty,
in that the documentary evidence for it is thin, although those who
remember him are in no doubt of it".[45] However, Webster is confident
enough to write of "the fact of [Hussey's] homosexuality".[46] He comments,
"It is highly likely that the warmth of the relationship between Britten
and Hussey, which seems to have been immediate, was in part due to
their shared sexuality,"[47] adding: "[Their] relationship was a mixture of
professional engagement between client and patron, pastoral concern
for the person, and simple mutual delight in each other's company."[48]

It would appear that *Rejoice in the Lamb* came about as a consequence
of many felicities. Hussey felt emboldened to contact a composer on the
basis of a minimal acquaintance with his music, but with a perception
of a shared taste. Britten's positive response was due to his wishing to see
"a closer connection between the arts & the Church", and may also have
been prompted by a felt need to "belong". The commission prospered
due to the free hand given to Britten in his choice of material; and the
relationship between the two men prospered thanks to each recognizing
a kindred spirit in the other. It is clear that a similar pattern underpinned
many of Hussey's other commissions. An initial approach on Hussey's
part might be prompted by an instinctive attraction to the work of the
artist in question: such approaches were also frequently facilitated by
the networks which Hussey was at pains to generate. Webster draws

---

[43]   Carpenter, *Benjamin Britten*, p. 328.

[44]   Carpenter, *Benjamin Britten*, p. 130.

[45]   Webster, *Church and Patronage*, p. 45.

[46]   Webster, *Church and Patronage*, p. 47.

[47]   Webster, *Church and Patronage*, p. 69.

[48]   Webster, *Church and Patronage*, p. 71.

particular attention to the role played here by Kenneth Clark, who "was uniquely positioned as a broker of contacts and information at the nexus of the social and political elites with the artistic world", and with whom Hussey established a long-lasting friendship which led to Clark contributing a "Tribute" to Hussey in a book celebrating the 900th anniversary of Chichester Cathedral.[49] Latitude was then given to the artist to explore their response to the commission, with a warm, personal and trusting relationship being built through the commissioning process.

All this being said, it is noteworthy that (with the exception of the *Prelude and Fugue on a theme of Vittoria*) Hussey's warm friendship with Britten did not produce any further Church music from the composer, despite Hussey's persistent requests. It is interesting to speculate on why this should have been the case. Britten accepted liturgical commissions from other sources (leading to the *Festival Te Deum* of 1944, the *Hymn to St Peter* of 1955, the *Missa Brevis* of 1959 and the *Jubilate Deo* of 1961, for example). Perhaps there was simply something about the situation of the composer in 1943, and the free hand given to him in the choice of a text, which gave rise to circumstances that were uniquely propitious.

Conclusion

Are there any lessons which may be learned from this episode? It would be foolish to attempt to generalize too much from the example of one individual, and still more from an analysis of one incident in the life of that individual. Hussey did things his way, and his example is not one that might simply be copied as a template. As Webster puts it, "Hussey's success was in large part due to his personal qualities; his work was not as a distant, demanding patron, but as a friend and collaborator, and as an unofficial chaplain to those with whom he worked. As such, his way of working was not easily codified into a model that could easily

---

[49]   Webster, *Church and Patronage*, p. 129, and see also Kenneth Clark, "Dean Walter Hussey: A Tribute to his Patronage of the Arts", in *Chichester 900* (Chichester: Chichester Press, 1975).

be transferred to other contexts."[50] This is what we might expect from "boundary" art, as we have seen: its expression is exquisitely sensitive to the initial conditions leading to its production.

To summarize: a reflection on the nature of a boundary indicates that it has the potential to be the locus of surprising occurrences, leading to fresh possibilities for communication between those on either side of the boundary. The analogy with chaotic systems suggests that such work is unpredictable, being highly contingent on the non-reproducible conditions which led to its production. We have further seen that, where boundary art is concerned, such work may be thought unconventional to the extent that it lacks taste, or even sense, when viewed through the lens of the perceptions of those on either side of the boundary; and yet it may still be found thrilling, captivating—and capable, perhaps, of expressing fresh and unexpected truths. Thus churchgoers might be offered an image, or a setting of a quirky yet thought-provoking text, to enlarge their liturgical perspectives, whilst those outwith the Church are similarly offered an invitation to reflect afresh on the very nature of worship. *Rejoice in the Lamb* serves as an example of all these aspects of "boundary art". Even if such art is, by its very nature, "one-off", reflection on this work and its inception may perhaps inspire further boundary art, however different it may be in terms of medium, form, content and expression to Britten's cantata.

Finally, what does all this have to say to us regarding "the end of the Church"? Only, perhaps, that any institution which can continue to engage with those at its boundaries to produce such work as described here remains a lively one. We may have to wait a while yet for that end to come to pass.

---

[50] Webster, *Church and Patronage*, p. 13.

2

Light in the Darkness of the Heart

Donald Orr

The Truth in Art is a notion that has involved the minds of philosophers, and others, who question if Art is a reflection of life or a mirror of the artistic concerns provoked by need, greed or ambition. Is Art, as Plato once asserted, an imitation of life, or does Art offer us a means to the acquisition of truth through consideration, contemplation and balance? Plato's concept of truth centred on an invisible, eternal sense of form beyond the physical manifestation of the object itself. If Art is mere imitation, a mimetic process in a quest for beauty, what of the darkness, the ugliness, barbarity and horror of life? What of the terror and dread, the fear and loathing? Aristotle argued that objects contain an internal eternal truth linked to their being and different from the notion of universal truth. Through Art the inner experience of the physical world might be reflected on, communicated and considered.

Humanity has always been concerned with itself, its forms, differences, systems and histories. The rise in, and development of, the representation of the body became paramount in the history of art. When it came to illustrating the Bible, there was an obvious gap between what the Church wanted to be present and what the artists' vision of a specific story was. The formal, stylistic and symbolic components of religious painting situate them in a socio-cultural and historical context where often it is the experience of the viewers and ritual usage that may be desired. What is clear is that the study of religion through the arts can create a more integrated cultural understanding of often complicated issues.

For some time now there has been a considerable drive towards intertextuality and further into other fields of communication. The problem of interpretation, negotiating an explanation whereby significance and intention may be conveyed through depiction or representation, moves us into the discipline of painting and also takes us into the field of commentary, which demands a degree of invention and imagination.

It can be argued that most artists, historically, have been involved in a process attempting to express mental content through visual objects, using raw materials to produce a new object, unknown even to the artist. The creative journey is one of discovery and is individual. Accepting Kant's notion that the aesthetic experience occurs in the gap between the viewer and the viewed is another individual experience but becomes meaningful through a collective understanding of the truth. This is the artist's focus on the world: their inner vision may not constantly be achieved but truth is their aim.

The movement between text and canvas presents a complex and fraught relationship between these media. The addition of vowels to consonants demonstrates a change in sound and meaning. Does this relate to movements of colour, tone and shape that may change the text further to the point of revelation, or confusion?

Meaning for us all is constituted by arranging what linguistic components we have available. We construct meaning, as opposed to objects having innate meaning themselves; in turn these constructs are affected by changing ideologies. Upon any canvas there are a number of different paintings operating within the frame. The nature of placement and positioning can radically alter the importance of what is depicted and may function as a challenge to any biblical text. Art may scandalize as it tackles areas that theology and tradition would rather avoid or will not enter into.

Black and white aspects of the truth

One of the singular peculiarities in dealing with paintings as theological resources is the contiguity of black and white. They are only opposites in linguistic terms, polarized by light and imagination, but their value on the palette is the same; they operate on the same plane dimensionally.

There exists a dread of whiteness, the strangeness of the albino, the terror of the great white shark, the fear of the albatross. We are aware of the pale horse whose "rider's name was Death, and Hades followed with him" (Revelation 6:8), and of the patriarchal figure of Captain Ahab confronting, again, the impenetrable whiteness of the great whale. Here whiteness bridges "the metonymic gap linking 'whale' to 'chaos'".[1] The whale represents a highly visible, chaotically mobile abyss; a whiteness that both attracts and repels. Whiteness too is a primal chaos; the mountaineer caught in a whiteout is in extreme danger. The whiteness itself is a warning of danger and death in an excess of motion and violence as it lures us to contemplate chaos as an aspect of order, part of the transformation of absolute disorder to the newly evolving natural world.

The whale, like the iceberg or the threat of the great white shark, is still with us—evolution has not been a shield we can rely on. Whitewashing is not something to be proud of and *Blanc* to blank is nothing but an empty openness devoid of colour. The polar caps are areas of blinding whiteness where only the distanced and uncomprehending Western visitor would be interested in going; in Inuit it is called "*Kingmersoriartor-figssuauq—* the place where you only eat dogs".[2] The Transfiguration of Christ outdoes any fuller for dazzling whiteness and terrifies the three disciples present, but it is not so much a colour event as the visible absence of colour, both chromatically and theologically. At the same time, whiteness remains the concrete, rather than the abstract, of all colours.

Darkness, for the Christian mind, may attest to an absence, but the writings and paintings only represent, they are not what they represent. The option of the represented aspect becoming merely a gap, a void, allows space for emptiness and accrues an element of time, and may generate fear, dread and the hidden causes of concern. The function of darkness is not unification but, in a sense, to assist in conveying the meaning of the new light, to begin a count or census of what exists. Darkness is colourless, a name for something that is void and is viewed

---

[1]   Catherine Keller, *The Face of the Deep: A Theology of Becoming* (London: Routledge, 2003), p. 141.

[2]   Jim Perrin, *Travels with the Flea and Other Eccentric Journeys* (Glasgow: The In Pinn, 2002), p. 63.

as movement and stasis; the problem is how to separate dark activity from the product of dark activity—what cannot be captured in symbols, the unshareable—the void being far greater than the sum of its parts. What we intuit about the black secret of Darkness is that it is not empty. Darkness, as a name, ghosts among us as the place we avoid, the place behind colour, the zero that corresponds to the empty grave. Darkness is the gap in the world, a sound enunciating behind colour, something we do not wish to be real—an ex-istence.

Culturally darkness has been exploited improperly, inaccurately where blackness has been used as a symbol. Darkness has peculiar connotations in Western culture where, on the one hand, it has adopted a self-righteous, puritanical quality and, on the other, where black has been seen as a "colour", it has accrued references to sin, evil and the feminine. The Bible and Shakespeare are full of references to darkness in terms of wickedness and the ungodly; similarly there is an entire film noir genre where the notion of "the baddie" is invariably enhanced by the dramatic irony of his dark attire accessorized by the ubiquitous black hat and/or gloves. Within the caste system and the apartheid system there was a colour coding; a division between blacks and coloureds that graded darkness. In art, this aspect of exploitation has invariably seen black being treated, mixed, varnished or coated, whereas the reality of black is of a dull, dark presence only feasibly represented by matt black. The darkness of the void is translated into formlessness; the unformed or maternal, thence to the hidden, the guilt and the origins lost in it. The ethos of the Plutonic suffers like negativity, which is closely linked to it, from cultural exploitation through social and ethnic meaning. Darkness is also resistance. Black is resistant to interpretation, to reproduction or duplication. It can resist exploitation in that it is unusable and un-reasonable. It is resistant to market forces or trade and commerce as it is price-less, unique but only of itself and therefore unmarketable.

Darkness, like Abstraction, resists qualification, definition and articulation, and links the two directly to the apophatic. Darkness and Abstraction resist attachment—colour has to do with life and is trapped in physical activity and assertions of its own. Darkness and Abstraction are not craft-related and resist emotional or aesthetic labels, or any that can be defined positively. Darkness resists perfection and is perfection. It is resistant to demythologizing despite being meaningless, spaceless and formless, since it maintains that capacity to attract and repel, sustaining the notions of hell, chaos, occultism and evil; it balances, yet destroys, the notions of void and myth. Darkness is aesthetic. Black is a non-colour. Colour is trapped by our physical recognition of it, our linkage of colour to aspects and objects of our world. Colour asserts itself in its correlation to aspects of life whereas that emotional content of colour is lacking in black—black is silent, and in its silence questions our ability to depict or picture it in any way since, no matter how dull a matt, non-reflective pigment is used, it will invariably appear as a very dark grey since we need light to see it. Darkness is truly neutral; it is glossless, textureless, non-linear and non-reflective. It is lustrous yet dull, holding its property in light or in shadow, its strength and interest lying in its non-colour capacity. Chiaroscuro, the artistic distribution of light and dark masses in a picture, is not immediately about colour, it is about dark and light expression but "expression is an impossible word. If you want to use it, I think you have to explain it further"[3]—black is expression—ultimate, voiceless and transcendent.

Darkness is also light. A luminous darkness, a brilliance within darkness—a numinous resonance which is an eternal condition, a perfection beyond being and virtue. It is inscrutable and indescribable in its undifferentiated unity, whose only characteristic is an undivided oneness. Darkness possesses no consciousness of anything and within it all distinctions disappear. It is apocalyptic and self-transcendent, having no before, or after, or remaining. It is the alpha and the omega; the beginning and, at the same time, the end, since it has neither extension nor recession, plane nor infinity; it is motionless, formless and nameless. Darkness allows us a perception of the unperceivable, and art cannot imitate text. The four "black and white" examples chosen here are a small selection from the history of Western Art and only touch lightly on the terms of the contemporary movements that surrounded them. "These paintings are truly 'darkness visible', dark nights of the soul that are at

---

3   Ad Reinhardt, "Black as a Concept and Symbol", in B. Rose (ed.), *Art as Art: Selected Writings of Ad Reinhardt* (Berkeley: University of California Press, 1999), pp. 86–9, here at p. 88.

the same time points of vision and enlightenment."[4] They are bound through time by their use of black and white to suggest equality and truth, and beyond that to forms of ultimate power. They provide a space, "even a sacred space, in which the task of theology may be challenged and renewed".[5]

Edouard Manet (1832–83)—*Olympia*[6]

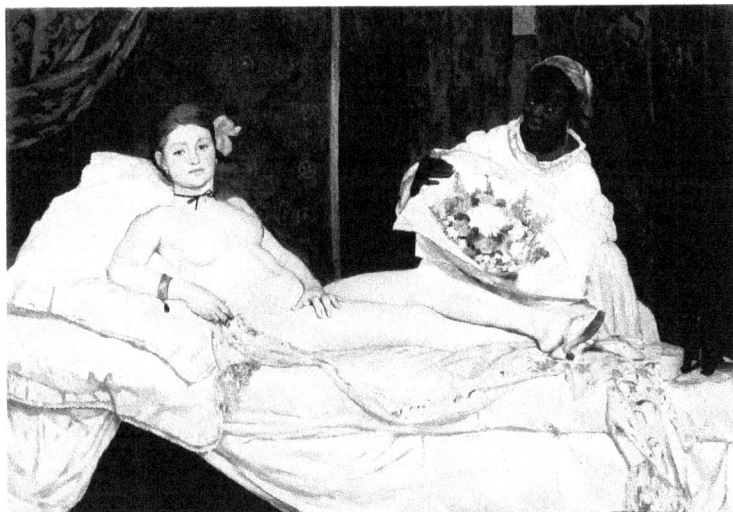

Figure 1: Edouard Manet, *Olympia*, 1863

This in many ways unique painting is essentially a black and white picture that flattened the painting space at a time when Impressionists were striving to deepen it through an examination of colour. Where most artists had used image as a key to the narrative in painting, and colour had been illustrative or informative, Manet's use of polarized tone is a unique portal to the parabolic narrative in art. Just as the language of

---

[4]   Jasper, *Sacred Desert*.

[5]   David Jasper, *Contemplations on the Spiritual* (Glasgow School of Art/ Glasgow University, 1997). p. 40.

[6]   Manet, E., *Olympia*, Oil on canvas, 130 × 190 cm, 1863. Musée d'Orsay, Paris.

Jesus in the Gospels is familiar and civil but conceals chaos, so Manet's *Olympia* is a search for modernity and honesty in the concealed aspects of Parisian society by establishing a cool, impersonal reaction distancing the audience. The vague stare of the model ignores the viewers yet draws them back to the reality of the model's profession. The black cat on the edge of the bed can be seen as a symbol of laziness and lust in art, but in Manet's framework black is upright and good and even the cat appears surprised at the girl's demeanour.

Beneath this the operation of black and white on the canvas reveals a truth that was shrouded and undiscussed: a truth about France's colonial history and contemporary attitudes to black French people—this at the time when the American Civil War raged across the Atlantic. In a scene where the contiguity of tone relates the black woman to the background, but technically, in terms of tone values, equates her with the white woman, a parity is established. The black woman is clothed, carrying flowers for the house symbolizing a desire for beauty and decoration. She is the bearer of gifts and ready to attend to the home. The juxtaposition of the black woman's modesty and the white girl's nudity, which bears all the emblems of harlotry, reveals her gifts and her readiness to provide a service. This provokes the viewer into moral judgements, and unpopular discussions in Parisian society at that time. The provocation of Manet's work exposes theological process and in its parabolic way demands an answer from us, and by that answer we will be judged.

El Greco (Doménikos Theotokópolous, 1541–1614)—*The Burial of the Count of Orgaz*[7]

Figure 2: El Greco, *The Burial of the Count of Orgaz*, 1586

This painting reveals El Greco's ability to combine complex political iconography, the medieval inheritance of the Spanish Church, and the aristocratic hierarchy of the Spanish Court in this densely packed arena

---

[7]   El Greco, *The Burial of the Count of Orgaz*, oil on canvas, 4.8 × 3.6 m., 1586 8, Iglesia de Santo Tomé, Toledo, Spain.

whose colour structure states far more than its forms. The painting portrays a fourteenth-century Toledan nobleman being laid to rest. He is surrounded by dignitaries of the Church and society, founding members of Holy Orders, and all the ritual and pomp of the period. Above, his soul passes through the strait gate to Heaven, where it will be welcomed by the Virgin and St John the Baptist, the communion of saints and Christ himself, who already awaits him with open arms.

The painting, densely packed with humanity, indicates he will have as many friends in heaven as he had on earth and will be just as dear to them, and welcomed by them as he was in life. The attentive faces in the funeral crowd are echoed in heaven, the attendance of the Church is resonated in heavenly dignitaries, both sets of which prepare him to meet Christ. This is echoed further by the role of angels in heaven, which is linked to the small acolyte in the left foreground, bearing a light in his hour of darkness. Similarly, the flow of vestments in the immediate foreground is matched by the shapes of the clouds, forming the barrier between life and death, heaven and earth.

This is truly a painting of two halves split between earth and heaven. The earthly portion is full of life, that is, it is compressed. Humanity is stacked in flat ranks of claustrophobic quality, enhanced by the boxed effect of the painting's edge, while heaven is light, spacious and airy under the arching dome of infinity. This is further emphasized by the dark hues used below and their opposites above. The earth is limited and dominated by men, while heaven is boundless and open to all.

With the small acolyte pointing inwards and the priest with his back to us indicating both ways, the artist has attempted to break up the flatness of the foreground composition with a ripple effect. Similarly, the attitudes of the bishop (St Augustine) and the vested priest (St Stephen) with the body of Count Orgaz cause a parallel movement in an otherwise uniform crowd. The fixed regularity of the aristocratic party is not accidental. They form a black fence, and their lost companion is very much within the pale, whereas their backs are turned to all: they bar all who are not eligible to take part. We, as viewers, are allowed into the scene as within the pale, and at the invitation of priest and acolyte. The darkness above their heads is indicative of the *Dies Irae*, and their uniform, sombre dress accentuates this, while the light of heaven allows low key colour and individuality.

The Virgin sits at the edge of heaven, waiting to welcome and supported by St Peter holding the keys of the Kingdom. Opposite her is the Baptist symbolizing new birth, and beside him is St Andrew facing his brother. The massed ranks of the saints sit at their ease in a diagonal formation as there is always room in heaven.

The vertical axis is the scene of the action. The body of the Count, supported by the Church, watched by the nobles, is transformed into a soul, and assisted by an angel into the narrow passage into heaven. On emerging, blessed by the Virgin and Baptist, it will rise to meet Christ. The vaginal/uterine nature of the passage, the symbolism of the child as a soul, and the Virgin midwife (and immediate baptism) all combine to make the birth/rebirth process of new life in Christ, to whom the Count is drawn.

Starting from the foreground the formal linear composition is not only enhanced by the colour structure, but the latter is also utilized symbolically to emphasize aspects of the Count's, the Church's and the aristocrat's status. The decoration on the Count's armour is a direct echo of the needlework on the vestments of the clergy. The dark/silver background of the armour relates to the colour iconography of the aristocracy and links to the light/silver background of the vestments. As the surpliced priest on the right prays, we are aware of the white over his black cassock and the fact that the Count, in his dark armour, is about to be draped in white to become "holy" and take his ordained place in heaven. The immediate wave of light colour, from the cope of the priest on the right to the figure in monastic habit to the left, creates a degree of recession before the wall of the noblemen. The symbolism of their closed ranks is clear but the contrast between their blackness and the white ruffs and faces, between the dark wall of bodies and the whiteness of heaven, is one of El Greco's finest subtleties.

Black and white are absolutes. One cannot mix dark black. Thus, these men are shadowless and impenetrable; the strength of their power as national statesmen and supporters of the Church cannot be broken. No background light shines through between these guardians of the

State and Church. They defend without having to brandish weapons or symbols of power; their massed ranks declare their status and might.

Immediately above is a range of clear, well painted, recognizable portraits in a ripple of light—the human face of authority. Above them hang the doom-laden clouds of the time. This is the only area of unsettled colour, indicating that under heaven is a region of chaos held in check by the Spanish aristocracy and Catholic Church. This single strip of disturbed tone has a degree of immediacy lacking in the staged format of the piece and differing from El Greco's usual use of colour, which is "often eerily strident, with sharp contrasts of blue, yellow, shrill green".[8] Similarly, the elongated limbs and nervous tension of his figures is absent, as is the haunted quality, where drapery can seem to have a life of its own. Nothing here is random or chance. This is a view of a well-ordered society that acknowledges the hierarchy of State and Church—a clear message that the divine order is reflected on earth in Spain and arguing against this position in Spain will lead nowhere, that is, into a greater darkness.

Henri Matisse (1869–1954)—*Porte-Fenêtre à Collioure*[9]

"To render time sensible in itself is a task common to the painter . . . It is a task beyond all measure or cadence."[10]

Matisse dealt with colour in his work and utilized his environment for innovative colour structures and design elements. His paintings of interiors and figures, or his fondness of the open window scene, trace his movements from Paris to the South of France's most popular resorts.

---

[8]   Peter Murray and Linda Murray, *A Dictionary of Art and Artists* (London: Penguin, 1964), p. 141.

[9]   Henri Matisse, *Porte-Fenêtre à Collioure*, oil on canvas, 117 × 93 cm, 1914. Centre Pompidou, Paris. See <https://www.centrepompidou.fr/en/ressources/oeuvre/5dq7dfI>, accessed 9 November 2022.

[10] Gilles Deleuze, *Francis Bacon: The Logic of Sensation* (London: Continuum, 2004), p. 64.

"The calm they radiate is not an expression of but a ploy against anxiety."[11] Matisse was 45 in 1914 and *Porte-Fenêtre à Collioure* was the antithesis of his contemplations on the sunny world beyond his balcony from the utter security of his room. This painting relates to a specific historical time/action where Matisse, perceiving the apocalyptic onset of the Great War, seeks to render it sensible by creating a notion of its end; its total cessation as the abyss engulfs the world and darkness reasserts itself.

In this canvas the filter between the outside and the inside has gone. It is through the *Porte-Fenêtre à Collioure* that he looks past the shutters of normality and out into the heart of darkness. Here Matisse acknowledges that the light is being overcome, the reclamation by darkness has commenced. For him, the apocalyptic vision is total, revealing the darkness but concealing its depths and horrors. It is depicted as a darkness that, despite its flat application, has palpability and depth. This is a darkness outside the window but already issuing into the room, on the point of dissolving into a deadly fog. This is an apocalyptic ending "that calls forth the deepest abyss, a truly absolute abyss effecting not only the end of history but the end of the world itself".[12] This ending will herald a new state, the creation of a new Europe.

Matisse changes the surface in such a way that it barely involves a shift of attention for the viewer to move from seeing the bare interior with a nightscape to seeing it as a mobile surface, threatening in its intentions. This surface is not an object, as it retains a subtle depth and a seeming mobility that engenders the enveloping feeling of primordial blackness.

This painting exerts a powerful sense of removal and extraction, and the loss of definition and depiction adds to the sense of desolation. The flat, dull half tones of the interior do not lighten but rather depress the scene dominated by the threatening blackness that fills the window space; a blackness one senses as being in motion. The dim landscape is just perceptible beyond the veiled rail of the French window, but the scene is drenched in darkness that infiltrates the room to attack the dimming light.

---

[11]   Robert Hughes, *Nothing if Not Critical: Selected Essays on Art and Artists* (London: Harvill, 1991), p. 172.

[12]   Thomas J. J. Altizer, *Godhead and the Nothing* (New York: State University of New York Press, 2003), p. 60.

By using an abstracted interior, he frames within the frame the intensity of darkness and what emerges is an emphasis on the surface, however this is not a nightscape, a view of Collioure in darkness, but a text of the shock of war. The Spirit about to move over the face of this darkness will unleash the apocalyptic vision of the Somme. Matisse's ability creates the seeming movement of the blackness promoting the invasive quality of a primeval darkness that will engulf France and all of Europe.

Annihilation beckons, annihilation by and of an absolute nothingness, the heart of darkness. It is Matisse's gift that this piece may provoke a theology of becoming, "for it would articulate a faith with which to face uncertainty, not a knowledge with which to eliminate it".[13]

Robert Motherwell (1915–91)—*Elegy to the Spanish Republic 34*[14]

Figure 3: Robert Motherwell, *Elegy to the Spanish Republic XXXIV*, 1953–4

---

[13]   Keller, *The Face of the Deep*, p. 203.

[14]   Robert Motherwell, *Elegy to the Spanish Republic 34*, oil on canvas, 203.2 × 254 cm, 1953/54. Albright-Knox Gallery, Buffalo, NY.

"Abstract Art is an effort to close the void."[15]

Throughout this series of paintings Motherwell dealt with the dark side of human nature outwith the creative realm of democracy. Motherwell "conceived of painting as something that demanded a wholesale reconstructive methodological solution".[16] This aspect of philosophical challenge differentiates Motherwell from his contemporaries. Newman, Rothko, Reinhardt and Pollock can all be seen as dogmatists, "but Motherwell was a criticalist in method and a pragmatist in everything else".[17] It was Motherwell who changed the polar definitions of spirituality in painting where the spiritual was seen as disdaining science, whose discoveries denied any hope of the divine or eternity. Spiritualism appeared as the opposite of Positivism, where natural science alone could explain existence. Positivism demanded the role of a higher revelation. This is a form of materialism and as such is severely limited.

Motherwell's drive for a spiritual resolution in the Spanish Elegies series was an effort to find evidence that refuted Positivism and enhanced the spiritual essence in humanity. This was Motherwell's "original creative principle", a phrase he used often and an aspect he deemed was lacking in American Modern Painting. This principle could not be a style or stylistic, nor an imposed aesthetic, but would be an original development unique to the individual who strove for this understanding. Here, in the Spanish Elegies, is the enactment of the abyss, "a transfiguration occurring in that very abyss itself".[18] In acknowledging the purely negative acts of humanity they are named, and in naming affirmed in a black positivism. In the solid black forms of the series, "darkness" and "void" are "coupled with the feelings of how material reality is".[19] In the elegies to the Spanish

---

[15]   George L. K. Morris, Willem De Kooning, Alexander Calder, Fritz Glarner, Robert Motherwell and Stuart Davis, "What Abstract Art Means to Me", *The Bulletin of the Museum of Modern Art* 18:3 (1951), pp. 2–15, here at p. 13.

[16]   Arthur C. Danto, *Philosophizing Art: Selected Essays* (Berkeley, CA: University of California Press, 2001), p. 15.

[17]   Danto, *Philosophizing Art*, p. 17.

[18]   Altizer, *Godhead and the Nothing*, p. 136.

[19]   Robert Motherwell, "The Modern Painter's World", in Charles Harrison and Paul Wood (eds), *Art in Theory 1900–2000: An Anthology of Changing Ideas*,

Republic, actuality has a historical basis and thus carries more than one set of values. They evoke a naming of the abyss; a structure from which they have evolved or emerged. This is the negative voice of humanity through history and across the globe, but it is these voices "that most deeply reveal or unveil our deep passivity",[20] for even if our passivity is part of an illusion, it is an illusion that has become universal in mankind, and Motherwell indicates the abyss and evil from which it came. "It is the artists who guard the spiritual in the modern world",[21] and this is a spiritual painting involving the initial aspect of creation, the separation of light from darkness.

While abstract the painting is highly figurative, a reality among realities, which has been felt and formed. It is the reflection of a pattern of choices made that gives the painting its form. The few pieces of bright colour—blue, a golden yellow and a bright red, new to this thirty-fourth version—can all be assimilated as a landscape shorthand partially excavated from the rubble of war, but also remind us of the national colours of Spain and the elegance of Spanish society. They can also appear as tattered fragments of a flag now broken and scattered, remnants of a true country now dominated by a colourless, faceless war. "There is an arid, tempered quality about these images that is not to be confused with blandness or faintheartedness."[22] Motherwell's use of black is similar to Reinhardt's but only within the density of his amoeboid shapes. Here blackness is total and featureless, the dead core of the abyss. There is an occasional surface movement that may denote a tension, a resistance to the void that seeks to dominate, but generally the darkness is impenetrable. The loss of culture, society, an entire way of life is painted out, buried and tarmac-coated. Not a shadow of it exists; it will never be seen again.

Motherwell, by his work and statements, found it impossible "to hang around in the space between art and political action"[23] without making

2nd edn (Oxford: Blackwell, 2003), p. 643.
20 Altizer, *Godhead and the Nothing*, p. 136.
21 Motherwell, "The Modern Painter's World", p. 644.
22 Max Kozloff, *Renderings* (London: Studio Vista, 1970), p. 169.
23 Herschel B. Chipp, *Theories of Modern Art: A Source Book by Artists and Critics* (Berkeley and Los Angeles: University of California Press, 1968), p. 490.

choices. He takes us to "the edge of violence, rather than violence itself".[24] The ripped edge of the black shapes represents the one area of hope. The final shape of a ripped edge cannot be predicted. Within the dominance of the blackness and its brooding sense of permanence there is an element of instability. This is the instability of a transfiguration of society and its translation of what we know as God. Here God is remodelled in a pathological way that damages humanity in its desire to remain close to the abyss. The abyss becomes extended, becomes external and internal to where humanity's darkness can be carried off. It allows the horror of war, the darkness of humanity, to be denied and simultaneously to be acknowledged. The interiorization of the abyss culminates in the loss of our interior, the destruction of our core humanity and a release of the chaos of the abyss. The violence of the physical process becomes imperative as an energetic outburst against indifference, revealing a stability dependent on a tension held within a structure relying on the establishment of balance from our own resources.

Motherwell's blackness is torn, not cut or moulded into shape. It is in the intimacy of this kind of area that abstraction may overlap theology in unknowing—"an absence of knowing in the sense that everything you do not know, or have forgotten, is dark to you".[25] While there is in its methodologies "conception, reason, understanding, touch, perception, opinion, imagination, name, and many other things",[26] there is still that cloud of unknowing between sight and understanding. Around its ragged edge, light permeates and blackness bleeds. This is not the smooth, machine cut of durability, but some chaos disguised as resilience. Its density and opacity may lend it strength, but its organic edge reveals the chance and impromptu gesture. The blackness is not permanent, it is present in a state of alteration and its "tearingness" is indicative of collage structures, which if stuck down can always be lifted up. It is the white areas that reveal their depth and signs of struggle. The light swallows

[24] Hughes, *Nothing if Not Critical*, p. 163.

[25] Anon, *The Cloud of Unknowing,* trans. A. Spearing (London: Penguin, 2001), p. 26.

[26] Colm Luibheid (trans.), *Pseudo-Dionysus: The Complete Works* (Mahwah, NJ: Paulist Press, 1987). p. 109.

darkness, floods the edges, creates shadow, and in its vertical structure displays a more rigid, organized format than the darkness. The light is disciplined and directed, as opposed to the black spillage of darkness.

The *Elegies* are "artistically excellent not simply because they are beautiful but because their being beautiful is artistically right".[27] Motherwell's stark forms allow their thought to be manifest and reveal the aesthetic beauty that remains internal to their meaning. These visual meditations on the death of a way of life are the broken abstract landscapes, scenes of suffering silence that hold the cadences of grief. Motherwell's *Elegies* approach the margins of human endurance. In their overlapping forms, we sense the intersection of endurance, that common ground where the unendurable overlies what can only be endured. The natural emotional response to elegy is sorrow, but Motherwell's abstract answer is an expression of deep regret that incorporates an aesthetic beauty in defining the mood of mourning that is "at once formally obtrusive yet thematically oblique".[28] The individual canvases are much greater than the sum of their minimal parts and their emotional momentum stems from an imperious pictorial logic. This beauty is not distant, nor has it distanced over time, "the blackness is not so much the patination of age and nature, but the charred effects of fire and dried blood".[29] The interiority of the *Elegies* connects their reference and their mood, which has come through darkness but not been overcome by it. The initial divine light in its creation erodes and abrades a physical darkness that is unprepared for such an onslaught. This is the instant of the word made light; art articulating the non-verbal theological experience. The translation of something new, the apocalyptic change, is translated into the structure of paintings. The decline of the figurative, of narration, of perspective, has in it all the resonance of that first creative, *kenotic* gesture

---

[27]   Arthur C. Danto, *The Abuse of Beauty* (Chicago, IL: Open Court 2006), p. 110.

[28]   David Craven, "A Legacy for the Latin American Left: Abstract Expressionism as Anti-Imperialist Art", in Joan M. Marter (ed.), *Abstract Expressionism—The International Context* (New Brunswick, NJ: Rutgers University Press, 2007), pp. 67–81, here at p. 77.

[29]   Danto, *The Abuse of Beauty*, p. 112.

that called forth light and is itself accomplished in the process of painting. "This notion of the reversal of beginning and end, the inversion of them . . . is accomplished through artistic work."[30]

Conclusion

If life imitates art, then art may imitate commentary, as the role of figurative art cannot be merely illustrative and art cannot imitate text. Text cannot illustrate itself despite figurative, descriptive language, but graphic painting can illustrate text and other forms may comment upon it. Painting exists beyond the bounds of the figurative, and as Robert Motherwell's *Elegy to the Spanish Republic* series offers an interpretation of, and commentary on, the trauma and loss of society in Spain in the 1930s, so Jackson Pollock's *Blue Poles* or Willem de Kooning's *Excavation* may be seen as a commentary on the initial part of Genesis.

What we see in paintings is often conditioned by the circumstances in which we view them, or the weight of art history can fix our attention on a chronology of development. There is a tendency in Western figurative art for the frozen gesture, usually situated in the foreground, to cause the loss of illusion. The static painted image cancels any sense of movement and reveals only flesh colour in the shape of a hand. It is within or behind that hand that the truth may lie. Art and its images have often been seen as inherently dangerous to society where the potential to read those concealed truths has become too apparent, and control has been exerted even, or perhaps especially, in subjects that were deemed "safe". If mirrors can distort, what might Scripture or Art reflect?

The paintings discussed in this article share a truth that is unobtainable in Scripture and yet their message may be deeply theological as, separated from text, they may force us to consider the nature of Scripture and humanity's continuing relationship with it. A different order of criticism is offered in Art. Art operates well beyond the confines of the picture and will of the artists. History may take over and blanket its effects, or

---

[30] Gottfried Boehm, "A New Beginning: Abstraction and the Myth of the 'Zero Hour'", in Marter, *Abstract Expressionism*, p. 101.

Art can be an influence. The recording of an event or the response to a narrative may be an image that expands and complicates the space/text of Scripture. They are not depictions of events nor simple illustrations, but paintings that offer a different hermeneutic of Scripture that may only supply a background narrative. This is the continuing work we are involved in: to examine the gaps in the texts and reveal how art has offered a commentary on them.

3

Rubble and Dust: A Sacrament of Ruins in Art and Theology

Heather Walton

Prologue

My first lecturing position was teaching practical theology at Northern Baptist College in Manchester. We were working with local churches to train ministerial students on an innovative, integrated programme of pastoral placements, theological reflection and community engagement. In many ways, this represented (and still does) my ideal mode of theological education. I gave myself to the work completely. I was up early each day for morning prayers and worked late most nights preparing my lectures. Sundays were spent visiting squat flat-roofed inner-city churches and the little black stone chapels of the neighbouring mill towns and valleys; hearing students preach or leading worship myself.

The work was compelling, but all was not well with me. I was disturbed by what seemed to happen when I brought radical perspectives into the ecclesial domain. They soon blunted and lost their purchase. Worse: I was finding it harder and harder to breathe in church. Too much dust? Was there sufficient ventilation? Were the efforts being made to preserve a different atmosphere inside the sanctuary preventing the free flow of air?

I needed to get out more—not that there was much relief to be found elsewhere. Those were the weary, wasted Thatcher years. All around us the dereliction of poverty and the degradation of communal life were starkly evident. But while we pondered, prayed and sought ways to offer comfort, we did not (yet) allow the ruination around us to emerge as a theological challenge. The heavy wooden doors still held, and we had sandbags to protect us from the flood. But what if the problems that afflicted our local communities were, as I believed, the latest local outworkings of a system that had produced a century of unprecedented violence? What if the evils we had failed to name were gestating future consequences we had not grasped? Was our guarded innocence really foolishness—or willed ignorance? And how could the fabric of the household of faith remain intact when the textile of our social life was being torn apart?

I still worked hard, I remained committed, but I was increasingly anxious that my labours might be misplaced. And then one morning after prayers, when I was lingering in the library with my strong coffee, I came across the journal, *Literature and Theology*, edited by David Jasper. It was everything that my ecclesiastically centred existence was not. It was unapologetically demanding to read, challenging, intellectual and creative. Artists and poets wandered around freely within it—although they would never be found in church. But more important than their seductive presence were the fierce warning blasts of indignation that blew through its pages. The atrocities of the age were named there and their implications for faith acknowledged. The foundations were being shaken and perhaps, very soon, temples would be crashing down. This encounter was a moment in which the trajectory of my life shifted.

I did not abandon ministerial training. To use the old term, it is my calling. But for many years I lived a divided existence. I was a practical theologian, doggedly seeking to resource those who would lead worship, pastor the faithful and maintain the shrines in a creditable working order. And I was also another sort of person entirely to this. One whose heart did not break as the altars were broken. Someone who remembered Jesus's words, "Do you see these great buildings? Not one stone will be left here upon another."[1] A sanctuary-curator who, nevertheless, fully assented to Jasper's assertion that faith in our time requires us to contemplate the dissolution of sacred forms. It entails "bearing to think the unthinkable:

---

[1]   Mark 13:1–2.

embodying … the unbearable so that embodiment and incarnation endures and embraces its own fragmentation and dismemberment".[2]

One of the most characteristic elements of Jasper's work is his affirmation of contraries. This is a cheerful contrariness he carries over into his personal life. He is content to contemplate the death of God and the desolation of religion over dinner with good wine in good company. However, he will then rise early to celebrate the Eucharist and go on to chair the committee on doctrine in the afternoon; stopping on the way home to sit quietly with a person who is sick or suffering in spirit. In his vicinity, it seems unnecessary to worry overmuch about the dissonances in my own discipleship. But acknowledging irreconcilabilities is one thing and theological indolence is quite another. In recent years, I have found myself challenged to carefully consider the implications of Jasper's prolonged insistence that the "unmaking" of theology and Church that takes place through serious encounters with creative making (poesis) is both necessary and now unavoidable.

**Figure 4: Anselm Kiefer *La Résurrection*
(photograph by Jean-Philippe Simard, 2019)**

---

[2] David Jasper, *Rhetoric, Power and Community: An Exercise in Reserve* (London: Macmillan, 1993), p. 161.

In what follows, I shall explore Jasper's challenge in the company of Anselm Kiefer. Kiefer is a provocative artist who figures centrally in Jasper's most "churchy" book: *The Sacred Community*.[3] Kiefer's disturbing but radiant making incarnates many core aspects of Jasper's own vision that through encountering the unthinkable and unbearable we might sense "in the darkness of God . . . a merest trace of a sense at the very end of the fingertips"[4] of what it might mean to be people entrusted with the holy mysteries of mourning and celebrating amidst the rubble and dust.

Betraying

Kiefer was born in Donaueschingen in Germany in 1945. On the night of his birth, the house next door to his own was destroyed in an allied bombing raid and Kiefer grew up playing amongst the ruins. He was aware that a disaster had once taken place but was reassured this was not something that little children these days should worry about. At his school, the war was rarely mentioned and fascism was not discussed. His first memorable confrontation with the concealed reality of the Nazi era occurred when he heard recorded speeches by Goebbels and Goering. These ghastly communications from the recent past assaulted his ears and so affected him that he felt as if their *shock* pierced "right through the skin".[5]

A further "shock" occurred when Kiefer uncovered his father's Nazi uniform in the attic of the family home—together with the rusty bathtub that the Hitler regime had distributed to German households as part of its "hygiene" programme. These relics enforced a realization that the ruins amongst which he dwelled were not simply formed of bricks and stone and broken glass. The intimate domestic life of his family was implicated in the devastation of fascism. His father had worn these clothes. This

---

3　　David Jasper, *Sacred Community* (Waco, TX: Baylor University Press, 2012).

4　　Jasper, *Sacred Community*, p. 13.

5　　Kathleen Soriano, "Building, Dwelling, Thinking", in Kathleen Soriano and Sarah Lee (exhibition curators), *Anselm Kiefer* (London: Royal Academy of Arts, 2014), pp. 20–9, here at p. 22.

was his grandmother's bathtub—she had bathed in it using her favourite lavender soap.

Reflecting on these traumatic incidents Kiefer was later to write, "Art begins in night after an intense experience, a shock. At first it is an urge, a pounding. You don't know what it is but it compels you to act."[6] Out of this pounding two challenges emerged. The first was how to bring the unquiet past into representation; for it is still actively present there in the attic. The second was, if fascism is so entangled in my own origins am I not somehow inextricably implicated in its continuing vitality? In this context there can be no assertion of innocent distance. "I cannot know today," he confesses, "what I would have done at the time . . . That is the explanation of my affliction."[7]

It was by tracing the "fault lines" in his own being that Kiefer's first major, and still most controversial, work emerged. "Occupations"[8] is a series of photographs taken by Kiefer in his early twenties as he travelled through Europe generating multiple images of himself wearing his father's uniform and making a Nazi salute. The work is disturbing on very many levels. To maintain that Kiefer's overriding concern was to confront people with a past that could not be cleanly disposed of and forgotten does little to mitigate either its offence or its challenge. A juvenile bravado (his gestures were illegal in Germany and elsewhere at the time) is evident in the work. However, "Occupations" remains significant. It embodies not only the "shock" of an encounter with a history that is both abjected and concealed but also the artist's (unsought but unavoidable) entanglement in the context, culture and common everyday commerce out of which this history was formed.

Engaging with such challenging art might appear to take us far from the realms of theology and ecclesiology but Jasper would insist otherwise. He maintains that it was the realization that the wounds of twentieth-century history were being neither acknowledged nor addressed which made him urgently seek the company of those literary scholars, theologians, priests

---

6   Soriano, "Building, Dwelling, Thinking", p. 22

7   Kiefer in Dominique Baqué, *Anselm Kiefer: A Monograph* (London: Thames and Hudson, 2015), p. 47.

8   For a discussion of "Occupations", see Baqué, *Anselm Kiefer*, pp. 44–7.

and poets who were exploring relations between art and faith. In the early conferences on "literature and theology" that took place from the early 1980s onwards, the passion to engage with literature was fuelled by many participants' personal experiences of evil—as survivors of the Holocaust or as witnesses to the later horrors of colonial wars and apartheid. In his reflections on these events, Jasper celebrates a litany of the great-souls-now-gone-to-glory who participated in these conferences.[9] They were united, claims Jasper, in their openness to being transformed by what was not being heard in the babble of religious life; what Jasper calls the deep silence of the tragic:

> It was this silence that brooded over our first conference of 1982. We met to talk of theology and literature precisely because of the failure, even the impossibility, of theology, its silence in the face of absolute tragedy . . . That is why we turned to literature.[10]

The turn to literature, in this frame, occurs not as a distraction from "real life" but because what is of most significance is being occluded from conventional discourse. The turn is made not to escape from suffering but "out of great sorrow"[11] that an accommodation has been made with evil in the form of forgetting. For Jasper, this forgetting is not limited to the conflicts of the last century, as he urges us to look behind these to the ancient *Christian* construction of anti-Semitism. Neither does it end with the trauma of these wars. The oppressive banality of contemporary cultural life, which powerfully constrains transformative vision, is also achieved through the anaesthetizing of memory. As Amitav Ghosh has powerfully argued, the "great derangement"[12] of climate change can be

---

[9]   For a full discussion of these events see David Jasper, *Literature and Theology as a Grammar of Assent* (London: Routledge, 2016).

[10] David Jasper, "Being Human in the European Tradition and the Post-Enlightenment Response", in Michel Fuller and David Jasper (eds), Made in the Image of God (Durham: Sacristy Press, 2021), pp. 125–37, here at p. 127.

[11] Jasper, "Being Human", p. 125.

[12] Amitav Ghosh, *The Great Derangement: Climate Change and the Unthinkable* (Chicago, IL: University of Chicago Press, 2016).

interpreted as a disastrous and willed effort to ignore those vital messages from past experiences that offer the means to comprehend current crises. The madness is a failure of re-cognition and our best hope in it lies in discovering the means to re-cognize; that is to "bring to mind" unspeakable histories and "imagine the unthinkable beings and events of this era".[13] For Jasper this happens supremely through the vehicles of art and literature which, as Kiefer claimed, are able to register the profound shocks that both wound and open space for transformative action.

But is it too late for this? In our jaded culture that has lost the capacity for engaging with extremities? And most particularly in the lives of our declining churches? For Jasper there is no merit to be found in denying that the outworn religious speech of our times seems unable to fulfil its vocation to incarnate the divine Word. Or that our religious institutions, still defending their innocence, are profoundly implicated in vicious forms of social injustice and abusive practices that have destroyed so many lives.

Bruno Latour, a major contemporary theorist who, like Jasper, does not flinch from reflecting on the wounds in his religious identity asks: "[What] metamorphosis makes what once had so much meaning become absolutely *meaningless*?"[14] "All together we pray in the shadows of this rubbish tip that's as high as a hill, ready to come streaming over us."[15] However, Jasper's work *The Sacred Community* does not take the recognition of faith's dereliction as the occasion for despair. Yes, he confesses, we believers are also the betrayers of faith. We have been mute witnesses to evil deeds and, compounding our mortal betrayals, so too have the silent heavens. Yet this is not the end. In the same move that Kiefer makes through his art, Jasper takes the recognition of betrayal, of blood at the roots, as the moment of genesis. Indeed, Jasper identifies the Church as a community that is constituted precisely at the moment of betrayal.

For it was on the night when He was being betrayed that He took bread . . .

---

[13]   Ghosh, *The Great Derangement*, p. 33.

[14]   Bruno Latour, *Rejoicing: Or the Torments of Religious Speech*, trans. Julie Rose (Cambridge: Polity, 2013), p. 2.

[15]   Latour, *Rejoicing*, p. 59.

The God Studio

In his major work on Kiefer, Dominique Baqué takes the opportunity to reflect on the significance of the attic in German culture.[16] It recurs in many differing representations. At first it was the place where poor people dwelt in their poverty. Romantics and radicals revisioned these associations and the attic became the location of artists and dissidents, its confined space, "removed", signalling their marginality and repudiation of bourgeois values. The rise of fascism and the events of the war resignified the attic once again as the place in which people hid or sought refuge—silent and separated from the visible social body.[17] Still later the attic (the place where Kiefer encountered his father's uniform and the old bathtub) is the place where dark and still dangerously animate histories exist concealed and waiting.

In 1971, Kiefer moved into the old schoolhouse in Hornbach and established his studio in the attic of the building. This place of rough wooden beams and a sharply sloping roof was reached by climbing a steep staircase and opening a sturdy wooden door. Drawing on the rich associations noted by Baqué, the attic became a key motif in many of Kiefer's works from this time. In what has come to be known as the "Attic Series" this rustic wooden space stages many important scenes. First, the attic becomes a place of rememorialization. Kiefer opposes its humble structure, sheltering to outsiders, to the huge classical monuments and arenas of fascism in which the heroes and myths of the German past were celebrated. Re-presenting these figures and stories through locating them within "the attic", a culturally significant but inglorious context, is a movement towards reclaiming a stained inheritance.[18]

Second, the attic is figured as a place for sacred encounters. Two pictures are particularly important in this regard. The first shows the Holy Trinity imaged as three fires burning (without consuming) on

---

[16]   Baqué, *Anselm Kiefer.*

[17]   Baqué, *Anselm Kiefer*, p. 50.

[18]   See "Germany's Spiritual Heroes", 1973. See also Parsifal I, Parsifal II and Parsifal III (1973).

the wooden floor of the studio.[19] It links artistic inspiration with Moses' revelatory encounter with the burning bush. The second joins these same three fires through a thin red line to a snake on the studio floor.[20] This work displays Kiefer's continuing engagement with the darkness he discovered in the attic and incorporated into his own genesis as an artist. It displays his recognition of the fallenness that constitutes the artist themselves, extends beyond them to the farthest reaches of the cosmos and is inextricably implicated in the divine creative process.[21]

Finally, in later works, the attic becomes a place in which a fire burns with dangerous force. Flames are engulfing the stairs and reaching the studio door. In a particularly striking version of this image, which is painted over a photograph of the entrance to Kiefer's studio, a blood-red fire has taken hold completely.[22] There can be no definitive interpretation of this work but, however it is viewed, the links between creative work and destructive energy are clearly embodied.

In *The Sacred Community*, Jasper reflects deeply on Kiefer's apparently paradoxical portrayal of artistic work as generative, reparative and holy as well as absorbed in what is dangerous and even destroying. For Jasper, the ambivalent work of the artist and, more typically for Jasper, "the poet" (he regularly uses this cipher to refer to all those whose business is the "act of making, or poiesis"[23]) represents nothing less than a participation in divine making. Their creative imaginings are the seeings of things unseen and they bring invisible things to form. However, at the furthest reaches of poetic making they also compel us to consider how forms disintegrate and are again embraced into chaos.

The fire that burns on Kiefer's studio floor represents a claim that the artist stands on holy ground. A space or clearing in which, following Heidegger, Jasper maintains that we are enabled to encounter things not

---

[19] "Father, Son and Holy Ghost" (oil, charcoal and synthetic resin on Burlap) 1973.

[20] "Quaternity" (oil and charcoal on Burlap) 1973.

[21] Kiefer is drawing here upon Jewish Kabbalistic traditions.

[22] "The Painter's Studio" (chalk, graphite pencil, acrylic and oil on photograph), 1980.

[23] Jasper, *Sacred Community*, p. 106.

comprehensible elsewhere.[24] Commenting on Kiefer's use of Kabbalistic symbols to incarnate a cosmology in which divinity withdraws in order to create and in which the uncontainable excess of divine creativity brings the created order to ruin, Jasper celebrates the blessing (or curse) of art which is able to contemplate "the moment of abandonment [as], the moment of creation . . . the moment of formation as the moment of despair".[25] Jasper states:

> Anselm Kiefer . . . describes this moment in this way: "It is the artist's job to imagine the most impossible things. These are not answers. They are just possible entries into hidden things." Thus, the artist calls us to stand before, to stand at, the vanishing point, the community at once in disintegration and fracture and at the same moment entering into the bliss of all creation: the gates of Auschwitz and the gates of heaven—the darkest of all entries into hidden things.[26]

Artists, who share in the transformative creativity witnessed in the birth and death of worlds, perform a function that Jasper, following his beloved Coleridge, argues makes them indispensable to the life of the

---

[24] Jasper states: "James C. Edwards has described such Heideggerian dwelling precisely: To dwell poetically on the earth is to live in awareness of the godhead, the clearing, the blank but lightening sky. It is to live so as to measure oneself against that Nothing—that No-thing—that grants the possibility of the presence of and the Being of the things that there are. Within that clearing, as Heidegger puts it, brightness wars with darkness. There we struggle with particular ignorances and incapacities to bring forth truth." David Jasper, "The Artist and the Mind of God", in David Jasper, Dale Wright, Maria Antonaccio and William Schweiker (eds), *Theological Reflection and the Pursuit of Ideals: Theology, Human Flourishing and Freedom* (Farnham: Ashgate, 2013), pp. 57–172. Jasper, *Sacred Community*, p. 106.

[25] Jasper here is particularly discussing Kiefer's artwork, "Zim Zum", 1990. This title refers to the Kabbalistic understanding that God withdraws Godself in order to enable the creation of the Universe.

[26] Jasper, *Sacred Community*, p. 115.

sacred community. They possess the founding vision of a burning glory "fundamental and anterior to all possible theological articulation".[27] And yet, he states, "the poet is to be feared . . . because the poet alone has returned to the Paradise Garden from which we have been banished" bearing not only knowledge but also death with them.[28] The sacred community must learn that it also is subject to the ruin that runs through all things.

Once again, such complex "poetic" thinking might seem to remove us far from the concerns of contemporary church life. However, a short poetic novel written by a woman whose idiosyncratic and ambivalent Anglicanism bears many resemblances to Jasper's own might help us grasp its implications in more concrete terms. Rose Macaulay lost her partner, her home, all her possessions and her own sense of identity and meaning during the blitz years of the Second World War. In her grief, she found herself drawn to the sites of ruin around St Paul's Cathedral and spent many days wandering through the wrecks of homes, offices and church buildings. These become the setting for her parabolic narrative, *The World My Wilderness*, in which a young woman, Barbary, who has been involved in the French resistance and complicit in many complex processes of bloody betrayal, is sent by her mother to London to become "normal" again and find a conventional place in the "peace time" world.[29] But Barbary's world has grown wild. She finds no place for herself in a context in which people appear determined to carry on as though oblivious to the devastation in their midst. Alienated and unmoored she is particularly drawn to spend her time in the ruined churches "with their towers still strangely spiring above the wilderness . . . all this scarred and haunted green and stone wilderness . . . the margins of the wrecked world".[30]

These churches, with their broken altars and roofless chancels now wide open to the sky, carry huge significance in the novel. They

[27] David Jasper, *Heaven in Ordinary: Poetry and Religion in a Secular Age* (Cambridge: Lutterworth Press, 2018), p. 6.

[28] Jasper, *Heaven in Ordinary*, p. 9.

[29] Rose Macaulay, *The World My Wilderness* (London: Virago, 1983).

[30] Macaulay, *Wilderness*, p. 73.

are mediators of faith broken, as it should be broken, by the betrayals Barbary has witnessed and participated in as well as by the greater betrayals of the post-war world. Yet their brokenness allows the incursion of a wild, stirring life that thrives in the "questionable chaos".[31] A green, creeping, burrowing, blossoming, buzzing life has entered where it was once excluded. In the novel Barbary's desire to be in sacred places where a "clearing" has been made almost destroys her—these ruins are dangerous places. However, claiming the broken churches as her rightful inheritance, and a holy space in which "death in life" and "life in death" are palpably present, also enables her regeneration.

I am particularly struck by one line in the novel. Barbary ponders, "Until you looked [closely] at them and saw they were ruins you would have thought the churches to be going concerns".[32] In many ways, I could echo this phrase in relation to the situation of the Church in contemporary Western culture. But does imaging Church as "ruin" mean the end of faith, the end of Christianity and the dissolution of the sacred community? When I was studying for my doctorate with Jasper as my supervisor, he pressed upon me Michel de Certeau's marvellous work, *The Mystic Fable*.[33] This explores the flowering of mystical Christianity in sixteenth- and seventeenth-century Catholicism, during a period in which the Catholic Church was deeply compromised, fragmented and broken. De Certeau images those spiritual mourners and ecstatics who were drawn to remain amongst the wreckage (in the place of a betrayal) as ruin dwellers: "The mystics do not reject the ruins that surround them. They remain there. They go there ... [to] the locus of a wound."[34] From this unroofed habitation unfamiliar and unexpected forms of spiritual growth emerged that, de Certeau's work suggests, might lead us to contemplate the possibility of generative stirrings within the questionable chaos of our own wreckage.

---

[31] Macaulay, *Wilderness,* p. 254.

[32] Macaulay, *Wilderness,* p. 57.

[33] Michel de Certeau, *The Mystic Fable, vol. 1, The Sixteenth and Seventeenth Centuries,* trans. Michael Smith (Chicago, IL: University of Chicago Press, 1995).

[34] de Certeau, *Mystic Fable,* p. 25.

Art in church

In 2019, an exhibition of Kiefer's work was held in Sainte Marie de la Tourette—a Dominican convent designed by Le Corbusier. In his early twenties, Kiefer had spent several formative weeks living in the community, attending worship, reflecting with the brothers, and seeking to comprehend the artistic vision manifest in Le Corbusier's work. Up to this point, I have considered how art challenges faith to contemplate its own "fragmentation and dismemberment".[35] However, Kiefer's glad return to this sacred place, where worship patterns the hours, and lives are lived in vowed dedication, leads me now to consider how art and religion coincide in seeking a continual commerce between the earthly and the heavenly.[36]

The exhibition at La Tourette was a stunning display of the fruits of Kiefer's lifetime of spiritual journeying through the ruins of faith and culture. It contained many iconic pieces, including exhibits from his Palm Sunday series named after the Christian festival which uniquely combines both celebration and mourning, triumph and tragedy. However, one work in particular forms my focus here. This is titled "Resurrection", and it was installed at the heart of the monastery in the chapel itself. Inge Linder-Gaillard describes the dramatic effect of encountering the work in this location:

> It is ... [met] in the church, in the space between the high altar
> and the east wall where a red screen, a sculptural gesture by Le
> Corbusier, signals the Passion. A field of petal-less sunflowers
> stand heavy with seed on a terrain of ruins. These plaster-covered

---

[35] Jasper, *Rhetoric*, p. 161.

[36] Wessel Stoker quotes Kiefer as saying, "The palette represents the idea of the heaven and earth. He works here but he looks up there. moving between the two realms ... the palette can transform reality suggesting new visions." Wessel Stoker, "Can Heaven Bear the Weight of History? The 'Spirituality of Concrete' in the Work of Anselm Kiefer", *Literature and Theology* 24:4 (2010), pp. 397–410, here at p. 397.

rods looming over four meters high seem to burst through broken
slabs of concrete that in fact hold them up.[37]

The giant sunflowers, held erect on long metal rods (typical of those
used to strengthen concrete constructions), are real seed heads covered
in plaster that petrifies their organic properties and unites them with
the ruins out of which they rise. It also bonds them with the concrete of
Le Corbusier's design. The walls and floor of the chapel and the great
slabs of the altar share the same colour and the same unyielding material
qualities. But what do these stone sunflowers that, despite their solid
stems, strain under the weight of their seeds, represent in Kiefer's spiritual
economy?

Kiefer has been painting and sculpting sunflowers for many years
and their associations are many. They are, firstly, a personal tribute to
his beloved Van Gogh and through him to the artists whose vocation is
the vivid and disturbing expression of spiritual visions. Second, they are
part of Kiefer's artistic translation of the alchemical thinking of the British
cosmological visionary, Robert Fludd (1574–1637). Fludd envisioned an
integral relation between the diverse figures of the trinitarian Godhead
and the cosmos emerging out of its chaos into multiple interacting forms.
Kiefer is particularly fascinated by Fludd's conviction that sacred threads
of connection holding all things together serve to co-join microcosmos
with macrocosmos; the flowers of earth to the heavenly bodies; the
sunflower seeds to the shining stars.[38] Each of these are caught up
together into a sacred spectacle that comprehends all things. Third, and
perhaps most significantly in relation to "Resurrection", the installation

---

[37] Inge Linder-Gaillard, "Anselm Kiefer at La Tourette" (2019), <https://go.gale.
      com/ps/i.do?p=LitRC&u=googlescholar&id=GALE%7CA616516402&v=2
      .1&it=r&sid=LitRC&asid=6f4cfb59>, accessed 17 March 2022.

[38] Stoker writes, "When Kiefer began to work with sunflowers, he saw a
      parallel between the black seeds in the flower and the night with its stars. He
      borrowed this parallel from . . . Fludd who pointed to a connection between the
      microcosmos and the macrocosmos and thus to a relationship between stars
      and plants . . . and between humankind and the cosmos. According to Fludd
      every plant has a corresponding star". "Can Heaven Bear", here at p. 403.

affirms the fundamental link between ruins and renewal; as Kiefer states, "Rubble is like the blossom of a plant ... It is the radiant high point of an incessant mechanism, the beginning of a rebirth."[39] In this frame, it is not that the fruitfulness of the sunflower heads transcends the ruination out of which they have emerged. Rather the seed heads are themselves sites of ruin—yet ruins "where hope is possible".[40] They are the glory of the flower transforming into a different substance. "This is the most triumphant saddest moment," Kiefer states. "They die and the flower becomes an urn for the seeds."[41]

Persistently and variously throughout his oeuvre Kiefer seeks to point towards the coincidence of destruction and regeneration within the spheres he represents. We might imagine that Kiefer is reaching through the devastation that Walter Benjamin famously described as history's catastrophe "which keeps piling wreckage",[42] towards something that is both integral and anterior to this. Kiefer himself asserts that he creates his images "to show what lies behind history. I make a hole and I go through".[43] His works are thus torn open and within them forms mutate and crumble away. Richard Davey names the realm brought into vision here as that of the "chaos that existed before the creation of the world ... [manifested] in the visual poetry of rubble and dust that inspires us to wonder rather than despair".[44] He further claims that Kiefer's art is sacramental, "constantly opening us to creative 'clearings' ... places of new beginnings and possibilities. Like the Spirit hovering over the waters of creation."[45]

As a sacrament is also the way in which Père Marc of La Tourette describes experiencing "Resurrection". He maintains that it mirrors in

[39] Richard Davey, "In the beginning is the end and in the end is the beginning", in Soriano and Lee, *Anselm Kiefer*, pp. 48–67, here at p. 49.

[40] Stoker, "Can Heaven Bear", p. 404.

[41] Stoker, "Can Heaven Bear", p. 404.

[42] Walter Benjamin, "Theses on the Philosophy of History", in *Illuminations* (New York: Schocken Books, 1968), pp. 253–64, here at p. 257.

[43] Baqué, *Anselm Kiefer*, p. 41.

[44] Davey, "In the beginning", p. 54.

[45] Davey, "In the beginning", p. 64.

art what the brothers perform through prayer as they gather each day between the altar and the sunflowers to celebrate the Eucharist.[46] This returns me to the work of Jasper and his reflections on the Church. Born at the moment of betrayal, forever broken and compromised, the Church displays its brokenness for all to see. Indeed, its wounds are perhaps most visible to the ruin dwellers themselves. As Jasper writes, our communities are "disintegrating and collapsing inwards on themselves".[47] "One cannot but be aware of the failings of those institutions which one loves most dearly".[48] And yet.

As I have sought to show in this chapter, Jasper's thinking on the sacred community engages in a profound dialogue with Kiefer's work because their spiritual visions are in many ways harmonious. Like Kiefer, Jasper, tutored by the "something of the pantheist"[49] Coleridge, perceives God in all things and encounters the divine in what appear to be irreconcilable experiences of bliss and horror that return us to the chaos which is the origin of all things. He affirms "the sense of divine unity in creation perceived in the life of words . . . and in the interweaving of images often in profound contradiction. You can be in heaven and hell at the same moment, and in a moment that is also outside time."[50]

Furthermore, Jasper's eucharistic vision does not focus, with common priestly conceit, upon the actions of one person at the altar but rather upon the ruined and broken people, the betrayers and betrayed, who gather in the clearing between seed heads and concrete slabs on earth and in heaven, in time and beyond it, to sing out the Sanctus: Holy, Holy, Holy. This is his vision of sacrament, of sacred community and indeed of resurrection itself. It entails acknowledging the silence of the utterly tragic and dwelling in the clearing this forms within the silence and without voice. There it happens. Jasper quotes Thomas Altizer:

---

[46]   Linder-Gaillard, "Anselm Kiefer at La Tourette".

[47]   Jasper, *Heaven in Ordinary*, p. 141.

[48]   Jasper, *Heaven in Ordinary*, p. 2.

[49]   Jasper, *Heaven in Ordinary*, p. 51.

[50]   Jasper, *Heaven in Ordinary*, p. 51.

The real ending of speech is the dawning of resurrection, and the final ending of speech is the dawning of a total present actuality. That actuality is immediately at hand when it is heard, and it is heard when it is enacted. And it is enacted in the dawning of the actuality of silence, an actuality ending all disembodied and unspoken presence. Then speech is truly impossible, and as we hear and enact that impossibility, then even we can say, "It is finished".[51]

We can join and say, Holy, Holy, Holy.

This vision can, of course, be phrased prosaically—and sometimes Jasper does speak more conventionally about the regenerative potential emerging out of institutional "rot"[52] and "the need repeatedly, to bring the community to a place of new birth from the ashes of the old, with eyes wide open to the contemporary, in memory of the past, and in firm and hopeful anticipation of that which is to come".[53] However, I cannot help but feel that the practical obligations required to address the challenges of renewal are not his chief concern. There will be those who seek to buttress what has become unstable, there will be others who seek to rebuild what is broken and even those who are able to imagine what might emerge in quite different forms out of our questionable chaos. Jasper, I think, stands with Kiefer, pointing us to that place of wonder where the altars crack and inciting us to a different kind of faith beyond this. Both expect that the falling of the temples will, *of itself,* call forth the architecture of the beginning. Kiefer describes the uncertain birth that is taking place among the ruins: "The end is the beginning—there is nothing more than residue. The beginning stumbles, it stumbles because of the many ruins, its impetus is constantly being interrupted. It tries to rebuild itself from what remains. From the relics."[54]

And, yes it does.

---

[51] Jasper, *Sacred Community,* p.110, quoting Thomas J. J. Altizer, *The Self-Embodiment of God* (San Francisco: Harper & Row, 1977), p. 96.

[52] Jasper, *Sacred Community*, p. 162.

[53] Jasper, *Sacred Community*, p. 153.

[54] Baqué, *Anselm Kiefer*, p. 272.

It does so.

It stumbles through the ruins of genesis into the passion of resurrection, which is the drama played out everywhere, in all things and everything, and in which the beloved and broken sacred community plays its own stumbling part.

Postscript

Kiefer uses many sunflowers in his art, attached to his pictures, included in collages and transformed into sculptures. The flowers are ubiquitously present; bending their heavy heads laden with seeds. But these sunflowers are not simply mystical symbols of death and rebirth. They are the remains of real plants. Kiefer grew them himself with seeds saved from the last flowering. Towering fields of sunflowers, metres high, planted each springtime in the grounds of his studio.[55] Golden, orange, amber, burnt ochre in the sunlight. Dark as the night under the stars. Tall, dry stalks each winter. Seeds for the birds. This is the sacrament of art.

In the last chapter of his book on the sacred community, Jasper turns from his discussions of art and poetry, ecclesiastical tragedy and transformation, from the "vast ... to the everyday",[56] to reflect upon a simple pastoral visit described by the poet-priest, David Scott.[57] Scott enters the house where a son has died on a parish visit. He has nothing to bring with him that will ease the loss, there are no texts that will comfort or explanations that can be offered. So he sits—empty—beside the mother as the fire in the grate becomes glowing ashes. Jasper links this precious, pastoral self-emptying, which he himself has undergone, to all that he has said before. Here on the rag hearth rug is the clearing that must be made for absolute tragedy. Here before the dying flames heaven and hell are acknowledged and something is being born. This common "act of care" comprehends everything about "being before the

---

55   This studio is located in Barjac, France.

56   Jasper, *Sacred Community*, p.159.

57   Jasper, *Sacred Community*, p. 160.

saving mystery".[58] Holding empty cups two people share in the sacrament through which "the sacred community of the Eucharist, like Isaiah of old, sees the glory of the Lord—the vision that prompts its endless hymn of praise".[59]

---

[58]   Jasper, *Sacred Community*, p. 160.
[59]   Jasper, *Sacred Community*, p. 172.

4

Abdiel—Or the Faithful Found in *Paradise Lost*

Tibor Fabiny

The end of institutional church in the emerging post-Christian culture in the third millennium might be a shocking reality to be lamented. But this is perhaps not entirely unexpected if one recalls the words of Jesus in the Gospel: "When the Son of Man comes, will he find faith on earth?" (Luke 18:8). The sixteenth-century reformers believed that, just as God is *deus absconditus*, so his church is *ecclesia abscondita*, as real saints are frequently hidden. With this essay, I invite the reader to find a hidden figure in Milton's *Paradise Lost*: an example of faithfulness and courage in the midst of a demonic world.

Who is the real hero of *Paradise Lost*? In the past centuries, various answers have been given. A traditional view is that the protagonist may be God or Adam. Since William Blake's famous dictum, "Milton was of the devil's party without knowing it," readers have enthusiastically followed the Romantics' fascination with the figure of Satan, claiming that it is neither God nor Adam but Satan who is the real hero of the epic. Marxist authors such as Christopher Hill have interpreted the figure of Satan as the mirror of Milton's own gigantic but frustrated struggle for freedom against the tyranny of traditional oppressive royalism and episcopacy, thus suggesting that Milton himself may be the real hero of his own epic.[1]

---

[1] Christopher Hill, *Milton and the English Revolution* (London: Faber; New York: Viking, 1977).

Stanley Fish's reader-response criticism offers the new argument that the real hero of *Paradise Lost* is the reader, whom Milton not only addresses but includes within the epic.[2] Fish argues that Milton aims to transform the reader by upholding, rewriting, and re-preaching the biblical message and his project of theodicy, thereby "justifying the ways of God to men".

However, if we consider *Paradise Lost* as a huge tapestry or a pictorial canvas, the so-called "real hero" should not necessarily be searched for only in the centre of the artistic composition, but also on the periphery. Applying this broader lens, I will argue that the "real hero" of *Paradise Lost* is the seemingly marginal, episodical figure of the angel Abdiel, who appears briefly in Books V and VI. Abdiel is not one of the great archangels such as Raphael, who is sent by the Father to admonish the yet unfallen Adam and Eve about the existence of their enemy and the danger of their temptation. Nor is Abdiel like Michael, the other significant archangel: the hero of the war in heaven and the one whom God sends to the postlapsarian couple to show them the consequence of their disobedience. Michael shows Adam both the tragic future of mankind and their chance of regaining "a paradise within", if they grasp the meaning and the effects of their restoration through the redemptive work of the Son.

I should clarify what I mean by the "real hero" of a literary work of art. For me, the real hero is not the most elaborate or even the most majestic character. On the contrary, one should be suspicious if a character dominates others by its mere presence, format or power. Our human senses very often cheat us into considering "great" what seems to be great only to our—perhaps—deceived, if not fallen, perception. Greatness can often be hidden in minute things. Beauty, glory is often hidden under the opposite of its appearance. Perhaps what a majority judges "perverse" (*PL* VI.37) is in fact true, real and beautiful.[3] As a proverb says, "The

---

2   Stanley Fish, *Surprised by Sin: The Reader in Paradise Lost*, Second Edition with a New Preface [1st edn 1967] (Cambridge, MA: Harvard University Press, 1997), p. 1.

3   References to *Paradise Lost* are taken from Alastair Fowler (ed.), *John Milton, Paradise Lost*, 2nd edn [1st edn 1968] (London and New York: Longman, 1997).

will of the majority if not necessarily the will of God". A hero may be quite "real", even in a fleeting appearance, because he/she has a striking, revelatory function and exerts a lasting impact on the reader, however short this actual presence is in the flow of the narrative. A hero is, in my interpretation, perhaps like a "star", though definitely not as in a modern popular register but in its original literal sense. For Shakespeare, love is such a star as it appears in Sonnet 116: "It is an ever-fixed mark . . . never shaken . . . the star to every wand'ring barque".[4]

Interestingly, two centuries after Shakespeare, the American religious thinker Jonathan Edwards (1703–58) in his rightly celebrated *Religious Affections* (1746) made a graphic distinction between hypocritical Christians who "are like comets, that appear for a while with a mighty blaze; but are very unsteady and irregular in their motion"[5] and the real stars. Says Edwards:

> [T]he true saints are like the fixed stars which, though they rise
> and set, and are often clouded, yet are steadfast in their orb, and
> may truly be said to shine with a constant light.[6]

This chapter explores Abdiel's hidden centrality in Milton's epic and argues that, with his steadfastness, he is ultimately the real hero of *Paradise Lost*.

4   William Shakespeare, Sonnet 116, lines 6–7. In Stanley Wells and Gary Taylor (eds) *The Oxford Shakespeare: The Complete Works* (Oxford: Clarendon Press, 1994). p. 765.
5   Jonathan Edwards, *Religious Affections* [First publication 1746], in John E. Smith (ed.), *The Works of Jonathan Edwards*, vol. 2 (New Haven, CT: Yale University Press, 1959), p. 373.
6   Edwards, *Religious Affections*, p. 374.

Satan's reaction to the elevation and
the anointing of the Son

Though Abdiel appears in Raphael's description of the war in heaven in Book V, Satan's reaction to the elevation of the Son is the first step to our understanding Abdiel's later role after the war as the first and most important foil to Satan. The chronology of the plot's major conflict in *Paradise Lost* begins with the elevation and the anointing of the Son as vicegerent by the Father in Heaven. This "exaltation" scene echoes Psalm 2:6–7 and Hebrews 1:5:

> This day I have begot whom I declare
> My only Son, and on this holy hill
> Him have anointed, whom ye now behold
> At my right hand; your head I him appoint;
> And by myself have sworn to him shall bow
> All knees in heaven, and shall confess him Lord. (V.603–8)

While the angels celebrate this solemn decree with harmonious "mystical dance" (V.620), Satan, who was the "first archangel", is "fraught / With envy" (V.661–2). His pride is hurt because he feels that his so far privileged status is undermined by the "new laws" (V.679, 680) of the Father.

Satan's essence is imitation and deception: just as the Father was elevating the Son on a "flaming mount" (V.598), Satan was also ascending a mount, "Affecting all equality with God / In imitation of that mount whereon / Messiah was declared in sight of heaven . . . ", "Pretending so commanded to consult . . . with calumnious Art / Of counterfeited truth thus held their ears." (V.764–71).

Satan's first speech

The Father's joyful and rhetorically majestic elevation of his Son occupies fifteen lines: "Hear all ye angels . . . without end" (V.600–15). It is formally imitated by Satan's address to his followers: "Thrones, dominations, princedoms, virtues, powers . . . not to serve" (V.772), but this speech is its subversion, inciting revolution and disobedience. The Father's command that "to Him [the Son] shall bow / All knees in heaven" (V.607–8) irritates Satan because he is unable to understand the integrative unity the Father envisaged: "Him who disobeys / Me disobeys, breaks union" (V.611–12), and Satan hears only threat in the voice of the Father. These very words, in the absence of the good will of obedience, literally provoke and bring forth his anger and rebellion.

We have seen that Satan had interpreted this proclamation as a "new law" (which means that it was the Father who changed the original order). Myers rightly notes that here "Satan draws on the assumption . . . that antiquity is a sign of truth and novelty is a sign of error.[7] Moreover, the "one" "doubled" himself in the Son, which means that the angels should bend not only their necks but also their knees. This appears a "yoke" to Satan which, he suggests, they should cast off. Satan appeals to their original free state, their status of liberty and equality on account of their heavenly nature. Originally, as he sees it, they were equals, "if in power and splendour less" (V.796). If law and "Monarchy" are imposed upon them, this means an arbitrary violation of the original order in which they were meant only to rule and not to serve.

Abdiel's appearance and his first speech

At Satan's moment of defiance Abdiel, one of the seraphim, stood up to oppose him:

---

[7]   Benjamin Myers, *Milton's Theology of Freedom* (Berlin and New York: Walter de Gruyter, 2006), p. 57.

Thus far his bold discourse without control
Had audience, when among the seraphim
Abdiel, than whom none with more zeal adored
The Deity, and divine commands obeyed,
Stood up, and in a flame of zeal severe
The current of his fury thus opposed. (V.803–8)

Who is Abdiel? He is the "humblest of angels" as Stella Revard has called him.[8] But there have been critics who have seen him as Milton himself.[9] Stanley Fish notes in a somewhat ironic reference to other critics, "In terms of the distinction between the epic heroism and Christian heroism, he is too easy to admire. (The fault of course is the observer's, not his.)"[10] Francis S. Blessington argued that Abdiel's figure proceeds from the classical epic convention of the "epic malcontent", whose function is to oppose the hero, in our case, Satan. Blessington compares Abdiel to Thersites in Homer's *Iliad*, who opposes Agamemnon by reminding him of the hierarchy. Blessington finds that "Milton changed the tradition so that the malcontent is the true hero who opposes the heroic code with the humility of Christianity".[11]

Abdiel's name, unlike Raphael's or Michael's, does not appear in the Bible. The only biblical instance of the name Abdiel is in 1 Chronicles 5:15, where he is said to be the ancestor of the Gadites. Abdiel's name means the "servant of God", and the seraphim are often pictured with flames. In the above quotation Milton uses four verbs to indicate Abdiel's nature: (1) he adored the Deity with more zeal than anybody else; (2) he obeyed the divine commands; (3) he stood up in a flame of zeal; (4) he opposed Satan with fury.

[8] Stella P. Revard, *The War in Heaven: Paradise Lost and the Tradition of Satan's Rebellion* (Ithaca, NY and London: Cornell University Press, 1980), p. 241.

[9] Perez Zagorin, *Milton: Aristocrat and Rebel: The Poet and his Politics* (Woodbridge and Rochester, NY: Brewer, 1992), p. 128.

[10] Fish, *Surprised by Sin*, p. 182.

[11] Francis C. Blessington, "Abdiel and Epic Poetry", *Milton Quarterly* 10/4 (1976), pp. 108–13, here at p. 109.

One chapter in Milton's *Christian Doctrine* (Bk II. Ch. VI) is devoted
to Zeal. It is defined there as follows:

> an eager desire to sanctify the divine name, together with a
> feeling of indignation against things which tend to the violation
> or contempt of religion.[12]

Abdiel calls Satan blasphemous (V.809) because he dares to condemn the
just decree of God, which was to claim and "confess" the Son "rightful
king" (V.817). Abdiel argues that Satan is false in saying that law is an
alternative to freedom. He points out his inner contradiction: Satan
wants to give God law to limit his freedom: "Shalt thou give law to God,
shalt thou dispute / With him the points of liberty, who made / Thee what
thou art" (V.822–4). Abdiel appeals to experience in arguing that God,
rather than desiring to make them less, wants to exalt their "happy state
under one head more near / United." (V.829–30). He also appeals to God
as their Creator and "the begotten son" (V.535)—as they are joined united
by degree "under one head" (V.830, 842). The last argument is pragmatic
common sense: "All honour to him done / Returns our own" (V.844–5),
which means that by blessing the Father and the Son, reciprocally they
are also being blessed.

We must see that however passionate and fierce Abdiel's first speech
is, it is first of all a voice of warning or admonishing. Abdiel finishes this
speech on a pastoral note, imploring the rebels to repent, assuring them
that they will find pardon:

> Cease then this impious rage,
> And tempt not these; but hasten to appease
> The incensed Father, and the incensed Son,
> While pardon may be found in time besought. (V.845–9)

---

[12] John Hale and Donald Cullington (eds), *De Doctrina Christiana, The
Complete Works of John Milton,* 8 vols (Oxford: Oxford University Press,
2012).

While keeping this unexpectedly gentle pastoral voice in our minds, we shall see that after Satan's hard verbal response, Abdiel will have to abandon this pastoral register for a harsh, prophetic condemnation.

Satan's reply

The "haughty" and "apostate" Satan's reply is sarcastic: he first denies the fact the angels were created ("strange point of view" V.855) and contemptuously dismisses the idea that this act of creation was the "work of secondary hands", "by task transferred / From Father to his son?" (V.854–5). Satan claims that no one can remember creation and thus they were "self-begot, self-raised" (V.860). He acknowledges only a blind and "fatal course" of circulation, a theory that C. S. Lewis considers to be "ridiculous and incoherent".[13] If they were not created, then, says Satan, "Our puissance is our own, our right hand / Shall teach us highest deeds by proof to try / Who is our equal" (V.864–6). Instead of "beseeching", they declare war by "besieging" (V.869).

Theological excursus 1: Abdiel the "Confessor"

In the quoted lines 805–8, two of the four expressions ("stood up"; "opposed") give a special Christian, even a Protestant, flavour to the identity of Abdiel which I would label as "confessor". I think this is a better term than Danielson's idea that Milton considers Abdiel the "first Christian commentator and apologist".[14] We should, though, clarify who a confessor is and when we should speak about the situation of the so-called *status confessionis*.

The twentieth-century Protestant theologian Karl Barth (1886–1968) in his *Church Dogmatics* argued that confession appears "when a man

---

13   C. S. Lewis, *A Preface to Paradise Lost* [1st edn 1942] (Oxford: Oxford University Press, 1984), p. 77.

14   Dennis Richard Danielson, *Milton's Good God: A Study in Literary Theodicy* (Cambridge: Cambridge University Press, 1982), p. 222.

realizes that his faith, or rather the faith of the Christian community, is confronted and questioned either from within or without by the phenomena of unbelief, superstition and heresy. Confession occurs when it is given to this man to lodge a protest against these with his word."[15] Barth adds: "Confession is always a protest against the utterance of a false faith that contradicts the glory of God. It is always a partial moment in the history between God and man in which the divine YES is set against the human NO, the divine truth against the human lie, the light of this truth against man's obscuring of it, its totality against the mass of human error which consists supremely in half and quarter and eighth of truths".[16]

Barth, who authored the famous *Barmen Declaration* in protest against the false theology of the Hitler-supporting "Deutsche Christen" in Germany in 1934, knew from personal experience that confession needs an extraordinary courage from the confessor, as he has to speak up "against the grain". *Status confessionis* is a situation where the integrity of Christian faith is seen to be endangered. In such a situation, the confessor is captive to his conscience, he "cannot do otherwise", even if he has to "stand alone", despised and mocked by others. For the sake of truth, he has to remain unpopular, or "out of season" (V.850) as Milton describes how Abdiel is seen by others. If somebody alone speaks out against a majority, he exposes himself as vulnerable and remains in isolation. Confessing is witnessing. The Greek word for witness is martyr: the confessor who dies for his belief is called martyr.

Confession, however, is not mere oppositionalism. Confession always begins by the zeal of affirmation ("we affirm") and it is only the second sentence which is opposition or rejection ("we condemn"). This was also the way the 1934 *Barmen Declaration* was structured. This is why Milton first stresses Abdiel's attitude of zeal, adoration and obedience. Opposition is only a consequence of faith in, and love of God. Opposition is, therefore, often furious, but passionate rhetoric should not cover up the logic and the reason of the argument.

---

[15]   Karl Barth, *Church Dogmatics* III/4 (London and New York: T. & T. Clark, 1936–1975), pp. 78–9.

[16]   Barth, *Church Dogmatics* III/4, p. 80.

Abdiel the prophet—Abdias?

Satan's blind and blunt response needs no comment. From this time on there is no place for admonition or appealing to God's pardon. With these words Satan alienates himself from God for good; his damnation is sealed. The so far passionate but pastoral Abdiel turns into a woe-telling Old Testament prophet. The prophet is a seer who predicts the harsh future not because has a supernatural power but because he knows the consequences of the choice of the created being. The powerful words of Abdiel's farewell not only echo images of Shakespeare's *Richard II* (II. iv.19) or the words of the Chorus at the end of Marlowe's *Doctor Faustus*, but also of a peculiar minor Old Testament prophet:

> O alienate from God, O spirit accursed,
> Forsaken of all good; I see thy fall
> Determined, and thy hapless crew involved
> In this perfidious fraud, contagion spread
> Both of thy crime and punishment: henceforth
> No more be troubled how to quit the yoke
> Of God's Messiah; those indulgent laws
> Will not now be vouchsafed, other decrees
> Against thee are gone forth without recall;
> That golden sceptre which thou didst reject
> Is now an iron rod to bruise and break
> Thy disobedience. Well thou didst advise,
> Yet not for thy advise or threats I fly
> These wicked tents devoted, least the wrath
> Impendent, raging into sudden flame
> Distinguish not: for soon expect to feel
> His thunder on thy head, devouring fire.
> Then who created thee lamenting learn,
> When who can uncreate thee thou shalt know. (V.875–95)

The above speech is more than a soliloquy of a faithful servant of God: it is in fact a prophecy. It was George W. Whiting who made the thought-provoking claim "that Abdiel is in fact Abdias, one of the minor prophets, and that Milton adopted and adapted the name of Abdias and his prophecy against Edom, altering both to suit his purpose".[17]

Abdias is the Greek form of the Hebrew Obadiah, and it also means the servant of God. The prophecy of Obadiah constitutes the shortest book of the Old Testament, containing only twenty-one verses. This prophecy, like that of Isaiah, is announced as a "vision" and has two distinct parts: a judgement upon Edom (descendants of Esau) for their share in the humiliation of Judah by the Babylonians in 586/7 BCE (Obadiah 1–16) and prophecy about the deliverance of the faithful (the descendants of Jacob) on the day of the Lord (Obadiah 17–21). Edom's sin is in fact almost identical with the sin of Milton's Satan: "Your proud heart has deceived you . . . Though you soar aloft like the eagle, though your nest is set among the stars, from there I will bring you down" (Obadiah 3–4). These words echo Jeremiah 49:15–16. Both the prophecy of Abdias and that of Abdiel predict the spectacular downfall of arrogance, whether it be Edom's or Satan's or both. Whiting's conclusion is that Milton "raised Abdias' oracle from the historical or legendary to the absolute and spiritual plane. He converted the Hebraic prophecy of vengeance upon a specific tribe (Edom, implacable enemies of Israel and type of the world, the flesh and the devil) into the servant Seraph's prophecy of the doom of Satan and his rebels".[18] Confessors are prophets, thus Whiting's perception makes sense.

The "faithful found" and free will fulfilled: Abdiel as example of steadfast faith

So spake the Seraph Abdiel faithful found,
Among the faithless, faithful only he;
Among innumerable false, unmoved,
Unshaken, unseduced, unterrified
His loyaltie he kept, his love, his zeal;

---

[17]   George Whiting, "Abdiel and the Prophet Abdias" *Studies in Philology* 60/2 (1963), pp. 214–26, here at p. 215.

[18]   Whiting, "Abdiel and the Prophet Abdias", p. 225.

ABDIEL

65

Nor number, nor example with him wrought
To swerve from truth, or change his constant mind
Though single. From amidst them forth he passed,
Long way through hostile scorn, which he sustained
Superior, nor of violence feared aught;
And with retorted scorn his back he turned
On those proud Towrs to swift destruction doomed. (V.896–907)

Book V ends with Raphael's summary of Abdiel's nature: "Among the faithless, faithful only he ... Unmoved, unshaken, unseduced, unterrified" (V.897, 899). He was the one "who kept loyalty", who had a "constant mind"; "Nor number, nor example with him wrought / To swerve from truth" (V.901–2).

Though scholars, fascinated by the figure of Satan as their real hero, have overlooked or diminished the dramatic role of Abdiel, for Milton and his reader Abdiel is the alternative way to Satan's behaviour. Mason Tung is entirely right in suggesting that "the Abdiel episode, therefore, is instrumental in substantiating the positive alternative that angels are free to stand, even at times when they are almost under overwhelming pressure to fall ... Abdiel acts as a foil to Satan".[19]

Abdiel's figure is crucial for Milton to justify his views on freedom; humankind's own responsibility for choosing to stand fast by remaining steadfast, or falling, i.e., letting themselves be moved by a pressure coming either from the demonic world above, or from the *Zeitgeist* of the outside world or culture, or from a hidden and repressed impulse within.

In the heavenly divine council between the "immutable" (III.373) Father and the Son in Book III, the Father reveals his theology of free will, which is valid for both the celestial and earthly beings:

I made him [the human creation] just and right,
Sufficient to have stood, though free to fall.
Such I created the ethereal powers
And spirits, both them who stood, and them who failed;

[19] Mason Tung, "The Abdiel Episode: A Contextual Reading", *Studies in Philology* 62/4 (1965), pp. 595–609, here at p. 599.

Freely they stood who stood, and fell who fell . . .
I formed them free, and free they must remain
Till they enthrall themselves . . . (III.98–102; 124–5)

In Milton's view, neither angels nor humans can blame God for their fall. There is only one alternative for them: either they remain obedient, true and faithful and "stand fast"; or, by being "self-tempted", "self-depraved" (III.130) they disobey, let themselves be lured and become "self-enthralled" (VI.181); i.e., they are "moved". Either remaining "immutable", "unmoved" by all the tempting pressures coming either from without or from within—or "yielding" (like Macbeth) to the magic suggestion, they let themselves be tempted, enthralled, moved—and fall. Boone is right to argue that "in a sense, Abdiel and Satan represent the two extremes of free will pertinent to the characters in *Paradise Lost*—the freedom to absolutely obey, versus the freedom to absolutely rebel . . . freedom itself is the central issue of Satan and Abdiel's debate, that is, to distinguish a 'freedom to' (Abdiel) versus a 'freedom from' (Satan)."[20]

Abdiel returns to heaven and to the Father who welcomes him: "Servant of God, well hast thou fought / The better fight" (echoing both Matthew 25:21: "Well done good and trustworthy slave" and 2 Timothy 4:7: "I have fought the good fight, I have finished the race, I have kept the faith") he praises him, "for this was all thy care / To stand approv'd in sight of God, though Worlds / Judg'd thee perverse . . ." (VI.30, 35–7).

These words make it clear that from a divine perspective the necessity to "fight" (in the Pauline sense) is encoded into the very nature of existence, and the criterion in the final judgement, both for angels and humans, is whether they were able to "endure", stand, remain firm or steadfast. No wonder that the motifs of "enduring" "overcoming" and "winning" are so frequently used in the apocalyptic passages of the New Testament, in the Gospels: "But anyone who endures to the end will be saved" (Matthew 24:13), and especially in the Book of Revelation

---

[20]   Randy Boone, *God-Like, or Ungodly? An analysis of Pluto and Proserpine marriage in Chaucer's Merchant's Tale*, unpublished dissertation (Bethlehem, PA: Lehigh Preserve, 1993), p. 53. <http://preserve.lehigh.edu/cgi/viewcontent.cgi?article=1174&context=etd>, accessed 13 July 2022.

(Revelation 2:11; 2:26; 3:5; 3:12; 3:21; 5:5; 6:2; 21:7). No wonder that the Greek word for enduring (*hüpomoneo*) is translated into Hungarian as "állhatatos"—"persistent" or "steadfast". God's people will be tried, will have tribulation, but the "faithful" (Greek *pistos*) will receive the crown of life (II.10). Abdiel's opposition, conflict and ultimate standing (*hüpomone*) is a dramatic condensation of the life of God's own people; for Milton definitely this attitude is the prototype of the real Christian. As a critic remarks, "Abdiel 'wins' due to his faith in entrusting God's will within himself and his own action . . . Abdiel represents everything that is most virtuous to Christians: obedience to God, faith, devotion through thought and deed, and humility."[21]

Abdiel is an "example" or type (in the sense of *typokoi* in 1 Corinthians 10) of the possibility of standing fast, while Satan remains a negative warning for Adam and Eve as well as for Milton's reader: do not transgress like Satan! However grandiose the figure Satan is in Milton, however peripheral or episodic is Abdiel's role in the plot, only at first sight is Abdiel a lonely figure in the Miltonic panorama. Mason Tung is again right that "we are impressed by Milton's fondness for and preoccupation with the idea of 'one just man' standing fast in the midst of tempting corruption".[22]

Abdiel as type of the "one faithful" (Enoch, Noah, Moses, Phineas, Elijah, Jesus)

The inherent biblical symbolism of figural interpretation or typology of Scripture, as well as of salvation history, is a dominant mode in Milton's *Paradise Lost*. The "type", or "figure" of the "one just man" always emerges in the dramatic moments when history is doomed to damnation. In Michael's visionary panorama of human history in Books XI and XII, Enoch is such a figure, "the only righteous in a world perverse" (XI.701). Noah is a similar figure. Goldman quotes a Midrash added to the Noah story, which suggested that "the antediluvian generation chided Noah,

---

[21] Boone, *God-Like or Ungodly*, pp. 60–1.
[22] Tung, *The Abdiel Episode*, p. 106.

mocking him for his steadfast loyalty to God but he, alone in the world, persisted adamantly and vociferously in his warnings that the iniquitous repent or suffer God's wrath".[23]

Some further biblical types could be added. Another critic compares the flight of Abdiel (V.888–92) to the attitude of Moses who was "urging the Jews to abandon the blasphemous rebels Korah, Dathan, and Abiram with the words, 'Depart from the tents of these wicked men, lest ye be consumed in all their sins' (Numbers 16:26)."[24] In Numbers we read about Phineas being praised by God, as he "hath turned my wrath away from the Children of Israel, while he was zealous for my sake among them ..." (Numbers 25:11).[25] The most striking similarity is between Abdiel and the prophet Elijah. Amidst the apostate Ahab and Jezebel and their four hundred priests of Baal, only Elijah remains the prophet of the Lord (1 Kings 18:22). "Alone and unattended, before the eyes of all the people, Elijah challenged the idolatrous priests to the test of truth betwen them and the God of Israel ... And the enemie met with their destruction ... and Elijah and Abdiel, with calm dignity and complete self-assurance, turned their backs on the wicked damned".[26]

Abdiel as a prefiguration of Jesus's "standing" in *Paradise Regained*

Finally, I wish to argue that Abdiel's exemplary steadfast "standing firm" and remaining "unmoved" anticipates the figure of Jesus in *Paradise Regained*. The major and the minor epic are related to one another typologically: as the first Adam, by being disobedient to God, lapsed and lost Paradise, Jesus, the second Adam, by being obedient to his Father and standing firm, managed to regain Paradise. While the story of *Paradise*

[23] Jack Goldman, "Insight into Milton's Abdiel", *Philological Quarterly* 49H2 (1970), pp. 249–54, here at p. 253.

[24] John Milton, *Paradise Lost*, ed. Kastan, David Scott (Indianapolis, IN: Hackett Publishing, 2005), note 890, p. 176.

[25] Goldman, "Insight into Milton's Abdiel", p. 253.

[26] Goldman, "Insight into Milton's Abdiel", p. 254.

Lost is the temptation of Adam and Eve in the Garden of Eden, the story of *Paradise Regained* is of the temptation of the second Adam, Jesus, according to the Gospel of Luke (Luke 4:1–12).

According to the sequence of Luke (which Milton follows), Jesus, while fasting in the desert after his baptism and presumably being hungry, was tempted to make stones into bread by Satan, who appeared as a desert-dweller. Jesus resisted the first temptation. Satan knows that Jesus has been committed to the freedom of his people throughout his youth, and thus offers him political power as fulfilment of his dreams. Let us observe then the luring of Satan and how the Son refuses the tempting offer, while remaining unmoved in Book III of the minor epic:

> By him thou shalt regain, without him not,
> That which alone can truly reinstall thee
> In David's royal seat, his true successor,
> Deliverance of thy brethren, those ten tribes
> Whose offspring in his territory yet serve
> In Habor, and among the Medes dispersed,
> Ten sons of Jacob, two of Joseph lost
> Thus long from Israel; serving as of old
> Their fathers in the land of Egypt served,
> This offer sets before thee to deliver.
> These if from servitude thou shalt restore
> To their inheritance, then, nor till then,
> Thou on the throne of David in full glory,
> From Egypt to Euphrates and beyond
> Shalt reign, and Rome or Cæsar not need fear.
>
> *To whom our Saviour answer'd thus unmoved.*
> Much ostentation vain of fleshly arm,
> And fragile arms, much instrument of war
> Long in preparing, soon to nothing brought,
> Before mine eyes thou hast set; and in my ear

Vented much policy, and projects deep
Of enemies, of aids, battels and leagues,
Plausible to the world, to me worth naught. (III.371–393. Italics mine)[27]

In Book IV, the third temptation is described: Jesus is taken up to the
pinnacle of the temple of Jerusalem where Satan is scornfully mocking his
standing still: *"There stand, if thou wilt stand; to stand upright"* (IV.551)
and tries to persuade him to show his divinity to his progeny: *"If not to
stand / Cast thy self down if Son of God"* (IV.554–5). But Jesus stands,
remains firm, steadfast, unmoved; he does not fall even if it is written in
Psalm 91 that angels would hold him up. At this very moment of victory
Satan falls from the pinnacle into the deep abyss:

To whom thus Jesus: also it is written,
tempt not the Lord thy God; *he said and stood.*
But Satan smitten with amazement fell. (IV.560–2, italics mine)

Theological excursus 2: Abdiel's *parrhesia* and deontologist ethics

In February and March 1984, just a few months before his untimely death,
Michel Foucault gave a series of lectures at the Collège de France. The
subject was "the courage of truth". Foucault rediscovered the significance
of the Greek and Biblical meaning of *parrhesia*, i.e., "truth-telling", the
boldness or courage to speak out when such a speech is risky and exposed
to vulnerability in an existentially dangerous context. Milton's Abdiel can be
seen as the illustration and embodiment of this attitude. In Foucault's words:

In parrhesia, the speaker is supposed to give a complete and
exact account of what he has in mind so that the audience is
able to comprehend exactly what the speaker thinks. The word

---

[27] References to *Paradise Regained* are taken from John Carey (ed.), *John Milton,
      The Complete Shorter Poems*, 2nd edn [1st edn 1968] (London and New York:
      Longman, 1997).

"parrhesia" then, refers to a type of relationship between the speaker and what he says. For in parrhesia, the speaker makes it manifestly clear and obvious that what he says is his own opinion. And he does this by avoiding any kind of rhetorical form which would veil what he thinks. Instead, the parrhesiastes uses the most direct words and forms of expression he can find. Whereas rhetoric provides the speaker with technical devices to help him prevail upon the minds of his audience (regardless of the rhetorician's own opinion concerning what he says), in parrhesia, the parrhesiastes acts on other people's mind by showing them as directly as possible what he actually believes.[28]

At this point, allow me a personal remark. In the 1990s, before the collapse of communism in Eastern Europe, I wrote an essay about Lajos Ordass (1901–78), a Lutheran bishop under communism, having read his autobiography published in Switzerland in 1985 and 1987. Ordass' unique and unparalleled ethical stance inspired me to write an essay entitled "A megállás szimbóluma" ("The Symbol of Standing Firm"). At the end of the essay, I quoted the episodes from Milton's *Paradise Regained* described above, about Jesus's remaining steadfast and standing firm, having been tempted three times by Satan. I found that Ordass remained unmoved in exactly the way Jesus did in Milton's brief epic.[29] Faithfulness in times of persecution (i.e., *in status confessionis*) allows no rational, pragmatic *modus vivendi* or compromise. This unmovable, steadfast faith becomes a powerful symbol, a source of energy and rejuvenation.

---

28 <https://parrhesiac.wordpress.com/2010/01/03/why-parrhesia>, accessed 13 July 2022. The Meaning and Evolution of the Word "Parrhesia": Discourse & Truth, Problematization of Parrhesia—Six lectures given by Michel Foucault at the University of California at Berkeley, October–November 1983, <https://foucault.info/parrhesia/foucault.DT1.wordParrhesia.en/>, accessed 13 July 2022.

29 Tibor Fabiny, *A megállás szimbóluma: Előadások Ordass Lajosról* (The Symbol of Steadfast Faith: Lectures on Bishop Ordass, Budapest, A szerző kiadása (Publication of the Author, 2001), p. 22. Tibor Fabiny, *The Veil of God: The Testimony of Bishop Lajos Ordass in Communist Hungary* (Budapest: Center for Hermeneutical Research, 2008), p. xi.

In 2006, an American ethicist and theologian, David H. Baer, wrote a book on the struggle of Hungarian Lutherans under communism. He considered Ordass a "real man" who "lived out his principles with a real life".[30] Baer introduced the ethical term "deontology" or "non-consequentialism" for Ordass's ethical behaviour. The way Baer defines "deontology" entirely fits the figure of Abdiel in my interpretation.

> Deontology means a commitment to duty that excludes from moral consideration the effects, even the most negative ones, that result from adhering to duty ... Deontology depends on a sense of hidden providence. For a deontologist of this sort, disregarding consequences makes sense because one believes that God controls history even when his providential care cannot be seen and, therefore, that God is responsible for the consequences, both good and bad, that result from adhering to duty. Without faith in hidden providence, keeping duty at great cost can appear foolhardy or irresponsible.[31]

Abdiel the faithful and obedient servant of God, we may conclude, was also a deontologist. Satan's cohorts called this attitude "out of season" (V.850) and Baer describes the world's opinion as "foolhardy".

Deontology is non-consequentialism. Milton personally experienced what has been described here as deontologist ethics. In *Defensio secunda*, he remembered his return to Rome and being warned by his fellow merchants not to speak openly about his own religious views, as the English Jesuits in Rome had laid a plot for him. Milton, however, insisted on the freedom of his conscience:

> I had laid it down as a rule for myself, never to begin a conversation on religion in those parts; but if interrogated concerning my faith, *whatever might be the consequence*, to dissemble nothing. I therefore returned notwithstanding to Rome; I concealed from

[30]   David H. Baer, *The Struggle of Hungarian Lutherans under Communism* (College Station, TX: A. & M. University Press, 2006), p. 76.

[31]   Baer, *The Struggle of Hungarian Lutherans*, p. 77.

no one, who asked the question, as before, the orthodox faith, for nearly two months there, even in the city of the sovereign pontiff himself.[32]

Conclusion—Abdiel's lasting imprint on the reader's heart

Abdiel also appears in Book VI, but the analysis of his "easier contest" (VI.37) would probably need another essay. With the beginning of the war in heaven Abdiel disappears from the plot. But like the Fool in Shakespeare's *King Lear*, who disappears in the midst of the tempest scene, Abdiel's withdrawal creates a presence. Abdiel's spirit is metaphorically present throughout the poem, just like the Fool's throughout the play.

As I have suggested, victory can only be achieved when one exposes oneself and stands entirely alone, when one is willing the take the risk of vulnerability or even defeat entirely on one's own, solely for the sake of truth and obedience. Abdiel is a great example of this unquestioning obedience, which often entails absurdity and loneliness. Abdiel is perhaps an even greater example of faith than Abraham. This is why his figure makes such a strong impact upon the reader, while his memory is still capable of haunting us long after we have read *Paradise Lost*. Once we have met him and learned about and from him, his lasting imprint cannot be erased from the reader's heart.

I have spoken much about free will and the freedom of choice. My free choice of choosing the protagonist in this essay has fallen not upon the spectacular central figure of Satan, but on one at the margin or the periphery of the plot, who appears briefly and only in Books V and VI. I found my hero, my "star" on the periphery. He is indeed "an ever-fixed mark . . . never shaken . . . the star to every wandr'ing barque". By way of a conclusion, and with the words of a perceptive critic, I wish to endorse my initial thesis that despite appearances, it is not Satan but Abdiel who is the real hero of Milton's *Paradise Lost*:

---

[32]   Quoted by Allan H. Gilbert, "The Theological Basis of Satan's Rebellion and the Function of Abdiel in *Paradise Lost*", *Modern Philology* 40:1 (1942), p. 39.

Abdiel's arguments and protestations jar Satan from the offensive
to the defensive, and in this way, Abdiel steals Satan's spotlight
... [B]y the time the debate is concluded, we identify Abdiel as
a truly virtuous character, and Satan as somewhat of an empty
trickster. At this point, it becomes difficult to accept Satan as a
hero (or perhaps even as a protagonist) any longer, for Abdiel has
stripped him of much of his glamour and apparently retained it
as his own.[33]

---

[33]   Boone, *God-Like or Ungodly*, p. 63.

5

"The Taste of Things Inconceivable": Spark, Proust and The Sacramental Way

Vassiliki Kolocotroni

In November 1951, the fortunes of Muriel Spark, minor poet, critic and newly retired editor of the *Poetry Review*, took a dramatic turn: "The Seraph and the Zambesi", her entry for *The Observer* short story competition, won first place (out of 6,700 submissions). The story "caused quite a stir" and set her on her way towards peer and popular recognition.[1] Nearly twenty-two novels and a few short plays later, Spark remembered that moment and her immediate reaction: "I bought myself a blue velvet dress for six pounds and a complete set of Proust's *À la Recherche du Temps Perdu*".[2] By then, Spark, a Scot of Jewish origin and Presbyterian schooling, was already "intellectually speaking" an Anglican;[3] she was baptized by Clifford Rhodes, the "belligerent modern churchman" and editor of the *Church of England Newspaper*, on 7 November 1952.[4] Writing for that publication on 27 November 1953, she put forward a prescient and intriguing thesis on the "sacramental view of the world

---

[1]   Muriel Spark, *Curriculum Vitae: Autobiography* (London: Penguin Books, 1993), p. 199.

[2]   Spark, *Curriculum Vitae*, p. 199.

[3]   Muriel Spark, "My Conversion", in Joseph Hynes (ed.), *Critical Essays on Muriel Spark* (New York etc.: Maxwell Macmillan International, 1992), pp. 24–8, here at p. 25.

[4]   Martin Stannard, *Muriel Spark: The Biography* (London: Weidenfeld & Nicolson, 2009), pp. 132–3.

in the writings of [Marcel] Proust", whose "labyrinthine work" she had "read deeply":[5]

> Lacking a redemptive faith, Proust's attempt was to save himself through art. And in refreshing our vision from a writer like Proust, we are following the tradition whereby a great amount of the most fruitful thought of the Church is derived from the efforts of inspired pagans to save themselves.[6]

The statement has personal resonance for Spark, as she clearly counted herself among the "inspired pagans" at the time; more poignantly, the "efforts [. . .] to save themselves" would reflect exactly what Spark was to go through a year and a half later, as she re-emerged after a serious breakdown, with renewed faith and a member of a different religious community. Following her recovery and the absorption of "great gusts of Catholic teaching", as her mentor Father Ambrose Agius, Benedictine monk and poet, put it, Spark was received into the Roman Catholic Church on 1 May 1954.[7] Already as an Anglican, however, Spark had strong views on a foundational issue. As she put it in her article on Proust, "One of the things which interested me particularly about the Church was its acceptance of matter. So much of our world rejects it";[8] but she had a bone to pick with "spiritual" creative pursuits:

> It could be abundantly demonstrated that present-day Christian creative writing, that which is most involved in an attempt to combat materialism, reflects a materialism of its own; this takes the form of a dualistic attitude towards matter and spirit. They are seen too much in a moral conflict, where spirit triumphs by virtue of disembodiment. This is really an amoral conception of

---

[5]   Spark, "My Conversion", p. 27.

[6]   Muriel Spark, "The Religion of an Agnostic: A Sacramental View of the World in the Writings of Proust", *Church of England Newspaper* (Friday, 27 November 1953), p. 1.

[7]   Stannard, *Muriel Spark: The Biography*, pp. 144, 150.

[8]   Spark, "My Conversion", p. 28.

spirit. For a corrective to this situation, for a representation of life which, by its very lack of moral concern, escapes the tendency to equate matter with evil, and for an acceptance of that deep irony in which we are presented with the most unlikely people, places and things as repositories of invisible grace, we have to turn to a most unlikely source—Marcel Proust, agnostic, hedonist, self-centred neurotic, exotic darling of the aristocratic *salons*, sexual pervert, columnist of *Figaro*, the hypochondriac turned chronic invalid, the insufferable hot-house plant [...][9]

The operative word here is "unlikely". It is the paradoxical, "deeply ironic", alarming, de-habituating, defamiliarizing, strange, other, difficult, negative, stirring effect of the acceptance of invisible grace, the belief in the unbelievable, that Spark claims on behalf of Proust's technique:

[Proust] reminds us that there is a method of apprehending eternity through our senses, analogous to our sacramental understanding of eternity by faith. We get from Proust's definition a richer conception of the verities we hold by faith, he releases them from their sentimental or habitual connotations. An involuntary act of remembrance, to Proust, is a suggestive shadow of what a voluntary act of remembrance is to a Christian.[10]

Spark's understanding of Proust's "richer conception of the verities" encompasses "unlikely" elements, at least in religious terms, the superstitious or pagan residue of the idea of the return of the dead being one of them. Proust's conviction of the reality of that return in *Swann's Way*, the first volume of *Remembrance of Things Past* (the title of the English translation by C. K. Scott Moncrieff that Spark read), will have struck a chord:

I feel that there is much to be said for the Celtic belief that the souls of those whom we have lost are held captive in some inferior

---

9   Spark, "The Religion of an Agnostic", p. 1.
10   Spark, "The Religion of an Agnostic", p. 1.

being, in an animal, in a plant, in some inanimate object, and so effectively lost to us until the day (which to many never comes) when we happen to pass by the tree or to obtain possession of the object which forms their prison. Then they start and tremble, they call us by our name, and as soon as we have recognised their voice the spell is broken. We have delivered them: they have overcome death and return to share our life.

And so it is with our own past. It is a labour in vain to attempt to recapture it: all the efforts of our intellect must prove futile. The past is hidden somewhere outside the realm, beyond the reach of intellect, in some material object (in the sensation which that material object will give us) which we do not suspect.[11]

The materiality of the object as repository of invisible grace is what Spark means to emphasize; fully to score the point against contemporary "immaterialism" or false dualities,[12] she calls in support an earlier definition of "sacrament":

Proust, who never once, so far as I recall, used the word "sacrament" in his novel, is enabled by the persuasive beauty of his language to convey to the world more about the nature of a sacrament than any modern treatise on the subject could hope to teach. In support of which I offer, for comparison with Proust, the definition of the seventeenth century Anglican Divine, Edward Reynolds: "The nature of a Sacrament is to be the representative of a substance, the sign of a covenant, the seal of a purchase, the figure of a body, the witness of our faith, the earnest of our hope, the presence of things distant, the sight of things absent, the taste

---

[11]   Marcel Proust, *Swann's Way. Remembrance of Things Past, Volume One*, trans. C. K. Scott Moncrieff (New York: Henry Holt and Company, 1922), p. 57.

[12]   Spark uses the term rather dismissively elsewhere in her writing, for instance via Hubert Mallindaine's contempt for "[a world] avid for immaterialism", in *The Takeover* (1976) or, the cognate slight aimed at Miss Jones, the journalist, who is reportedly "avid for symbolism", in *Symposium* (1990).

of things inconceivable, and the knowledge of things that are past knowledge".[13]

Reynolds's definition could indeed be a gloss on Proust's technique and the tropes that guide the reader through his novel's extraordinary maze of memory and forgetting. In the following, famous passage from *Swann's Way*, lines from which Spark cites in her article, "the presence of things distant, the sight of things absent, the taste of things inconceivable, and the knowledge of things that are past knowledge" are in evidence:

> Many years had elapsed during which nothing of Combray, save what was comprised in the theatre and the drama of my going to bed there, had any existence for me, when one day in winter, as I came home, my mother, seeing that I was cold, offered me some tea, a thing I did not ordinarily take. [. . .] She sent out for one of those short, plump little cakes called "petites madeleines", which look as though they had been moulded in the fluted scallop of a pilgrim's shell. [. . .] No sooner had the warm liquid, and the crumbs with it, touched my palate than a shudder ran through my whole body [. . .] An exquisite pleasure had invaded my senses, but individual, detached, with no suggestion of its origin. And at once the vicissitudes of life had become indifferent to me, its disasters innocuous, its brevity illusory—this new sensation having had on me the effect which love has of filling me with a precious essence; or rather this essence was not in me, it was myself. I had ceased now to feel mediocre, accidental, mortal. Whence could it have come to me, this all-powerful joy?[14]

When young Marcel's mother offers him a "little madeleine" (*petite madeleine*) soaked in a spoonful of tea, a "new sensation" transforms the sense of taste into a sudden revelation of the richness of his unconscious memories of Combray and of his childhood vacations there. In Reynolds's terms, here is "the presence of things distant, the sight of things absent";

---

13 Spark, "The Religion of an Agnostic", p. 1.

14 Proust, *Swann's Way*, p. 58.

in Samuel Beckett's expression, a "visitation", as he called the motif of such
sudden turns that in his reading of Proust, "may be considered as forming
a single annunciation".[15] One may see here a still more direct evocation
of a sacrament, that is, as Steven F. Walker puts it, of "that moment in
the Mass when the Host is broken and the priest puts a particle of the
Host into the Chalice".[16] Walker goes on to trace a number of religious
associations, in the first instance with Mary Magdalene (*la Madeleine*),
though as he notes,

> not so much the figure of the New Testament but what she
> became in later Christian mythology, that is, the saintly repentant
> courtesan. Via such an association the madeleine can be taken as
> suggesting and symbolizing the complex relationship of affinity
> in Proust's novel between such apparent opposites as depravity
> and virtue, the life of the senses and the life of the spirit, the
> *côté de Méséglise* and the *côté de Guermantes*—for that matter,
> between taking tea and taking Communion."[17]

In the final volume of Proust's novel (*Time Regained*), the m/Madeleine
will be re-tasted through a different evocation—before entering the
Guermantes' salon, browsing around the library shelves, Marcel is struck
by a title and a recollection: *François le Champi*, a children's book by
George Sand, which his mother had read to him almost for an entire

[15] Samuel Beckett, *Proust and Three Dialogues with Georges Duthuit* (London:
John Calder, 1987), p. 42.

[16] Stephen F. Walker, "The Name of the Madeleine: Signs and Symbols of the
Mass in Proust's *In Search of Lost Time*", *Religion and the Arts* 7:4 (2003), pp.
389–411, here at p. 393.

[17] Walker, "The Name of the Madeleine", p. 394. As Walker points out, "Proust
spent the first thirty years of his life in Paris in an apartment at 9 Boulevard
Malesherbes two blocks from the Church of St. Mary Magdalene, which
Proust would glimpse through the trees to his right every time he walked out
onto the sidewalk. Constructed between 1757 and 1842, the church was and
is commonly referred to simply as *la Madeleine*. The reliquary in the church
allegedly contains a bone fragment of the saint" (p. 395).

night. Recalling the story of an abandoned child, rescued by Madeleine, a miller's wife-cum-foster mother, and many years later beloved, of the adult François, reanimates both the sensation of Marcel's unresolved longing for his mother and his own "child self", reappearing to him suddenly as a familiar ghost.

By association, then, the madeleine offers "a taste of things inconceivable", as well as conjuring both the Oedipal desire and the ghost of the self, consumed with regret and nostalgia. But there is a further incarnation—this time in volume three, *The Guermantes Way*: Marcel is about to meet Saint-Loup, a close friend, whose obsessive passion for an unworthy woman Marcel finds hard to accept:

> While I waited I strolled up and down the road, past these modest gardens. [. . .] A cold wind blew keenly along it, as at Combray, but from the midst of the rich, moist, country soil, which might have been on the bank of the Vivonne, there had nevertheless arisen, punctual at the trysting place like all its band of brothers, a great white pear tree which waved smilingly in the sun's face, like a curtain of light materialised and made palpable, its flowers shaken by the breeze but polished and frosted with silver by the sun's rays.
>
> Suddenly Saint-Loup appeared, accompanied by his mistress, and then, in this woman who was for him all the love, every possible delight in life, whose personality, mysteriously enshrined in a body as in a Tabernacle, was the object that still occupied incessantly the toiling imagination of my friend, whom he felt that he would never really know, as to whom he was perpetually asking himself what could be her secret self, behind the veil of eyes and flesh, in this woman I recognised at once "Rachel when from the Lord," her who, but a few years since—women change their position so rapidly in that world, when they do change— used to say to the procuress: "Tomorrow evening, then, if you want me for anyone, you will send round, won't you?"[18]

---

[18] Marcel Proust, *The Guermantes Way. Part Three of Remembrance of Things Past*, trans. C. K. Scott Moncrieff (New York: T. Seltzer, 1925), p. 211.

Marcel's realization that the mistress his friend venerates is a common prostitute, a "Rachel when from the Lord", (his own, sarcastic phrase suggesting a perverted gift from God, because offered to all) brings on an emotional response:

> It was not "Rachel when from the Lord"—who seemed to me a small matter—it was the power of the human imagination, the illusion on which were based the pains of love; these I felt to be vast. Robert noticed that I appeared moved. I turned my eyes to the pear and cherry trees of the garden opposite, so that he might think that it was their beauty that had touched me. And it did touch me in somewhat the same way; it also brought close to me things of the kind which we not only see with our eyes but feel also in our hearts. These trees that I had seen in the garden, likening them in my mind to strange deities, had not by mistake been like Magdalene's when, in another garden, she saw a human form and "thought it was the gardener"?[19]

As J. Hillis Miller, who has commented on the episode, notes, "the reference is to that episode in The Gospel according to St. John (20:11–18) in which Mary Magdalene, the sinner whom Jesus cured of her devils and whom he loved, comes to the tomb of the crucified Jesus, finds the sepulchre empty and guarded by two angels in white. She then mistakes the risen Jesus standing in the garden for the gardener. When Jesus speaks to her, she suddenly recognizes him and hails him as 'Master'".[20] For Miller, the scene's "turnings" (as Mary Magdalene first turns away from the empty sepulchre and then turns again when she recognizes Jesus) "mime the reversals of conversion and of spiritual insight. Each of these turnings is a trope (that is what trope means: 'a turning'), a redefinition

---

[19] Proust, *The Guermantes Way*, p. 215.

[20] J. Hillis Miller, "Reading Proust's 'Rachel when from the Lord': Interpretation of the Wholly Other". *LiterNet* 2 (15), <http://liternet.bg/publish1/dzhmiller/index.html>, accessed 13 July 2022.

of meanings by performative language".[21] A final transfiguration ensues, this time to close the circle, and re-convert the image:

> Treasurers of our memories of the age of gold, keepers of the
> promise that reality is not what we suppose, that the splendour
> of Poetry, the wonderful radiance of innocence may shine in it
> and may be the recompense which we strive to earn, these great
> white creatures, bowed in a marvellous fashion above the shade
> propitious for rest, for angling or for reading, were they not rather
> angels? I exchanged a few words with Saint-Loup's mistress. We
> cut across the village. Its houses were sordid. But by each of the
> most wretched, of those that looked as though they had been
> scorched and branded by a rain of brimstone, a mysterious
> traveller, halting for a day in the accursed city, a resplendent angel
> stood erect, extending broadly over it the dazzling protection of
> the wings of flowering innocence: it was a pear tree.[22]

In Miller's reading, here is "a passionate celebration of the human imagination for its power to reach a hidden truth, accessible not to reason but to performative speech acts".[23] This reach requires and generates tropes of conversion and redemption, as well as conflation. As Miller argues, the redemption and transformation of Mary Magdalene into a Christian saint and the conflation by early and late Christians of "the various Marys in the gospels" into a single name "parallels the transformation of Rachel into Saint-Loup's beloved mistress and exemplifies the same power of the linguistic imagination".[24]

Spark's communion with Proust's work and her proposal of it as an exemplar of the sacramental understanding of time suggests a poet's intense awareness of the salutary, revelatory powers of that linguistic imagination. The conflation in a sudden moment out of time of figures of sin and redemption, loss and recollection, absence and presence, has

---

21 Miller, "Reading Proust's 'Rachel when from the Lord'", n.p.

22 Proust, *The Guermantes Way*, p. 215.

23 Miller, "Reading Proust's 'Rachel when from the Lord'", n.p.

24 Miller, "Reading Proust's 'Rachel when from the Lord'", n.p.

a generative but also inscrutable quality that is important to Spark. She identifies it in the work of another writer she admired, the Poet Laureate John Masefield, whose biography she published in 1953:

> I think it is easy to recognize in the moment of illumination which every artist experiences at times, a kinship with that primitive order of religious revelation which is described in *The Everlasting Mercy*. These are the moments which Shelley, in his Platonic way, declared could never be expressed in their entirety: the most perfect poem would be but a shadow, and which Proust describes as connecting with an earlier experience in a quite illogical way which can only be described as mystical.[25]

The Everlasting Mercy (1911), the long narrative poem that made Masefield's name, tells the story of the conversion of hapless sinner Saul Kane from "contrary son" to "brother [to] all souls on earth", in his own "downright honest English speech".[26] As a contemporary reviewer enthused, what Masefield rendered in his poem was "not the 'interesting' conversion of some cultured and introspective Agnostic, full of wise saws and modern instances, but the sensational, primitive, catastrophic conversion of a village wastrel, violent alike in body, mind and soul".[27] Similarly, in Spark's terms, Masefield's poem is powered by its access to a "primitive order" of revelation, an analogy for which she once again finds in Proust's secular sacramental method that in its inscrutable, "illogical way" approximates the mystical. In *Robinson* (1958), a Swiftian fantasy with nods to *Robinson Crusoe* and *The Tempest*, and the second novel she published after her conversion, Spark accords that prerogative to the heroine, January Marlow, the precocious Eve/Miranda figure who finds sustenance in the exercise of serendipitous, surreptitious transfiguration:

---

[25]   Muriel Spark, *John Masefield* (London: Pimlico, 1992), p. 87.

[26]   John Masefield, *The Everlasting Mercy* (London: Sidgwick & Jackson Ltd, 1911), pp. 1, 67, 43.

[27]   Evelyn Underhill (orig. in the *Daily News*), cited in Masefield, *The Everlasting Mercy*, p. 81.

It is not that I judge people by their appearance, but it is true that
I am fascinated by their faces. I do not stare in their presence. I
like to take the impression of a face home with me, there to stare
at and chew over it in privacy, as a wild beast prefers to devour its
prey in concealment. […] Most of all, I love to compare faces.
I have seen a bus conductor who resembles a woman don of my
acquaintance, I have seen the face of Agnes throwing itself from
side to side in the pulpit; I make a meal of these.[28]

January's savage, associative mental habit is triggered early on in the novel
by a commonplace sacramental scene presided over by Robinson, owner
of the island where she is stranded. Having served food at the dinner
table, he says a prayer for grace, "and when we had finished he gave
thanks according to the form used by English Catholics, following it with
that usual prayer for the faithful departed which frequently suggests to
my mind that we have eaten them".[29] January, another of Spark's converts,
is particularly receptive to the signs of "transfiguration" via the kind of
literal, linguistic imagination lacking in those born in the faith. A case
in point is Ian Brodie, January's brother-in-law, a cradle Catholic "rather
aggressive in his religion, [who] was always using that word, danger, in
connexion with Our Blessed Lady".[30] In thrall to misconceived, badly
digested dogma, Ian "frequently wrote to the Catholic newspapers letters
of concerns about the Marian excesses he had witnessed at feast-day
processions in Italy or Spain, and their danger".[31] Here Spark sets up,
satirically, the ancient insult or double devaluation of *matter* and *mater*
which the false dualism between spirit and substance perpetuates.
She had already used the fallacy as a cue for her reading of Proust as
a "corrective to […] the tendency to equate matter with evil",[32] and
returned to the matter often in her work. In a commissioned essay on
Piero della Francesca's fresco *Madonna del Parto*, published in *Vanity*

---

[28]   Muriel Spark, *Robinson* (Harmondsworth: Penguin Books, 1964), p. 137.

[29]   Spark, *Robinson*, p. 45.

[30]   Spark, *Robinson*, p. 78.

[31]   Spark, *Robinson*, p. 78.

[32]   Spark, "The Religion of an Agnostic", p. 1.

Fair in December 1984 under the title "Spirit and Substance", she delivers
in ekphrastic mode a serene riposte to Ian Brodie's fixation:

> Piero della Francesca was a humanist with a deep sense of the
> sublime. His Madonna (Our Lady of Childbirth) is a substantial
> country woman and at the same time a majestic, archetypal
> figure. [...]
>
> In Piero's time there was great theological controversy. The
> Renaissance questioned everything. What was the nature of the
> Virgin? Was she just an ordinary woman or was she of the divine
> essence? Questions about the spirit and substance were argued
> endlessly. What is spirit? What is substance? Today we know
> more about substance than ever before, but the more we know
> the more it is recognised that we know nothing. Five hundred
> years have taught us nothing new about the life of the spirit.
> Piero della Francesca, like all great artists, did not accept any
> dichotomy between spirit and matter. There is no spirit without
> substance; the whole of nature is impregnated with spiritual life.
> His *Madonna del Parto*, one of the few pregnant Madonnas, is
> both human and touched with divine revelation. It is a work
> that reposes in its own mystery: Life emerging into the life of the
> world, Light into its light.[33]

The "first Christmas Eve", as Spark names Piero's Madonna, in her
"marvellous condition",[34] is indeed a figure of marvellous portent but also
of proud and practical materiality. The magical, mysterious simultaneity
of the two aspects is a version of the Proustian transfiguration that Spark
appreciated. In *The Public Image* (1968), Spark features another such
pregnant figure. At the end of the novel, Annabel Christopher, the English
actress turned Italian film star, idolized for her performances on screen
as "the English Lady-Tiger", at last abandons a life lived through the

---

[33]   Muriel Spark, "The First Christmas Eve", in *The Informed Air: Essays*, ed.
        Penelope Jardine (New York: New Directions, 2014), pp. 223–5, here at pp.
        224, 225.

[34]   Spark, "The First Christmas Eve", p. 224.

mediation of her public image and the pernicious emotional legacy of her self-destructive husband for an unspecified future that sounds more like a half-forgotten past:

> Waiting for the order to board, she felt both free and unfree. The heavy weight of the bags was gone; she felt as if she was still, curiously, pregnant with the baby, but not pregnant in fact. She was pale as a shell. She did not wear her dark glasses. Nobody recognized her as she stood, having moved the baby to rest on her hip, conscious also of the baby in a sense weightlessly and perpetually within her, as an empty shell contains, by its very structure, the echo and harking image of former and former seas.[35]

Given the Italian setting and the novel's concern with iconicity, the likening of Annabel to a shell (twice in as many sentences) might be a visual echo of Sandro Botticelli's *The Birth of Venus*, or perhaps too Proust's shell-shaped *madeleine* and the "taste of things inconceivable". Headed for Greece, perhaps to return to ancient shores and a mythical assumption, Annabel is an ambivalent, timeless Madonna, "both free and unfree", mother to herself, or like Piero's Lady, "as if, about to deliver her child, she is herself about to be delivered from a vaster, cosmic womb".[36]

Self-creation as a kind of salvation, and the perils of transfiguration in a world of bad faith, are explored in *The Prime of Miss Jean Brodie* (1961). The novel features the most iconic (and perhaps the most hubristic) of all Sparkian "spinsters", formidable figures of inscrutability. Miss Jean Brodie's rise and fall as a leader of "young girls in flower"[37] is a tale of failed instruction imbued with "that deep irony in which we are presented with

---

[35]   Muriel Spark, *The Public Image* (New York: New Directions, 1993), p. 144.

[36]   Spark, "The First Christmas Eve", p. 224.

[37]   From the title of the second volume of Proust's *À la recherche du temps perdu*: *À l'ombre des jeunes filles en fleur*. In C. K. Scott Moncrieff's translation, the title appears as *In the Budding Grove*; more recently, for the 2003 Penguin edition, James Grieve renders it in the literal *In the Shadow of Young Girls in Flower*.

the most unlikely people, places and things as repositories of invisible grace",[38] as Spark put it in her reading of Proust. A cipher for the authorial figure, reconstructing events and meting out justice, is Sandy Stranger, leading member of Jean Brodie's *crème de la crème* girl army and latter-day nemesis of her mentor. Sandy, or Sister Helena of the Transfiguration as she is known after she converts to Catholicism and takes vows, becomes unexpectedly famous for publishing "her odd psychological treatise on the nature of moral perception, called 'The Transfiguration of the Commonplace'".[39] We will never know what wisdom the treatise purveyed, but there are mini insights strewn proleptically in the girls' recollections of "the happiest time of our lives", as the mantra-like phrase has it. Most revelatory for Sandy is the realization that they, she, may be but copies of a fantastic, impossible image:

> Teddy Lloyd's passion for Jean Brodie was greatly in evidence in all the portraits he did of the various members of the Brodie set. He did them in a group during one summer term, wearing their panama hats each in a different way, each hat, adorning, in a magical transfiguration, a different Jean Brodie [...][40]

The budding writer Sandy, heretofore authorized teller of imaginary tales of vicarious adolescent fantasy, enters that fictional universe to become a real-life lover of Teddy Lloyd. To complete the plot, Sandy "betrays" Jean Brodie, who is forced into retirement, to the end ignorant of the true agent of her fate. In turn, Sandy's conversion and cloistered existence remains a riddle, at least in terms of its causal relationship with her Brodie set formation, and its banal sense of predestination. Like Annabel, Sandy/Helena is ultimately "both free and unfree".

The ambivalence of that strange, transfigured innocence recurs in Spark's writing. A literally intriguing later example is Alexandra, Abbess of Crewe, protagonist of the eponymous 1974 novel. Wildean aesthete and

38   Spark, "The Religion of an Agnostic", p. 1.
39   Muriel Spark, *The Prime of Miss Jean Brodie* (Harmondsworth: Penguin Books, 1965), p. 37.
40   Spark, *The Prime of Miss Jean Brodie*, p. 113.

Machiavellian schemer at once, the Abbess is the Richard Nixon alias in what is usually read as a Watergate satire, or a parable about the power-crazed behaviour of people in insular and institutionalized environments—but she is much more besides. At the end of the novel, having overstepped the mark by her control-freakish ways, and sailing to Rome to face the wrath of the Pope, this outrageous anti-heroine is "converted" by Spark into an evocative emblem—again iconic or "fresco-like":

> Our revels now are ended. Be still, be watchful. She sails indeed
> on the fine day of her desire into waters exceptionally smooth,
> and stands on the upper deck, straight as a white ship's funnel,
> marveling how the wide sea billows from shore to shore like that
> cornfield of sublimity which never should be reaped nor was ever
> sown, orient and immortal wheat.[41]

True to the style of the novel, which is a collagistic "treasury of English verse", recited, almost like a tape on a loop, mechanically in the Abbess's mind, the conclusion cannibalizes literary utterances—*The Tempest*, but also the following extract from the meditations of seventeenth-century Anglican clergyman and mystical poet Thomas Traherne:

> 1. […] Certainly Adam in Paradise had not more sweet and
> curious apprehensions of the world, than I when I was a child.

> 2. All appeared new, and strange at first, inexpressibly rare
> and delightful and beautiful. I was a little stranger, which at
> my entrance into the world was saluted and surrounded with
> innumerable joys. […]

> 3. The corn was orient and immortal wheat, which never should
> be reaped, nor was ever sown. I thought it had stood from
> everlasting to everlasting. The dust and stones of the street were
> as precious as gold: the gates were at first the end of the world.

---

[41] Muriel Spark, *The Abbess of Crewe* (Harmondsworth: Penguin Books, 1975), p. 107.

> The green trees when I saw them first through one of the gates
> transported and ravished me, their sweetness and unusual beauty
> made my heart to leap, and almost mad with ecstasy, they were
> such strange and wonderful things [...][42]

The effect is magical and slippery—it is not clear whether the lines rendering the Abbess's final poise are ventriloquized, spoken in automatism, "carried", as if through a medium or a conduit (another Sparkian staple),[43] or whether the fadeout, as it were, is not a return to innocence (individual and collective), an acknowledgement of the transfigurative potential of language, and the dreams that humanity has stored in it. Crucial here is the figure of the child, Traherne's "little stranger", that may indeed be the provenance for the name of the precocious Sandy of *The Prime of Miss Jean Brodie*, but also a glimpse of the Proustian perspective that so attracted Spark. As Theodor Adorno observed, "Proust looks at even adult life with such alien and wondering eyes that under his immersed gaze the present is virtually transformed into prehistory, into childhood."[44] Adorno continues in terms that resonate with Spark's approach:

> Proust's fidelity to childhood is a fidelity to the idea of happiness
> [...] The polarity of happiness and transience directs him to
> memory. Undamaged experience is produced only in memory,
> far beyond immediacy, and through memory aging and death
> seem to be overcome in the aesthetic image. [...] Total

---

[42]   Thomas Traherne, "The Third Century", *Centuries of Meditations*, ed. Bertram Dobell (London: Published by the Editor, 1908), pp. 156–237, here at pp. 156–8.

[43]   I have discussed the affinities between and implications of such instances in Spark's work in "Poetic Perception in the Fiction of Muriel Spark", in Michael Gardiner and Willy Maley (eds), *The Edinburgh Companion to Muriel Spark* (Edinburgh: Edinburgh University Press, 2010), pp. 16–26.

[44]   Theodor W. Adorno, "On Proust", in Rolf Tiedemann (ed.) *Notes to Literature. Volume Two*, trans. Shierry Weber Nicholsen (New York: Columbia University Press, 1992), pp. 312–17, here at p. 315.

remembrance is the response to total transience, and hope lies only in the strength to become aware of transience and preserve it in writing. Proust is a martyr to happiness.[45]

Spark's fidelity to Proust may or may not stretch to such a definition of martyrdom, but she does share his deep faith in memory. As Barbara Vaughan, one of the "passionate pilgrims" to the Holy Land in *The Mandelbaum Gate*,[46] puts it:

> [...] my mind is impatient to escape from its constitution and reach its point somewhere else. But that is in eternity at the point of transfiguration. In the meantime, what is to be borne is to be praised. In the meantime, memory circulates like the bloodstream. May mine circulate well, may it bring dead facts to life, may it bring health to whatever is to be borne.[47]

In Spark's 1965 novel, Barbara, an English, half-Jewish Catholic convert, is embroiled in personal and political intrigue while on a visit to the holy sites of Israel and Jordan, against the backdrop of the 1961 Eichmann trial. Her faith in humanity is tested in the face of "the banality of evil",[48] and the palimpsest of competing claims on the land and its history, but mental and emotional order is ultimately restored in a secure happy ending that Spark reserves for those characters with whom she shares a sacramental sense of the miraculous: "For [Barbara] was gifted with an honest, analytical intelligence, a sense of fidelity in the observing of observable things, and, at the same time, with the beautiful and dangerous gift of faith which, by definition of the Scriptures, is the sum of things hoped for and the evidence of things unseen."[49]

---

[45] Adorno, "On Proust", pp. 316, 317.

[46] Muriel Spark, *The Mandelbaum Gate* (Harmondsworth: Penguin Books, 1967), p. 191.

[47] Spark, *The Mandelbaum Gate*, p. 31.

[48] Hannah Arendt, *Eichmann in Jerusalem: A Report on the Banality of Evil*. Rev. and enlarged edn (New York: The Viking Press, 1964).

[49] Spark, *The Mandelbaum Gate*, p. 23.

6

Poets, Professors and Priests: Reflections on Poetic and Pedagogic Vocation in the Work of Seamus Heaney and David Jasper

Alison Jack

David Jasper has been a generous supporter and friend to me over several decades. He has encouraged me in my own research and in the development of the field of religion and literature in the School of Divinity at the University of Edinburgh where I am based. Most recently, he has taken part in seminar sessions on the Core Course for our newly launched MTh programme in Religion and Literature, which has given me a welcome sense of reassurance that we are proceeding along the right lines. His breadth and depth of knowledge, combined with his ability to communicate the complexities of the field in straightforward terms, have been invaluable as we have all, students and staff, been finding our way.

Last year, a Master's student on a different programme chose to write a book review on one of David's recent publications, *Heaven in Ordinary: Poetry and Religion in a Secular Age*,[1] as one of the tasks on their Approaches to Research course. Marking the review took me back to the book, and as I was working on the poetry of Seamus Heaney at the time, I was struck by the connections between David's understanding of poetry and Heaney's. I am not aware of David having written on Heaney's work, but their shared fascination with poets of the Romantic period is striking, as is the influence of both Thomas Hardy and Gerard Manley

---

[1] David Jasper, *Heaven in Ordinary: Poetry and Religion in a Secular Age* (Cambridge: The Lutterworth Press, 2018).

Hopkins on the early development of their appreciation of poetry.[2] The Christian traditions which formed them are very different, Anglican in David's case and Roman Catholic in Heaney's, and the extent to which they have understood themselves to be committed to these traditions is avowedly divergent. However, in their assessment of the sacramental power of poetry they are remarkably similar. In this short contribution, I shall draw out the significance of these connections and particularly the ways in which reading and teaching poetry has a vocational aspect for them both.

As David Jasper continues to be, Heaney was by all accounts a fine and committed teacher, taking personally his responsibilities towards his pupils at all levels. In his reflections on the "Poet as Professor" for *The Poetry Ireland Review*, he comments that "teaching is as much a mystery as it is a technique, and the aura of the person, his or her intellectual radiance or moral verity, is going to have as much to do with the poet/ professor's impact as the size of the reputation or the intrinsic quality of the poetry itself".[3] He goes on to warn against a teacherly overbearance towards students, and to encourage instead a "protectiveness on the part

[2]   David Jasper devotes a chapter to the significance of Hardy's work in *Heaven in Ordinary* (pp. 13–36), and Hopkins is referred to in Chapters 3 and 7 of the same book (pp. 52, 126–7). Hardy's ongoing significance to Heaney is summed up by Tara Christie in "'Something to Write Home about': Seamus Heaney at the Hardy Birthplace", *The Thomas Hardy Journal* 20:2 (2004), pp. 35–45, <http://www.jstor.org/stable/45274722>, accessed 13 July 2022: "From as early as 1954, when he was a fifteen-year-old student heading into his final year at St Columb's College, Heaney's fifty year engagement with the works of Thomas Hardy plays a central, complex, and ever-changing role in Heaney's poetic vision" (p. 35). Heaney describes himself as a "slave to Hopkins" by the time he was a student at Queen's University, and goes on to describe the effect of Hopkins's poetry on his own early work at length in Dennis O'Driscoll's *Stepping Stones: Interviews with Seamus Heaney* (London: Faber and Faber, 2008), pp. 36–40.

[3]   Seamus Heaney, "Poet as Professor", *The Poetry Ireland Review*, 31 (1991), pp. 10–13, here at p. 10. <http://www.jstor.org/stable/25577051>, accessed 13 July 2022.

of the empowered figure of the teacher" which communicates the merits of students' work with a concern for their "emotional tissues" and without crushing their aspirations.[4]

In his two collections of poetry for children, edited with Ted Hughes,[5] and earlier in his radio programmes from 1974 for the BBC Northern Ireland Schools Service, *Explorations*, Heaney combines this concern for the nurture of the learner with a commitment to allowing children to engage for themselves with poetry at every level. In his Foreword to *The School Bag*, Heaney describes the collection as "a kind of listening post, a book where the reader can tune in to the various notes and strains that have gone into the making of the whole score of poetry in English".[6] The contributions in *The Rattle Bag* are arranged alphabetically according to the first line of each poem, so the work of finding themes and connections is handed over to the reader entirely. In the Teacher's Notes to *Explorations*, Heaney writes that the aim of the series is not to "service" the Literature syllabus, but to present "enriching material that will stir the imagination in the conviction that children's sensibilities can be opened to the experience of language as literature".[7] Literary language is envisaged as having its own power when it is experienced appropriately and its readers are "open" to engaging with it.

David Jasper makes a similar claim for such poetic language in *Heaven in Ordinary* when he argues that "as living, unifying things, words can never be merely a means to an end, for they are, in all their poetic mystery, an end in themselves". He goes on to assert that "it is the vocation of the poet to speak words that are themselves part of the mystery: language as sacramental, the words of the poet irreplaceable, irreduceable, being

[4]   Heaney, "Poet as Professor", p. 12.

[5]   Seamus Heaney and Ted Hughes (eds), *The School Bag* (London: Faber and Faber, 1997); Seamus Heaney and Ted Hughes (eds), *The Rattle Bag* (London: Faber and Faber, 1982).

[6]   Heaney and Hughes, *The School Bag*, p. xv.

[7]   Seamus Heaney, *Teachers' Notes: Explorations* (London: BBC, 1973), p. 1. Quoted in Rosie Lavan, *Seamus Heaney and Society* (Oxford: Oxford University Press, 2020), p. 86.

what they are".[8] For Jasper, the Church may not grasp this in its drive
to make liturgy more comprehensible; for Heaney, it is an education
system which may close off this mysterious freedom of words to mean
and signify, and which he has sought to influence through his teaching
and his poetry. Jasper quotes approvingly Austin Farrer's conviction that:

> poetry and divine inspiration have this in common, that they are
> both projected in images which cannot be decoded, but must be
> allowed to signify what they signify of the reality beyond them.
> In this respect inspiration joins hands with poetry.[9]

In the text by Heaney that I want to focus on here, which originates in
an educational rather than religious setting, there is a surprising and
significant connection made to very similar convictions about poetic
language.

In 2003, Heaney was invited to give a lecture in the "Greatest Minds"
Lecture series, which was delivered at the Celebration of Graduation
at the University of Dundee. It was published under the title "Room to
Rhyme" by the University in 2004.[10] In this address to new graduates,
Heaney opens up the power of poetry both to help make sense of life in
the past and to make change for the future possible. His starting point
is the memory of seeing a mummers' play in his youth, which begins:

> Room, room, my gallant boys,
> And give us room to rhyme.[11]

The memory of these words "transports" him back to that experience and
"restores" something that was missing. The poetry is "its own reward"[12]
for the one who remembers it, as it was for the one who performed it,

---

8   Jasper, *Heaven in Ordinary*, p. 137.

9   Austin Farrer, *The Glass of Vision* (Westminster: Dacre Press, 1948), p. 148,
     quoted in Jasper, *Heaven in Ordinary*, p. 137.

10   Seamus Heaney, "Room to Rhyme" (Dundee: University of Dundee, 2004).

11   Heaney, "Room to Rhyme", p. 4.

12   Heaney, "Room to Rhyme", p. 8.

Heaney's own father, from the later perspective of the man who was then the child. Heaney brings a new understanding to the memory of the poem as it was performed by his father: he integrates the memory with his later experiences of the power of poetry, and sees the otherness of his father afresh:

> It was as if he took a swim in his inner man and came out refreshed. As if he went through the eye of the needle of his inner self and entered the kingdom of rightness. Because that, especially, is what rhymed and rhythmical speech can provide: a sense of rightness.[13]

The biblical image of going or seeing through the eye of a needle is a favourite one of Heaney's.[14] It expresses something apparently impossible, miraculous, and transformative when it occurs. The "kingdom of rightness" is a secularizing of the more familiar biblical pairing of the kingdom of God with righteousness, but it brings a universal sense of resolution to the effect of the performance of the poem on Heaney's father. Heaney the son imputes this integration of his father's inner and outer selves through the expression of poetic language almost as if the words were a liturgy. His explicit association of poetry with "mantras", and identification of poems as "manifestations"[15] of something beyond themselves adds to the liturgical heft he obliquely ascribes to poetic expression here.

---

[13]   Heaney, "Room to Rhyme", p. 12.

[14]   See, for example, his description of George Mackay Brown as transforming everything "by passing it through the eye of the needle of Orkney", which appeared on the dust jacket for Brown's *Selected Poems 1954–1983* (London: John Murray, 1991). The reference to the Gospel story about how difficult it is for a rich man to enter heaven (Matthew 19:23–6; Mark 10:24–7; Luke 18:24–7) is more explicit in Heaney's "The Rain Stick", although the transformative image is itself transformed into "the ear of a raindrop" rather than the "eye of a needle". See *New Selected Poems 1988–2013* (London: Faber and Faber, 2014), p. 61.

[15]   Heaney, "Room to Rhyme", p. 8.

Heaney makes the further observation that it is poetry which has the power to give meaning to a memory which was not available at the time the event took place. Just as Thomas Hardy in his poem, "The Self Unseeing", revisions a memory of dancing for his parents into a "system of signs", so Heaney presents the ordinary event of folding sheets with his mother into a moment which "in retrospect was emblazoned with blessings" in his poem "Clearances".[16] As Jasper suggests at the end of *Heaven in Ordinary*, poets continue to express the "living mystery of words", perhaps because they "speak in the language of the imagination, a repetition in the finite mind of the eternal act of creation in the infinite I AM".[17] It seems unlikely that Heaney would have made such an openly confessional claim about his self-understanding as a poet, although his ongoing relationship with the belief systems of his youth is the subject of much speculation.[18] As he explained to Dennis O'Driscoll, his loss of faith, "intellectually speaking . . . occurred offstage, there was never a scene where I had it out with myself or with another". He cannot now "make the act of faith", but theologically charged language and images retain their "potency" and their "undying tremor and draw", which means he cannot "disavow" them.[19] The "blessings" with which the new creation of the memory of the folding of sheets in his poetic utterance "Clearances" are "emblazoned" attest to the "draw" of this language of faith, and are perhaps an acknowledgement of the mystery of the language of the imagination which is shared in some sense with the divine.

More explicit connections are evidenced between theology and poetry in Heaney's second argument in his lecture to graduates, which focuses on the role of the poetic Muse to initiate and enable change. He identifies

---

16 Heaney, "Room to Rhyme", p. 17. The poem is found in *New Selected Poems 1966–1987* (London: Faber and Faber, 1990), pp. 224–32.

17 Jasper, *Heaven in Ordinary*, p. 141.

18 For two recent attempts to clarify Heaney's religious convictions at every stage in his life, see Gail McConnell, *Northern Irish Poetry and Theology* (New York: Palgrave Macmillan, 2014) and Kieran Quinlan, *Seamus Heaney and the End of Catholic Ireland* (Washington, DC: Catholic University of America Press, 2020).

19 O'Driscoll, *Stepping Stones,* p. 234.

this Muse as that aspect of the self which seeks "room to rhyme". It is "the voice of your truest self, the voice of your most inward recognitions and intuitions",[20] and he associates its recognition with the story of the call of the first English poet, Caedmon. It is this voice which is called forth by the angel sent by God to inspire and challenge the reluctant Caedmon. When Caedmon is persuaded to express himself in this voice, the result is startling in its vernacular integrity and directness, a newly minted hymn to the Creator God. Heaney finds himself "intimately and immediately" connected to the story of Caedmon, which he identifies as archetypical of all who fulfil a calling to express themselves after initially seeking to avoid their destiny. The story "gives an overall order to the accident of my discovery that poetry was a vocation that I myself might follow".[21] He then describes his own calling which came in his early twenties after he had begun to read poets such as Norman MacCaig and George Mackay Brown, who wrote in the language of their place and time. He was thus inspired to believe his "own experience was fit material to work with".[22] The revelation involved hearing in the mummers' language he remembered an unbroken link with languages of the past, including both the voice of Shakespeare and the Irish culture which more dominant, English tongues had replaced.

Heaney's situating of himself in this poetic tradition, with its roots stretching back into a mythic world with deeply religious foundations, is told here as a story to inspire others to hear their own calling within. He offers his well-known poem, "Digging" as an expression of the balance to be found between "memory and meaning", continuity and change, which poetry is uniquely able to prompt its readers to seek. The poem is a stalwart of school curricula in English Literature, and Heaney might well be appealing to the prior knowledge of his graduate audience, for whom "Digging" may enable the opening of new understanding which the mummers' poem enabled for him. He presents the poem as that which "brought together the country-child self who had vanished in

---

[20]   Heaney, "Room to Rhyme", p. 22.

[21]   Heaney, "Room to Rhyme", p. 24.

[22]   Heaney, "Room to Rhyme", p. 25.

the course of [his] education and the graduate self who took his place".[23]
In doing so, he is taking on the role of poet, professor and priest, in
many ways, or perhaps the angelic role in Caedmon's story, mediating
the message from God to the ones reluctant to voice their Muse. But it is
the poem which is the message, the power of its language which Heaney
trusts to give his hearers "room to rhyme".

The waiting, watchful poise of the poem is one aspect of its particular
effectiveness, and its attentiveness to the moment in spatial and temporal
terms. The speaker is still and elevated, watching the activity of his father
in the garden below digging potato drills, while the "squat pen rests"[24] in
his hand. The sight provokes the visceral memory of holding potatoes
in the past of his childhood which this activity, repeatedly, enables, and
the more distant memory of his grandfather and his legendary, frenetic
skill at digging peat. The speaker has access to these memories and this
heritage, but he is not equipped to follow them, and is distanced in more
ways than merely time: "But I've no spade to follow men like them". The
moment of realization is arrived at after the opening lines are repeated
and resolved with the assertion "I'll dig" not with a spade but with the
pen already resting, poised, in his hand. Change is anticipated and
accommodated through the recreation of memory into patterns and signs
which bring blessings rather than judgement. The expert "handling" of
generative things becomes a heritage within which the speaker is proud
to belong, despite the distance of his new calling.

The poem is a perfect choice for the occasion and for the argument
presented in the lecture to new graduates, forging a connection between
the poet and his listeners through the shared experience of this significant
moment in life. The poems which open and close the lecture perform
the function of a call to worship and a benediction, both reaching back
into distant memories while offering the language of imagination as
a powerful source of comfort, inspiration and encouragement. In the
lecture, Heaney has inhabited one of David Jasper's insights into the
reason for the continuing importance of poets: "They are the ones who

---

[23]   Heaney, "Room to Rhyme", p. 25.
[24]   Seamus Heaney, "Digging", in *New Selected Poems 1966–1987*, pp. 1–2.

do not so much speak, but truly listen".[25] This, Jasper implies, is a gift put into poetic form by the poet-priest R. S. Thomas in the extract from "Kneeling" with which Jasper closes *Heaven in Ordinary*. At prayer, the one who is to bring the message to the people asks for the prompting of God, but only after an acceptance is reached of what is lost in the mediation. For, as Thomas writes, "The meaning is in the waiting."[26] Heaney, like Jasper and Thomas, has a keen sense of an acceptance of this "waiting" and listening within the mystery that is for him at the heart of teaching and memory and calling, which poetry expresses and acknowledges.

I have argued here that just as David Jasper holds together the callings of professor and priest with grace, so Seamus Heaney, professor and poet, gracefully demonstrates some of the callings of priest also. It is in their shared understanding of poetry that these callings are held together. It is professors, poets and priests who know, as Heaney acknowledges in his poem "On His Work in the English Tongue", written in memory of Ted Hughes, that there are:

> . . . Things not to be said.
> Things for keeping, that can keep the small-hours gaze
> Open and steady. Things for the aye of God
> And for poetry.[27]

---

[25] Jasper, *Heaven in Ordinary*, p. 141.

[26] R.S. Thomas, "Kneeling", in *Not That He Brought Flowers* (London: Rupert Hart-Davis, 1969), p. 32, quoted in Jasper, *Heaven in Ordinary*, p. 141.

[27] Seamus Heaney, "On His Work in the English Tongue", in *Electric Light* (London: Faber and Faber, 2001), pp. 61–3.

7

The End of the Church

Elisabeth Jay

In a piece entitled "Where are all the great thinkers of our time?", the *Times* columnist Iain Martin deplored the inability of the Church of England's senior figures to offer a public platform for debating the moral and ethical implications of the Covid-19 pandemic.[1] The Archbishops of Canterbury and York might have felt this particularly unfair in the wake of their joint letter to the nation of 26 January 2021, marking the passing of 100,000 Covid-related deaths. In it, they remarked that "poorer communities, minority ethnic communities and those living with disabilities have been afflicted disproportionately", reminded us that all lives, and deaths, counted with God, and recommended that, however difficult, we keep following the government guidelines. Before finally expressing Christian hope in the resurrection, they besought us all, "Whether you're someone of faith, or not, we invite you to call on God in prayer". For those humanists, atheists and agnostics not unreasonably puzzled by this invitation, its theological implications were spelt out thus: "Prayer is an expression of love. A number of resources will be made available at www.ChurchofEngland.org/PrayerForTheNation."

All doubtless well-intentioned, but lacking in spiritual gravitas, theological depth and a sense of visionary leadership; or, as Iain Martin put it, by comparison with today's senior Anglican figures, "The clerics of 30 or 40 years ago seemed much more muscular and intellectually confident". Even the leader in the *Church Times* of 4 February 2021 complained that their Graces had failed to find a place either for the expression of a nation's

---

[1] *Times*, 4 February 2021, p. 25.

anger at the perceived mismanagements leading to the worst recorded death rate per head of population in the world, or for a global perspective upon the debates about priorities in the vaccine roll-out.

It is all too easy to find fault with this seemingly rather naive attempt to provide spiritual leadership. Might it have been worth pausing to reflect upon the Prayer Book's prayers "for Deliverance from the Plague, or other Common Sickness", and contemplate what they have to teach of our weakness or "humiliation"?[2] I am not suggesting a return to National Days of self-flagellation, though many viewers seem happy to indulge in the secular equivalent on Sunday evenings at the hands of Sir David Attenborough. Yet instead of being bidden meekly to follow "the advice of the Chief Medical Officer and Chief Scientific Adviser", could we not have been asked to think a little about the nature of science and whom it serves, or the tricky matter of weighing economic interests against preserving the vulnerable? If we are to avoid a future in which identity politics reigns and binary values are all we have on offer, it is worth recalling the words of the Communion Prayer that reminds us that government exists to preserve us "in wealth, peace and godliness"; a judiciously weighed Cranmerian triplet rather than binary alternatives.[3]

Rather than berating the two archbishops, it is worth briefly considering how the Anglican Church and its leadership reached this abject position and whether a gradual decline in its authority and ability to speak truth to power has been observable over the last half century or so. It is certainly true that today, when voices from many quarters look askance at the number of seats taken by the Lords Spiritual in the House of Lords, many parishes and churches lack a resident priest, and rumours abound of reducing their salaried number yet further, the Church of England is less confident of its place at the establishment table, and nervous in presuming that it any longer speaks on behalf of a majority of believers in a nation of many faiths and none. Moreover,

---

2   Brian Cummings (ed.), *The Book of Common Prayer: The Texts of 1549, 1559, and 1662* (Oxford: Oxford University Press, 2011), p. 270.

3   The second of the collects for the Sovereign in the Order for Holy Communion of 1662. See Cummings, *The Book of Common Prayer: The Texts of 1549, 1559, and 1662*, pp. 391–2.

when the churches are closed—the advisability of this is an argument best pursued elsewhere—where are church leaders to speak? Thrown to the mercy of the *Today* programme's terrier-like interrogators,[4] or venturing onto social media, they find themselves unmoored from the quietness of the study, or the pulpit's monologic status, and cast adrift upon a sea of sound bites, one-liners and instant news. Is it any wonder that a certain timidity has developed when the media, hungry for today's new villain, hero or victim, light briefly but devastatingly upon a word or phrase uttered without pause for reflection? The previous Archbishop of Canterbury, Rowan Williams, was frequently mocked for his lengthy pauses in responding to interviewers, but although he was sometimes wrong-footed by the press, he managed on the whole to convey the impression that complex problems deserved careful consideration. Within the few years since his return to academia, the cultural landscape has changed quite swiftly, affecting what it is possible or permissible to say both in public debate and within universities. As Canon Professor Nigel Biggar found to his cost, an academic project established "to measure apologias and critiques of empire against historical data from antiquity to modernity across the globe", so as to "raise ethical questions of urgent public importance, which the history of empire can illuminate",[5] fell victim to the very over-simplifications it had been designed to combat. It is perhaps, then, no wonder that, faced with the multiple dilemmas raised by a global pandemic, the current Archbishop of Canterbury has thought it better by and large to be seen serving in a practical capacity as a hospital chaplain than leading public debate.

No one would doubt that hospital chaplaincy calls upon many priestly gifts, especially in the intensive care wards occupied by dying Covid patients, but is it the best use of a Church of England primate? Recently

---

[4] A regular radio programme that runs before 9 a.m. from Monday to Saturday on the BBC's Radio 4. The programme covers national and international news and conducts a number of searching live interviews with individuals concerned in current events.

[5] These quotations are taken from the University of Oxford's website for the project "Ethics and Empire", <https://www.mcdonaldcentre.org.uk/ethics-and-empire>, accessed 13 July 2022.

the Church of England has shown a penchant for fast-forwarding to senior roles those whose early successes lay in other professions: Justin Welby in the oil business, or Dame Sarah Mullally, the Bishop of London, in nursing, are two prominent examples. This has the appearance of an institution inclined to value and fast-track managerial skills over the painstaking development of spiritual discernment and the ability to articulate unpalatable truths. Similarly, it is alleged that, while some dioceses are contemplating considerable reductions to the stipendiary parish clergy, they are simultaneously advertising better-paid administrative roles, disparaged by one disenchanted rector as "spending its scarce resources on middle management".[6] These developments are both symptomatic of an institution looking elsewhere than to its fundamental *raison d'être* to remedy its sense of dwindling congregations and loss of vision. The irony, of course, is that in its attempt to bolster an institutional presence by concentrating on managerial aspects it is egregiously failing the tests by which most modern organizations are judged. Few professionals enjoy the almost ubiquitously mandatory courses on safeguarding, or unconscious bias, but few come away without learning something. Clerical appraisal schemes met with the kind of mixture and outrage they encountered in universities when they were first introduced, but in academia, when sensitively handled, they have increasingly proved a useful annual review point when concerns or training needs could be flagged up: all the more important to feel that there is systematic support of this kind in the church, where parish clergy especially can sometimes feel lonely or even beleaguered. Perhaps, given the notable changes in the distribution of church attendance across the nation, and the feeling that the church has responded by appointing more

---

[6]   Lucy Bannerman, "Clergy eased out as Church of England puts its faith in managers", *The Times*, Saturday, 6 February, 2021: "'Oversight' roles advertised by the church include: four associate archdeacon 'mission and transition' enablers in Sheffield, each with a salary of £35,000; a vision programme manager in the West Midlands, £45,000; a part-time justice, peace and integrity of creation office coordinator in Southwark, £30,000; a mission enabler in Oxford, £30,000; a growth officer in St Albans, £40,000, and a director of church revitalisation in Leeds, £52,000."

chiefs while overseeing the decline of its regular clergy, there is a case
for a root-and-branch investigation of the way in which the Church of
England organizes itself. The length of time apparently taken to resolve
some accusations against clergy suggests it has proved difficult to roll out
standardized procedures across an institution which includes the very
different spaces of parishes, cathedrals and clergy homes.

Meanwhile, during the pandemic especially, many parish clergy have
been truly valued for, *inter alia*, their willingness to visit the dying and
the bereaved and to conduct meaningful funerals and weddings under
the difficulties imposed by lockdown legislation; their willingness to
learn fresh ways of preaching the Word; and their engagement in local
practical programmes designed to help those, whatever their faith, who
have lost out so badly economically. They have, in short, been perceived
as something more than the auxiliaries to the social services that an
increasingly secular society has sometimes cast them as.

How does the diatribe above serve to help us consider this volume's
central motif: "the end of the church"? As so often with the Church, it is
worth taking a longer and broader perspective. First, and perhaps most
importantly, it has always been a great mistake to confuse the numerical
strength of a religious institution with its spiritual intensity and power.
Second, the Anglican Church is an organic institution, throwing out
limbs here and there, suffering harsh prunings, but constantly evolving.
At home, the parochial model with a priest living in every parish has been
superseded in many places, as populations have shifted, by the concept
of team ministry. Furthermore, the congregations and priesthood of
urban churches in particular have been refreshed by successive waves
of immigrants. Abroad, the shape-shifting Anglican Communion forms
new provinces and enters into full communion with churches at both
ends of the Protestant–Catholic spectrum.[7]

It may by now seem that I am in danger of mistaking the Church of
England for "the church". The Church of England is simply the Christian
community in which I grew up and have grown old: the last point has

7   These structures and developments are explained on the website of the
     Anglican Communion: <https://www.anglicancommunion.org/structures/
     member-churches.aspx>, accessed 13 July 2022.

especial relevance. Office-holders in the Church of England are required to retire at 70, though they may continue to serve in a number of non-stipendiary roles. I have been struck by how many of the clergy of my acquaintance, either retired or about to retire, are so disillusioned with the institution that they question whether they wish to continue serving within it. I suspect that it is customary for retirees in many organizations to look back over a long career and express the view that the golden age has long passed. It is certainly true of universities, where the levers of government funding have encouraged a Stakhanovite approach to research and teaching; yet there most old hands would also agree that the last fifty years have also witnessed improvements in areas as diverse as gender equality, the development of new curricula, and students now drawn from a greater cross-section of the population. None of the dispirited clergy I have met have faltered in their faith or their pastoral inclinations: it is just that they no longer feel the Church of England today bears much resemblance to the one in which they were ordained. The complaints are surprisingly uniform: poor leadership; the worst aspects of a "professionalized" ministry; the loss of a sense of direction; and all too often a culture of bullying by senior clergy, both male and female, who seem increasingly remote from and ignorant of the daily challenges experienced at parish level.

Perhaps a longer period of retrospection is required. The pandemic has certainly accentuated a feeling that it will not be possible for some of our institutions simply to resume life as if we had simply skipped a year since 23 March 2020. Universities, for instance, will struggle to convince students that a communal "experience" justifies graduate debts of over £50,000, when teaching can be accessed through the internet and accommodation costs saved. Many church buildings, deprived of regular offerings, may have to be closed down for good, and those who have lost the weekly habit of attendance may find it difficult to pick up the routine again. Yet we should not despair: the cry of "the church in crisis" has been heard before, and should not in any case be confused with the notion that humanity has abandoned all interest in religion: the thesis of the inexorable rise of secularism at the turn of the twentieth century has long been exploded. Apparently, indeed, the first lockdown saw a surge in sales of the Bible, although as the biblical scholar and Anglican priest, John Barton, wisely reminds us, the explanations for this could range through treating it as a talisman, hoping to find confirmation for apocalyptic predictions, and wishing to find words of hope and comfort.

John Barton, having rightly reminded us how open to individual interpretation the Bible is, recommends 1 Thessalonians and Galatians to believers, as a vivid picture of the early church, demonstrating "how argumentative Christians already were, just as bad then as they are now", while also showing how Christians "regarded the current state of the world as a place of suffering but also of hope".[8] The recent pandemic has certainly brought "the current state of the world as a place of suffering but also of hope" sharply into focus, while also encouraging the investigation of fundamental values and concentrating the minds of so many on what "a good death" might mean in these circumstances.

"Spirituality", as a generic term indicating metaphysical longing, or a sense of the transcendent not easily aligned to, or confined within, particular histories of institutionalized affiliation, seems likely to have been stimulated by the extraordinary circumstances created by the pandemic. Just as the Victorian age witnessed movement away from the orthodoxies of Bible, Church tradition and shared liturgy when confronted with aeons of geological change, the theory of natural selection, imperial encounters with alternative cultures, and technological advances that challenged previous conceptions of the possible, so we too, without "the Church" are in imminent danger of drifting away from "the community of saints" and into more and more privatized belief systems.

At the very least, the Church and its liturgies drag "believers" back week after week from our inner world of theological speculation, personal musings and frank disbelief, to inspect whether we still retain any identification with the doctrines and hopes they spell out. Variously the week's appointed Gospel or epistle might reignite belief, while a psalm may lead to repudiation and refusal to mouth the unintelligible or frankly vicious sentiment. This sort of sifting process is, I suspect, not uncommon among worshippers. More than that, however, the church's services, encoded in the 1662 Book of Common Prayer and

---

[8]   "Why lockdown has inspired a surge in Bible sales" <https://www.penguin. co.uk/articles/2020/05/lockdown-reading-bible>, accessed 13 July 2022.

later iterations, provide a rhythm and rhetoric, sometimes rising to the state of poetry, drawing worshippers together into a sense of a shared experience. The liturgy absorbs the various private anxieties, anguish, regrets, aspirations and wonder of those gathered there and pours them into a mould capable of containing these but also extending our prayers to encompass our fellow worshippers, and beyond them the separate worlds to which they will return. The purest expression of this is in the Communion service's "comfortable words", offered to "all that travail and are heavy laden",[9] but the consolations of a liturgy which repeatedly modulates from the individual state to the sense of a common humanity is felt most poignantly in the funeral service, which rehearses for all present the journey from birth to death and its aftermath. It does this in such a way as to draw mourners together in the recognition that, however difficult the personal circumstances, this is to be faced as a common and thus unifying experience. This resolution is in complete contrast to the pathos of a last attempt to assert singularity suggested by the increasingly frequent playing of Frank Sinatra's "My way" as the final "processional".

It was something of this sense of a loss of commonality that Philip Larkin sought to express in his poem, "Church Going".[10] Pondering what purpose churches would serve when all attendance had ceased, he imagined a future follower in his footsteps, wondering, as he tended to:

> this cross of ground
> Through suburb scrub because it held unspilt
> So long and equably what since is found
> Only in separation—marriage, and birth
> And death—and thoughts of these—for which was built
> This special shell?

Larkin himself recognized:

---

[9]   Cummings, *The Book of Common Prayer: The Texts of 1549, 1559, and 1662*, p. 400.

[10]   All further quotations from Larkin in this piece come from this poem and are to be found in his collection, *The Less Deceived* [1955] (Hull: The Marvell Press, 1977), pp. 28–9.

A serious house on serious earth it is,
In whose blent air all our compulsions meet,
Are recognised, and robed as destinies.

The archaism "blent" just avoids the anticipated "blessed" but speaks
to the co-mingling of our most urgent needs, while also suggesting a
continuity from the past to the emphatic present of "Are" in the third
line. "Robed" pays nodding allusion both to ceremonial clerical garments
and the "designed" nature of churches. Church buildings, architecture
and adornments also help to confirm and make sense of our part in
something greater, whether this is a local community, the global church
or "the communion of saints". The pandemic has acutely sharpened our
sense of our need to feel the fellowship of other human beings. While a
communion celebrated in one kitchen and received by Zoom in another,
or a funeral service streamed to mourners prevented from attending
in person by the exigencies of lockdown may have their own validity,
they are second best to being actually present in the physical building
of the church. Not only do churches feel "serious" because they have
borne witness to the chief rites of passage in people's lives over many
generations, but also because the church and its furniture are designed
to bear symbolic significance, from the baptismal font positioned at the
rear of the church at the foot of the main aisle to indicate the welcome
provided to those embarking on their Christian life, to the eastward
disposition of the sanctuary, suggesting either the church's looking
forward to the resurrection, re-enacted daily in the sun's course, or the
looking towards Jerusalem of the early Western churches.

Like all good symbols, over time these artifacts have grown beyond
any simple one-for-one translatability, and so require reinterpreting for
each generation. Such teaching is a responsibility of the Church and its
leaders. George Herbert, the seventeenth-century poet-priest, recognized
this, turning his poetic gifts to realizing and explicating the devotional
value of such artefacts as "The Altar". Herbert too stood at a turning point
for the Church: recently untethered from its Roman Catholic heritage,
the Anglican Church was potentially free to repudiate traditional
understandings, or to rework the metaphors it had inherited so as to
embrace a Reformed theology. The impulse to destroy, as idolatrous,

understandings of church architecture and decoration which invested the material with a degree of the sacral would shortly result in the iconoclastic sacking of many a parish church during the Civil War, and different understandings of the Eucharist or Communion embodied in references to the altar or the Lord's Table rumble on to this day.

> A broken ALTAR, Lord, thy servant rears,
> Made of a heart and cemented with tears:
>   Whose parts are as thy hand did frame;
>   No workman's tool hath touch'd the same.
>   A HEART alone
>   Is such a stone,
>   As nothing but
>   Thy pow'r doth cut.
>   Wherefore each part
>   Of my hard heart
>   Meets in this frame,
>   To praise thy name:
>   That if I chance to hold my peace,
>   These stones to praise thee may not cease.
> Oh, let thy blessed SACRIFICE be mine,
> And sanctify this ALTAR to be thine.[11]

Herbert's theological inclination towards either position has long been the subject of academic controversy, but as befitted a parish priest more anxious to save souls than win arguments, his poem is a model of theological tact. It contrives to suggest that the serious business of the spiritual life occurs inwardly in the individual heart, while also allowing that at moments when this is in abeyance, the physical presence of the altar continues the act of worship. Simultaneously he invokes memories of the Edwardian "stripping of the altars", asserts an unmediated relationship with God the sculptor, and punningly rebuilds "the broken altar" of the first line in the shape of his "concrete" poem.

---

[11] Louis L. Martz (ed.), *George Herbert and Henry Vaughan* (Oxford and New York: Oxford University Press, 1986), p. 22.

Larkin suggested that the swift decline of churchgoing already evident in the mid-1950s would lead to such knowledge becoming arcane and then gradually receding into a part of superstitions whose origins are long forgotten. Eventually he foresaw empty shells of churches visited by those knowledgeable about "rood-lofts . . . Some ruin-bibber, randy for antique". Not an unfair description of the professional art historians favoured by the media to present churches and cathedrals as part of the English cultural heritage while actual religious observance is hived off into watered-down community hymn-singing, or banished to more remote frequencies, or unpopular timeslots, save for Christmas when we are allowed to count upon "A whiff / Of gowns-and-bands and organ pipes and myrrh".

There is no good reason why this should be so. The Church of England cannot be devoid of qualified art historians, nor, for that matter, of "intellectually confident" theologians capable of communicating with a largely non-church-attending population. Perhaps, despite much talk of "mission", the Anglican Church at state level has become too inward-looking in its desire not to cause offence in a society of many faiths and none.[12] It may be that the move to non-stipendiary clergy, hastened by the cuts to the salaried clergy, may encourage the growth of an equally respected lay ministry moving back and forth between their secular and religious tasks. Moving regularly between different worlds can help to produce a greater awareness of the concerns of the larger parish beyond the immediate congregation.

Congregations, comfortable with their well-honed sense of churchmanship, and where certain families have grown used to rotating positions of responsibility between them, too easily become inward-looking and keener to defend their own particular culture than welcome newcomers or those who do not obviously fit the mould. Parishes

---

[12]   Nevertheless, news in February 2022 of a consultation launched by the archbishops together with the Bishop of London to consider "significant changes to the shape, structure and number of dioceses and bishops" certainly set the cat among the pigeons of the secular press. The notion of a cadre of senior bishops with special topical briefs raised fears of the creation of an alternative shadow government with a pronounced radical tendency.

should regularly ask themselves whether their patterns of worship, and especially their "break-out groups" for Bible study or prayer, have become a perfect fit for a particular lifestyle or whether they could be tweaked to accommodate the single parent or the shift worker. The proliferation of new housing estates devoid of church, church hall or pub makes it increasingly difficult for neighbours to form a community, especially if they do not belong to the nuclear family model often favoured by the speculators. The pandemic has taught many of us, especially those who live alone, of the value and pleasure of getting to know our immediate neighbours better rather than relying entirely on our closest friends and family who, not unnaturally, tend to share our outlook and presumptions. It has been customary to mock much American piety as Bible-belt fundamentalism, but many church traditions there offer us an impressive model in the way that they produce a welcoming first port of call for newcomers, who often find themselves many hundreds of miles away from the place where they grew up.

In England, we may well be approaching the point, yet again, when the notion of an established church no longer seems viable or, perhaps worse, remains viable only because it seems potentially so revolutionary to start deracinating it from our unwritten political constitution. The lingering potency of the myth of a Christian nation where personal spirituality finds its natural expression in a national system of parochial worship was in any case fully exposed 150 years ago in the 1851 Religious Census: this demonstrated the effect of a previous demographic drift, brought about by the industrial revolution, which saw a population migration from agricultural parishes, where squire and parson exercised power, to urban centres where the Church was under-represented and many labourers attended neither church nor chapel. The Anglican Church of the day was less rocked than it might have been by these findings, in that its Catholic wing had been taught in the 1830s by the initial leaders of the Oxford Movement that the clergy drew their spiritual authority not from the state, but by virtue of ordination into a church which traced its direct descent from the body instituted by Christ and his apostles. The Evangelical wing of the Church, then as now, could draw theoretical comfort at least by reminding itself of its part within the wider church invisible. Perhaps the church, as a nationally sponsored facility for

THE END OF THE CHURCH

spirituality, will save itself again by imaginative re-incarnation, not by pandering to entertainment add-ons such as helter-skelters in the nave, but by opening its doors wide.[13] The cathedrals that recognized a way of ministering to body and spirit by offering sanctuary for Covid vaccinations to take place have been widely praised for their response to a national need. The church—as an institution or as a series of buildings in use for regular services—may not survive in the form my generation has known it, but that may be for the best.

Perhaps only those who have broken whatever ties they may once have had with the church are best able to describe the sense of loss they have experienced. Larkin's semi-flippant allusion to the church graveyard is a kind of whistling to keep up his courage in the face of his recognition that death brings with it a need to feel part of "the communion of saints":

> . . . someone will forever be surprising
> A hunger in himself to be more serious,
> And gravitating with it to this ground,
> Which, he once heard, was proper to grow wise in,
> If only that so many dead lie round.

Thomas Hardy, who continued intermittently to attend church services, claimed that his critics had "cast slurs upon him as Nonconformist, Agnostic, Atheist, Infidel, Immoralist, Heretic, Pessimist or something else equally opprobrious" but they had never "thought of calling him what they might have called him much more plausibly—churchy".[14] Both he and George Eliot, whose novels were largely devoted to the search

---

13   In August 2019 Norwich Cathedral temporarily installed a helter-skelter as part of an initiative towards making the cathedral a welcoming place in a way less formal than usual. This received a mixed reception, reflected in journalism at the time, e.g., <https://www.bbc.com/news/uk-england norfolk-49292493> and see the Cathedral's own web page https://www. cathedral.org.uk/about/news/detail/2019/08/18/seeing-it-differently-farewell-service. Both websites accessed 13 July 2022.

14   Michael Millgate (ed.), *The Life and Works of Thomas Hardy* (Basingstoke: Macmillan, 1984), p. 407.

for a way to live the moral life beyond the confines of the Church, were attracted by the shared worship and liturgical ritual developed by the Positivists, though neither actually became formal members.[15] I can in fact think of few better ways of finishing this brief piece about "the end of the church" than by offering the tribute paid by George Eliot to the institution she had left. *Adam Bede* (1859), the novel in which this passage occurs, is retrospectively narrated, allowing Eliot to suggest that though he is not in a position to recognize this, the form Adam's observance of his faith takes is already obsolescent. Nevertheless, as Eliot broadens her commentary from the particular to the general, she finds herself reaching back to the church's long history of continuity and distancing herself from "the unsympathizing observer". In pinpointing the inherently conservative nature of most older worshippers' attachment to the Church, this passage also awakens us to the counter notion that if the Church is to survive we may need to open ourselves to the possibility of major change:

> And to Adam the church service was the best channel he could have found for his mingled regret, yearning, and resignation; its interchange of beseeching cries for help with outbursts of faith and praise—its recurrent responses and the familiar rhythm of its collects, seemed to speak for him as no other form of worship could have done; as, to those early Christians who had worshipped from their childhood upwards in catacombs, the torch-light and shadows must have seemed nearer the Divine presence than the heathenish daylight of the streets. The secret of our emotions never lies in the bare object, but in its subtle relations to our own past: no wonder the secret escapes the unsympathizing observer, who might as well put on his spectacles to discern odours.[16]

---

[15]   T. R. Wright, *The Religion of Humanity: The Impact of Comtean Positivism on Victorian Britain* (Cambridge: Cambridge University Press, 1986), pp. 176 and 196.

[16]   George Eliot, *Adam Bede*, ed. Valentine Cunningham (Oxford: Oxford University Press, 1996), p. 199.

8

The End of Church? An Experiment in Beauty Refracted

Margaret Masson

I do not know David Jasper well, but I will always be grateful to him for establishing the study of theology and literature in Durham back in the 1980s. This, along with the presence of Ruth Etchells, who offered to supervise my PhD, was a key reason for my coming to study in Durham, and that decision set the course of the direction of the rest of my life.

I have fond memories of those early Durham Theology and Literature conferences—the camaraderie, the intellectual energy and excitement at the emergence of this new combined discipline, conversations and ideas spilling over from seminars into the Hatfield College bar or worship in the chapel where David was chaplain. And beyond the annual conferences, David ensured a regular programme of papers and conversations around the University including, from time to time, in the home he shared with Alison. For anyone interested in theology and literature as I was, Durham in the 1980s felt like the place to be—certainly in the UK—and David was the strategist, the host, the curator, the enthusiast who brought this all together, and through it all, he was kind and encouraging to the young scholars like me who were drawn to Durham thanks, at least in part, to his energy and focus.

Sadly, I never did carry forward as much of the kind of scholarly work in theology and literature as I had hoped to. My post PhD saw me busy as a young college lecturer in the USA, and in 1992 I returned to Durham to continue my career as Senior Tutor in one of Durham's colleges—St John's. Nearly three decades on, I find myself Principal of another—St

Chad's—where David himself was Principal for a short time. Although I
was able to carry on my teaching in the University's English Department,
I never managed to detach myself sufficiently from the business of college
work to write as I had hoped. But I have loved the alternative creativity of
helping to shape a college community, and it has been here that my own
scholarly vocation has found expression—not primarily in conference
papers and scholarly articles and book chapters, but in helping to work
out a vision for a multi-disciplinary residential academic institution in
all the materiality, spirituality and intellectual vitality of its life.

What drew me to the intersection of theology and literature is also
what drew me to immersing myself in the life of a college—my enjoyment
of meaning embodied, insight en-fleshed, lived experience given shape
and texture and rhythm. It's also no accident that I have found myself
working in the two Durham colleges that have their roots in the Church
and which define themselves within the Christian tradition. St Chad's,
which stopped training ordinands for ministry in the Church of England
in the 1970s, has had particular need to ask itself through the years what,
if anything, this foundation continues to mean as its relationships with
the Church, the University and indeed its students have changed hugely
since its foundation. This search for meaning, texture, shape—not within
a literary text, academic discipline or typical scholarly vocation, but in a
living, changing, complex institution—has certainly been an intellectual
task which has drawn on my literary and theological imagination every
bit as much as on my experience in pastoral care and leadership.

The world in which these colleges live has, of course, changed
significantly and often rapidly in recent years and in 2016, at the time
I was thinking about applying to be the next Principal of St Chad's, the
College's identity as a Christian or church institution was under lively
scrutiny. Many students and governors, who loved the College, did
not see a need for any continuing mooring to its Anglican foundation.
Indeed, to their eyes, the Church represented many things that they
abhorred including homophobia, misogyny, racism and bigotry, and
many believed that the College continued to flourish despite its Christian
heritage, not because of it. For them the relevance of the Church had all
but ended—certainly as it pertained to a college like St Chad's. And not
before time.

I disagreed. I understood these critics' distrust of Christian values and the institutional Church. I understood that to many of our members, the Church was accepted—sometimes tolerated—as part of our history but had no significant place as an ongoing inspiration: why would any forward-looking institution like St Chad's hold itself back by continuing to define itself in relation to outmoded, sometimes offensive, affiliations and associations? Yet in my own imagination—shaped through the years in the edgelands of theology and literature—the possibilities and resonances of rich untapped seams that still ran deep in the College's Anglican bedrock convinced me that there was much in the tradition that could and should continue to resource the identity of this small and lovely Durham college. For us, in our time and context, this was not the end of Church; I did not believe its possibilities had all been played out in the life of St Chad's. Rather I believed this small university college with its Christian foundation could be an end of church in the sense of being one of its possible outworkings or extrapolations. At the very least, I hoped it could be an arena in which much that had remained rich, resonant and true through millennia of Christian theology and experience—traditions around hospitality, truth, justice, beauty, for example—could still be fruitfully explored and expressed in the context of our modern College. I believed that these Christian resources could help us, whatever the mixture of faith and beliefs of current members, to co-create a community that was able to interpret and be defined by its heritage in a way that gave it integrity, purpose and vision whilst also being true to its current identity, membership and aspirations. As Principal, I wanted to see if we could continue to draw on Christian tradition and insights to help animate an institution that was not church, and not inhabited mostly by Christians.

One of the features of Christian theology that makes it endlessly fascinating as well as infinitely resourceful is its core belief in the Incarnation. The God of all creation comes to live as a human being—embodied, enfleshed, enculturated and thus able to identify with beautiful, flawed, particular humans—and their institutions. The implications of this root understanding radiate through all of Christian theology and practice, which means that Christian belief must always be interpreted, translated, embodied within whichever particular context it finds itself. The Truth, the Word, can never be understood as fixed, distilled essence, but is always improvised. Literature likewise—along with each of the arts—carries its meaning in its expression. "A poem should not mean but be," as Paul Valery maintained; the same is true of institutions and communities.

So, what might this being, this form actually look like when expressed as a college? Not long after I assumed the role of Principal of St Chad's, its governors rightly agreed it was time for a new strategy, a fresh sense of direction and purpose. It was not that they were unhappy with where the College found itself—far from it—but after Joe Cassidy's long and transformational principalship had come to an abrupt end with his untimely death, this was a good and necessary time to take stock and work out where the College should be heading in the years to come. We needed an articulation of who we were now, what we were about and what we wanted to aim for.

Formulating the strategy was very much a community effort, with students and staff as well as governors given the chance to contribute their thoughts. From all the conversation and debate of that time, a strategy emerged which tried to articulate our hopes and intentions as St Chad's College for the foreseeable future. It was an energizing, occasionally fraught, but ultimately fruitful process. One of the words that raised the odd eyebrow—it sat oddly, even discordantly, amidst the usual language of Strategy—was Beauty. For reasons I could not entirely articulate at the time, it felt important to have this word near the heart of any attempt to define what the College was about, and, looking back, I think part of what I wanted it to convey was our commitment to our Strategy not just being an ideal articulation of abstract virtues to which we aspired, but something that had shape and form and was dynamically alive.

Beauty

In part and most obviously, Beauty expresses something about the institution as a physical place—its buildings and sense of space, its bricks and mortar, its grounds, its fabric. St Chad's as a set of buildings has an innate beauty. Its location alone, set on a world heritage site just across the road from Durham's impressive cathedral, ensures that its lovely physical presence is at the heart of its identity and what it means to its members. It is one of the things that draws people to want to be part of the College, and one of the things that they remember so fondly.

In recent years, I felt we had become more utilitarian in our work on the fabric of the College; while we had a rolling programme of refurbishment, we had not always paid sufficient attention to aesthetics, and a kind of carelessness and clutter had come to characterize our estate—a misjudged choice of paint or carpet tile here, a riding roughshod over a beautiful feature there, an occasional pile of timber (or row of toilet cisterns) half abandoned in the grounds . . . I was sometimes embarrassed when I stumbled across such lack of care in the course of showing visitors around the College, and I believed strongly that this inattentiveness did not express the meaning of who we were. I wanted each decision about our buildings and grounds to consider beauty, not just price and utility, the kind of beauty (I argued) that did not need to mean more expense, but rather more thought and care. I also understood beauty as part of St Chad's' theologically catholic DNA, integral to a heritage that was worth honouring, part of a sensibility that valued the aesthetic as embodying, reflecting and bearing witness, ultimately, to the beauty of God.

This sense of the importance of beauty, then, goes far beyond the physical and geographical. It also encompasses the kind of beauty that philosophers, poets and theologians through the ages have seen as connecting us with the deepest truths and joys of human existence, and it felt important to try to restore the thread of this meaning as core to our aspirations as a college. What might it mean to try to be an institution that saw beauty as quintessential to what we wanted to express, to try to draw out and reflect this in our gardens and buildings, our intellectual life, our characters, our relationships, our outreach—in fact, in the whole of our life together? Could this be a community that could inspire, express and nurture all that was beautiful in its members and the world in which we lived?

Does this sound fanciful? Perhaps! However, after thirty years of involvement in college life, and responsibility for, among other things, the pastoral care and discipline of a wonderful array of characters, I have a very clear sense of the challenges of collegiate life. I have lived through the dramas, the moments of tragedy, the celebration, the banality, and I am acutely aware of the many ways in which communities and the individuals within them can be far from beautiful—disfigured by cruelty, cynicism and fear. I have seen the damage inflicted by dysfunctional families and racism and sexual violence and entitlement and abuse of power and all the rest. But I have also seen the beauty of a place in which people can find the kind of acceptance and friendship and love that liberates them, a space in which they can be truly seen—both as they are now but also as they have the potential to be. This dual recognition is transformative, and in its moments of radiance it offers glimpses of what beauty embodied in a community can look like.

Gerard Manley Hopkins' understanding of his poetic vocation depends on this kind of notion of beauty. His term "inscape" describes the quintessential "thisness" of something or someone—that moment of recognition when a creature or person or movement is so utterly and irreducibly itself that there is an overflow of presence which results in joy and wonder. This attentiveness to inscape is an intellectual as well as a spiritual perception, long celebrated by artists, poets, mystics, theologians; I believe this kind of recognition and receptiveness can also characterize an institution.

Hans Urs von Balthasar, believed by some to be one of the last century's most brilliant theologians (and one whose name I first heard at one of the early Theology and Literature Conferences in Durham), set Beauty at the heart of his great trilogy. In *The Glory of the Lord*, the first set of its volumes, he restates the relationship between truth, love and beauty by reordering the transcendental virtues and placing beauty first:

> Whoever . . . confronts such wholeness of truth desires to choose as his first word one which he will not have to take back . . . but one which is broad enough to foster and include all words to follow, and clear enough to penetrate all the others with its light.[1]

---

[1]   Hans Urs von Balthasar, *The Glory of the Lord: A Theological Aesthetics*, vol. 1: *Seeing the Form* [1967] (San Francisco, CA: Ignatius Press, 1982), p. 17.

Balthasar, who cared very much that thought and theory should be thoroughly integrated with lived experience, believed that recognizing and restoring the primacy of beauty helps us see the kind of transformative trinity in which truth and goodness find their being and wholeness in a dynamic relationship that truly expresses their mutual interdependence:

> For von Balthasar, beauty is a dynamic event: what is objectively beautiful "apprehends" and transforms the beholder, drawing him or her into a kind of union with itself. "Beauty" therefore refers both to something given and to a personal response, and embraces both the objective and the subjective. When confronted with beauty's revelation, people are drawn to it beyond themselves. Something good and true has taken place in this experience.[2]

Balthasar was referred to in his time as "the most cultured man in Europe". Certainly, he was an intellectual giant, but not, interestingly, one who ever accepted an academic appointment. Some would argue that the strengths and weaknesses of this freedom from institutional academic constraints mark his theology, and his analogical model is not unproblematic for those of us grappling with the perplexities of contemporary gender politics. However, many appreciate the way Balthasar's theology sets thinking (truth) and action (goodness) firmly in the context of the desiring that lies at the heart of beauty—we must be captivated by beauty's simultaneous longing and recognition before truth and goodness can find their full expression.

So, what does this dynamic of the aesthetic calling out, this giving shape to the ethical and the truthful, look like in the context of the life of a place like St Chad's? Quite a number of our students describe arriving at St Chad's for the first time—often on an Open Day visit— and experiencing a sense as soon as they walk in the door that this is the college for them. It is an intuitive sense: they have been grasped by something that I like to think of as the beauty of St Chad's at its best. It

---

[2] Joan L. Roccasalvo, "Hans Urs von Balthasar: Theologian of Beauty", *The Way* 44:4 (2005), pp. 49–63, here at p. 56.

is variously expressed: some comment on the welcome they received, others on the beauty of the place—our Cassidy Quad, perhaps, right at the heart of the College with its unexpected light and space. Some refer back to the glimpse they catch of our aspirations as we've talked about the kind of college community we hope to be. What I think they are responding to is that simultaneous sense of longing and recognition that we experience when we are captivated by something beautiful. It is a kind of homecoming, perhaps even a kind of falling in love.

Of course, the reality, when they have been Chad's students for a while, does not always live up to this initial perception, and our new students must learn along with the rest of us how to live with the compromised messy and sometimes disappointing reality. If they challenge us (and, hopefully, also themselves) to live up to what they first saw in the college, and the clarity of their initial hopes, this can be bracing. If we can hear this and along with them resist the slip-sliding into defensiveness or disillusion or cynicism, if we can nurture a mature commitment to the work of co-creation, then something really worthwhile can emerge— something closer to what we're aiming to be—a college community that students from all kinds of backgrounds and beliefs can call home, a place where intellectually and personally they are supported and challenged in equal measure, given space to understand and grow into their own "inscape", and know themselves to be known, seen and accepted. Such a community is transformative, mostly in countless small ways, but occasionally recognized in moments of epiphany—that experience of everything coming together, and a transfigured reality is glimpsed.

It is these glimpses, I think, that make successive generations of students want to hang at each and every welcome event a large (and not particularly beautiful) banner which boldly proclaims "Chad's: the happiest place on earth". Much of the time, of course, it isn't, and our students know this. But for many of them, it is a place where they have experienced a sense of integration and happiness that binds together so much of what they value. It is this I want to express as Beauty.

If this kind of integrating energy, this fulfilment of form and being in which truth and goodness find their expression, is a kind of Beauty, I'd like to sketch out just a few examples of how this finds tangible expression in the life of an institution like St Chad's College.

Justice and inclusion

The College had its beginnings in 1902, when a vicar in Hooton Pagnell near Doncaster wanted to make it possible for young men of slender means to follow their vocation to be priests in the Church of England. To do this, they needed to be educated, and thanks to various generous benefactors, this led to the foundation of St Chad's Hall in Durham in 1904, which grew into St Chad's College, which continues to be a recognized college of Durham University. Throughout its history, and certainly since the beginning of Joe Cassidy's Principalship, St Chad's has been very conscious of these roots and has worked hard—through bursaries and scholarships—to make it possible for students from lower income backgrounds to be find their place and thrive here. There has also been a conscious emphasis on outreach and service (including in a rural school in South Africa for a number of years) as a way of trying to live out and put flesh on the College's founding commitment to what we now tend to call justice and inclusion.

The St Chad's motto—*Non Vestra Sed Vos*—is very much understood within this context and much quoted and hash-tagged: "Not what you have but who you are", "Not yours but you". This is often taken to mean that, as a college, we want to look beyond a person's wealth, whether material or social, and welcome people from all backgrounds regardless of what they bring with them. It is easy to be glib or naïve about such aspirations, and in reality trying to work them out can be complex and disruptive and involve us in all kinds of demanding reflection: what is the fairest way to select scholarship or bursary recipients? If we are serious about diversity, how open are we as a college to having some of our cherished traditions questioned, transformed, possibly even dismantled? Such negotiations take time, honesty, generosity and humility but are essential if we aim to be a more just and inclusive community, and if we aim to be a place of hospitality and welcome.

Hospitality

Above the high table in St Chad's hang three paintings by Kirril Sokolov, a Russian artist who was a resident of Durham for many years; his widow (and distinguished Russian scholar) Avril Pyman is a member of the St Chad's Senior Common Room. The paintings form a kind of triptych that can be read as a meditation on hospitality. The central image, the smallest, was painted from a scene in a village in Russia where the artist enjoyed the daily ritual of a woman, fortunate enough to own a cow, sharing its milk with her friends. From this image, Sokolov painted a number of images inspired by Rublev's icon of the Holy Trinity, and two of these hang in the Chad's dining room on each side of the Russian friends.

Together, these images express some distinctively Christian understandings of hospitality. In a religious tradition with a trinitarian concept of God, human identity is understood in the context of relationship, and hospitality is seen as intrinsic to the notion of community. Just as Rublev's icon draws on the story of Abraham and Sarah welcoming the stranger and so entertaining God's angel unawares, the importance of hospitality for the stranger, of ensuring a welcome for everyone and especially those in need, is deep rooted in a tradition that gave rise to hospitals and hospices. We see it enshrined in the Rule of St Benedict with its matter-of-fact instruction teaching us how this tradition of welcome and inclusion has been managed in the context of monastic communities for hundreds of years—radical, inclusive, practical, sustainable: God's invitation grounded and made tangible.

Of course, a college like St Chad's is far from being a monastic institution or a radical intentional Christian community. Among other things, it is a university college and a business that needs to make ends meet. The beautiful vision of hospitality has to be worked out, as it is in Benedict's Rule and with Sokolov's women, in the gritty materiality of community life—in the case of St Chad's, the reality of accommodation charges, aging boilers, food budgets, debates about the ethics of meat-eating, and the sometimes jagged politics of class and gender and race. Negotiating all this is as bracing as it is illuminating. Yet the Sokolov paintings above the place where we eat together serve as a reminder that the call to justice and inclusion that lie deep within the seams of the rock from which we were hewn has imaginative hospitality and generous welcome close to its gut. It also brings joy and beauty when we manage to live it faithfully.

Community

It is easy to feel warm and high-minded about community in the context of a wonderful feast. Certainly, entertaining guests on high table at our formal dinners is something that is hugely enjoyable. Getting on with those that one lives with day in, day out can be a little harder. It is easy to think of college "community" as a catch-all shorthand for a rather romantic sense of the fun of having an extended house party with one's friends. However, building a community takes hard work and a lot of grace, and when members feel let down by some lack of collegiality, when we fail as a college to live up to our billing as inclusive and friendly, it hurts.

The kind of hospitality and community envisaged in the Christian tradition assumes a kind of radical profligacy that reflects the unconditional grace and love of God. As a college within one of the UK's elite universities which demands high academic grades as a condition of entry, and often assumes so many of the privileges associated with this kind of academic success, we are, of course, very far from the kind of total inclusivity of access of a Benedictine monastery. But within the daunting limits of the highly competitive hierarchical system of UK higher education, we do our best to ensure as diverse a cohort of students as we can—in terms of social background, ethnicity, religious tradition, nationality and gender. And once students settle in, we encourage them not just to gravitate towards others who look and sound and dress and vote and believe more or less as they do. We hope that they will—and they usually do—befriend and begin to see the world through the eyes of others who bring a very different perspective.

This kind of engagement takes us back to the kind of beauty that Hopkins's concept of inscape suggests—this piercing sense of the particularity of someone or something, the recognition of someone as they are—not as one wants them to be or simply imagined as an alternative version of oneself or even as a type. This attention to the other's particularity invites a certain spaciousness and welcome and respect—a kind of hospitality.

These moments of engagement and exchange may be glimpsed often in the course of college life—in the bar or dining room, on the sports field or stage or at choral Evensong, in a college seminar or discussion or a volunteering project. Some of the most significant expressions of this kind of hospitality, inclusion and community have, for me, been in the hard, risky college conversations we have held in St Chad's over the years. Two in particular stand out, perhaps because in both we had students deeply invested in one particular side or the other and for whom the stakes felt high. One was a conversation about the politics of Israel–Palestine, and involved students who were Muslim, Jewish (some supportive, some critical of Israel), and others of us simply there to understand more about this fiercely contested land. The second was a series of conversations we called *China and the World* culminating in the sensitive topic of the relationship between China and Hong Kong. Involved in this series were students from mainland China, Hong Kong, and indeed from at least seven or eight other different nations, all keen to understand more. What felt most important about these conversations— freighted with risk as well as possibility—was the way that members of the same college community, who had never had this opportunity before, listened deeply and talked from various sides of a fraught geopolitical divide and so helped us all to understand a little of what it looked and felt like, through other eyes.

There are many other examples of ways in which a college like St Chad's can draw from the wellsprings of its Christian heritage to resource its current members—vocation, service, discipline, friendship to name just a few. One of the challenges is how one holds these together with integrity. How can Christianity continue to resource an institution when most of its members are no longer Christian, and no longer united in a common purpose or set of beliefs?

It is important that the values that resource an institution with a diverse membership must be ones that are generally agreed to be for the common good, widely shared and owned. Values like justice, inclusion, hospitality and community are not, of course, the property of one faith but have common referents in all great belief systems. When an institution draws from its own particular understanding of such values in the light of its particular religious heritage, this should not feel exclusive to those who do not share this heritage. It is important that everyone is part of the conversation around interpretation and contextualization: the kind of dialectical scrutiny that should be part of the life of any learning community.

An institution like St Chad's may see the fruits of its Christian heritage as gifts to be shared for the flourishing of all, shared in a way that embraces the risk that incarnation assumes in letting go of any sense of protective ownership of *our* cherished values; do we have the confidence and humility not only to see them burnished and polished in the exchange, but also handled and questioned and changed—sometimes even tarnished?

Although prayer and worship still resource its heart and help sustain its continuing Christian inspiration and identity, a college like St Chad's is not a church. The values that it draws from the tradition must be translated in such a way as to make sense and ring true for and hopefully inspire all its diverse members so that everyone may feel invested in the community and all can flourish. The stories of who we are as communities are vital in helping us find shape and meaning together and one of my most important jobs as Principal is to articulate our structuring narrative in a way that is aspirational and true and inclusive. It will be constantly tested in the crux of the community, and with each new generation, new and creative variations will emerge.

The use of rhetoric in religious settings is a key strand in David Jasper's work and often explored with a large dose of critical scrutiny. In *Rhetoric, Power and Community*, he warns of the manipulative potential of religious rhetoric, the risks of the assurance of its own certainty and objectivity and truth. Jasper's acute sensitivity to the seduction of language and especially religious language, and the "manipulation and persuasion which lie at the heart of all kinds of community and community action" is a reminder to all who see their vocation as the building of communities— especially those that draw from the powerful rhetoric of religious texts. Jasper warns of the dangers of "complicity in the imposition of power" and the particular need in such contexts for responsible readings—and, presumably, the prior need for responsible articulations.[3]

One of the bracing realities of articulating any kind of vision in the context of a college like St Chad's, with its diverse cohort of young people as intelligent as they are invested (not to forget an engaged community of alumni and senior members), is that the kind of scrutiny involved in what Jasper calls "responsible reading" is a given. If the rhetoric feels false or manipulative, students will soon sense this and find ways to tell you. If the gap between aspiration and practice is too wide, they will be quick to point this out. Hopefully they will also be willing to join in the work of responsible deconstruction and creative reimagining that contributes towards a truer articulation and brings practice and aspiration closer together.

This kind of co-creation is at the heart of what shapes a college community like St Chad's. It is a continual exercise in hermeneutics and translation every bit as demanding of subtle intellect as more conventional scholarly vocations require. And interpreting St Chad's alongside others generates fresh insights and practice, sometimes unexpected, as community is contextualized in a fresh matrix of meanings, truth and goodness refracted in new ways in the life of a community buzzing with curiosity and potential.

For individual students, as is the case in most educational institutions, the invitation to live an examined life is made real not just in the public articulation of the vision and values but in the way these are lived out in each member, offering both invitation and challenge.

In a college like St Chad's, we hope that our members take some of the many opportunities to explore the foundations of their beliefs—the religious claims of Christianity and other religious traditions, as well as what they might too easily take for granted as the self-evident truths of Western secularism. And if together we have managed to live by the values that underpin our community life—including intellectual curiosity, justice, inclusion, hospitality—in a way that has integrity and

---

[3]   David Jasper, *Rhetoric, Power and Community: An Exercise in Reserve* (London: Macmillan, 1993; Louisville, KY: Westminster/John Knox Press, 1993), p. 150.

resonance, then we hope that students will carry these with them into the rich variety of their lives beyond St Chad's.

In the gardens of St Chad's stands an old, low-slung, whitewashed wooden building: the Chad's chapel. It was meant to be temporary, but it's stood there for almost a hundred years. It is easy to miss. It is not ancient or spectacular like some college chapels. It is cold in winter, and we have to put buckets out to catch the leaks when it rains. The choir sings the Sunday Eucharist and regular Evensongs as they have been sung for generations but now to a tiny congregation. Prayers are said on weekdays, whether anyone turns up or not. Yet here, in the margins of the college, we find the wellspring from which the values, the identity and vision of St Chad's flow. The result is the co-creation of a lively, diverse community, most of whose members would no longer identify as Christian, yet still, these timeless values find their resonance afresh in each generation.

Is this an end of Church? If by this we mean that the truths and values that the Church has embodied for centuries are a spent force, then clearly not. They continue to be a rich resource for an institution like St Chad's which, although not Church, is sustained and nourished by the fruitful interaction between its founding inspiration and its emerging life. And more than this: in those moments when I catch a glimpse of St Chad's living its best life, I see it as a kind of extrapolation, a fulfilment, a refraction of that beauty in which what we know to be both good and true, what we simultaneously recognize and long for, finds a home.

9

Imaginary Homelands'
Legends and Ghosts

Lori A. Kanitz

Over thirty years ago, under the supervision of David Jasper at Durham University, I wrote a Master's degree thesis on Salman Rushdie's novel *The Satanic Verses*. Published in 1989, the novel, a postmodern work of fiction about two Indian immigrants' experiences assimilating (or not) to life in England, set off a theological and political firestorm. Because the novel, more broadly, explores questions about how one constructs national, religious, cultural and personal identities—and what it means to be faithful to those—it inadvertently and tragically uncovered just how perilous those questions can be. A *fatwa* was issued calling for Rushdie's assassination, translators were murdered, Rushdie himself was forced into hiding. The novel became notorious, and its plot forgotten. "The Rushdie Affair", however, lingered for nearly a decade, and was brought back to our attention by the attack on Salman Rushdie in August 2022.

When I began the thesis in 1990, the UK was still deeply embroiled in debates the novel had engendered. How does one construct an identity? What is the balance between fixity and change? And how are these identities informed through "the stories we live by"—religious, national, cultural? In short, the immigrant experience became a macrometaphor for how one responds to life's exigencies that demand one adapt, rescript one's story and remain nimble—or descend into irrelevance and madness by insisting on a fixed and brittle fantasy. Rushdie terms these fantasies "imaginary homelands" in his collection of essays by the same name.

Never could I have dreamed that thirty years later, as Brexit, Trumpism and populist leaders touting virulent nationalism gain footholds in seemingly robust democracies, that this novel's prophetic warnings about how we construct our identities would seem more relevant than ever.[1] What is even more astonishing, however, is the book's theological power to speak truth to the manifold identity crises of the early twenty-first century in ways the Christian Church seems to have abandoned. The Church, and I speak as an American, seems also to be engaged in a doomed attempt to realize imaginary homelands, rather than embrace the ephemerality of all but the one Homeland.

With great gratitude and indebtedness to David Jasper's legacy, this chapter will take up Rushdie's metaphor of "imaginary homelands" in an effort (1) to suggest that both the theological right and left are perhaps ghosted by a dangerous nostalgia for a fantasy; and (2) to re-examine the Church's prophetic call to manifest "amazing grace", as the means by which one holds in loving embrace conflicting identities wherever we find them—whether our own souls, communities, or nations—and learns to sing a love song to our mongrel selves.

Imaginary Homelands: A reprise

In his 1992 essay entitled "Imaginary Homelands", Rushdie explores the unique challenges emigrant writers, specifically Indian writers living in the West, face navigating the challenges of living and writing from within a culture that is both "home" and not home: "Our identity is at once plural and partial. Sometimes we feel that we straddle two cultures; at other times, that we fall between two stools."[2] Rushdie begins autobiographically, describing a 1946 black and white photo of his childhood home in "Bombay, which is my lost city",[3] that rendered

---

[1] See, for example, Anne Applebaum's recent analysis "The Bad Guys are Winning", *The Atlantic* (15 November 2021), accessed 15 November 2021.

[2] Salman Rushdie, "Imaginary Homelands", *Imaginary Homelands* (London: Granta Books, 1991), p. 15.

[3] Rushdie, "Imaginary Homelands", p. 9.

all memories of his early life in India in monochrome. After being away from the city for over half his life, Rushdie returned and on impulse drove to his childhood home. Standing before it, he was astonished by its vibrant colours and living presence. It was at that moment, he observes, there awakened a longing "to restore the past to myself",[4] to reclaim all the living colour, both real and metaphorical, that had leeched out of his memories. If Bombay was a city "built by foreigners upon reclaimed land", he had been away long enough nearly to qualify as one and was seized by the impulse to reclaim his version of its history.[5]

Importantly, he suggests that this impulse is not just his own but a universal experience that immigrant writers are uniquely qualified to help their audiences perceive. All writers, he surmises, who are "exiles or emigrants or expatriates are haunted by some sense of loss, some urge to reclaim [the forgotten country], to look back, even at the risk of being mutated into pillars of salt".[6] However, he warns, the past we reconstruct should never be confused with the lost homeland itself. Any time we attempt to reconstruct the past, "we will, in short, create fictions, no actual cities or villages, but invisible ones, imaginary homelands . . . ".[7] In short, when we construct or reconstruct an identity—whether cultural, national, or personal—we "are obliged to deal in broken mirrors, some of whose fragments have been irretrievably lost".[8]

What is most fascinating and theologically fertile about Rushdie's thinking here is his dogged insistence on the fecundity of these "in-between" spaces, of occupying and constructing narratives from within them. "However ambiguous and shifting this ground may be," Rushdie asserts, "it is not infertile territory for a writer to occupy. If literature is in part the business of finding new angles at which to enter reality, then once again our distance, our long geographical perspective, may provide us with such angles."[9] This is certainly "part of the business"

---

4   Rushdie, "Imaginary Homelands", p. 10.
5   Rushdie, "Imaginary Homelands", p. 10.
6   Rushdie, "Imaginary Homelands", p. 10.
7   Rushdie, "Imaginary Homelands", p. 10.
8   Rushdie, "Imaginary Homelands", pp. 10–11.
9   Rushdie, "Imaginary Homelands," p. 15.

of *The Satanic Verses*. The narrator in the first pages of the novel asks, "How does newness come into the world? How is it born? Of what fusions, translations, conjoinings is it made?"[10] However else the novel might be read or remembered, it is Rushdie's postmodern manifesto to the creative power of ongoing cultural and personal metamorphosis by fusion of often conflicting and disparate realities through what he terms "translation", a central theme in both *The Satanic Verses* and Rushdie's work at large. While acknowledging that English has been and must be recognized as one of many instruments of colonization, he asserts that Indian writers must begin forging a new identity *within* the English language, in short, they must assent to being translated:

> [English] must, in spite of everything, be embraced. The word "translation" comes, etymologically, from the Latin for "bearing across". Having been borne across the world, we are translated men. It is normally supposed that something always gets lost in translation; I cling, obstinately, to the notion that something can also be gained.[11]

He goes on to observe that the existential difficulty which makes translation—both linguistic and cultural—such a contested notion is that, at bottom, it foregrounds questions of identity:

> To be an Indian writer in [English] society is to face, every day, problems of definition. What does it mean to be "Indian" outside India? . . . What are the consequences, both spiritual and practical, of refusing to make any concessions to Western ideas and practices? What are the consequences of those ideas and practices and turning away from the ones that came here with us? These questions are all a single, existential question: How are we to live in the world?[12]

---

[10]   Salman Rushdie, *The Satanic Verses* (London: Viking, 1988), p. 8.

[11]   Rushdie, "Imaginary Homelands", p. 17.

[12]   Rushdie, "Imaginary Homelands", p. 18.

The question is, of course, a universal one. Rushdie notes that "it may be argued that the past is a country from which we have all emigrated, that its loss is part of our common humanity".[13] However, the writer, the person, who experiences living outside his or her home country and gives voice to that experience in another language knows concretely the sense of "discontinuity"[14] with the past and feels acutely the necessity and difficulty of translation in ways that can perhaps uniquely inform this universal human experience.[15] The term "translation" creates implicitly the metaphor of the self and world as text. Indeed, the process of selecting, excluding and interpreting the events and memories that forge an identity is essentially the process of meaning-making through story. One assembles the bits and pieces into a more or less cohesive narrative that explains and gives shape to one's perception of self, the world and others.

Importantly, for Rushdie, because historical knowledge is partial and fragmentary and memory is fallible, the stories we live by must continually undergo translation as new experiences invite us to reimagine and rewrite the stories we live by. So to return to the foundational question, "How are we to live in the world?", we return to Rushdie's vision of being, summarized in his defence of *The Satanic Verses* in his 1990 essay, "In Good Faith":

> [*The Satanic Verses*] celebrates hybridity, impurity, intermingling, the transformation that comes of new and unexpected combinations of human beings, cultures, ideas, politics, movies, songs. It rejoices in mongrelization and fears the absolutism of the Pure. Mélange, hotchpotch, a bit of this and a bit of that is *how newness enters the world*. It is the great possibility that mass migration gives the world, and I have tried to embrace it. *The Satanic Verses* is for change-by-fusion, change-by-conjoining. It is a love song to our mongrel selves.[16]

---

13   Rushdie, "Imaginary Homelands", p. 12.
14   Rushdie, "Imaginary Homelands", p. 12.
15   Rushdie, "Imaginary Homelands", p. 12.
16   Salman Rushdie, "In Good Faith", in *Imaginary Homelands*, p. 394.

In short, we are to live in the world as joyful mongrels, as "translated" individuals who humbly acknowledge that though we construct our realities as faithfully as we can, we do so with broken mirrors of memory, tradition, texts and communities. As creatures whose lives are narratives situated within a historical context and shaped by a multitude of experiences, intellectual and spiritual integrity demands we acknowledge that no person is a homogenous entity. Paradoxically, to become more authentically oneself, and more humane, means to be always creating and recreating, reshaping and remoulding oneself with each new experience. For Christians, to use a Pauline metaphor, it means undergoing the often painful and deconstructive process of being "conformed to the image" of Christ (Romans 8:29). In short, one is continually undergoing a translation of identity, bringing newness into the world by fusing the old and the new.

Unholy ghosts and fixity's fury

For Christians, the question of how to live in the world, specifically how one negotiates the tension of being "in the world but not of it", is an old one. Jesus's prayer for his disciples the night before his crucifixion includes a prayer for God's protection over them, since they (and we) like him "do not belong to the world, just as I do not belong to the world" (John 17:16). Within the New Testament canon is a seemingly wide spectrum of options for engagement with and appropriation of the culture at large.[17] Countless scriptures allude to, or state explicitly that there

---

[17]   For example, Paul's address to the Greeks on the Areopagus in Acts 17 reflects deep cultural knowledge and appropriation. Paul often speaks of freedom in Christ from the law, the very means by which Jews in Roman Palestine carved out a distinctive identity. To the Corinthian church he claims, "I have become all things to all people, so that I might by any means save some." (1 Corinthians 9:22) Yet he also admonishes the Roman church, "Do not be conformed to this world, but be transformed by the renewing of your minds, so that you may discern what is the will of God—what is good and acceptable and perfect" (Romans 12:2).

are two worlds—a spiritual kingdom and earthly powers—at war with one another, and Christians are but aliens and strangers in this present age (Hebrews 11:13). Perhaps the most well-known treatise outlining broadly the Church universal's various responses to this question is H. Richard Niebuhr's *Christ and Culture*. These responses range from total withdrawal from and rejection of the prevailing culture ("Christ against Culture") to the conversionist position Niebuhr identifies as "Christ Transformer of Culture".[18] These questions remain perplexing. What does it mean to be distinctively Christian in a pluralistic society? How do Christians in democratic societies defend religious liberties unique to and crucial for them without insisting on a theocratic state? When Christianity has been complicit in a nation's sins, how does it acknowledge and repent of them without negating the belief that the gospel still offers the best hope for healing and unity?

---

[18]   H. Richard Niebuhr, *Christ and Culture* (New York: Harper, 1951). Niebuhr's description of culture wars in the book's opening paragraphs seems as prescient and relevant as when first published. It could very well summarize the current intra-church culture wars ranging from debates about Covid-19 vaccinations to Critical Race Theory. Niebuhr writes, "A many-sided debate about the relations of Christianity and civilization is being carried out in our time . . . It is carried on publicly by opposing parties and privately in the conflicts of conscience. Sometimes it is concentrated on special issues . . . . Sometimes it deals with broad questions of the church's responsibility for social order or of the need for a new separation of Christ's followers from the world." "The debate is as confused as it is many-sided. When it seems that the issue has been clearly defined as lying between the exponents of a Christian civilization and the non-Christian defenders of a wholly secularized society, new perplexities arise as devoted believers seem to make common cause with secularists, calling, for instance, for the elimination of religion from public education . . ." "In this situation it is helpful to remember that the question of Christianity and civilization is by no means a new one; that Christian perplexity in this area has been perennial, and that the problem has been an enduring one through all the Christian centuries." (pp. 2–3).

These questions are not new. However, something in the tenor[19] of the religious culture wars seems to have shifted since the American presidential election of 2016, when white evangelicals helped elect Donald Trump as president.[20] This shift, at least, is something everyone along the breadth of the political and religious spectrum can agree upon. In the section that follows, I want to explore very briefly two positions that in general terms outline responses in the Protestant American Church to culture wars that seem to have escalated—or at least to have made the fault lines more visible—as virulent, populist rhetoric has been normalized, and America's cultural clashes over issues such as racism, abortion, immigration and pandemic responses have led not only to unprecedented violence at the nation's capital on 6 January 2021, over "whose" and what kind of America this is, but that have also engendered worldwide protests, emboldened autocrats and further eroded democratic norms.[21]

---

[19] See Peter Wehner, "The Evangelical Church is Breaking Apart: Christians Must Reclaim Jesus from His Church", *The Atlantic* (24 October 2021), accessed 24 October 2021. Wehner, senior fellow at the Ethics and Public Policy Center, notes that the "aggressive, disruptive, and unforgiving mindset that characterizes so much of our politics has found a home in many American churches". After interviewing over a dozen pastors, Wehner was alarmed at the consistent note they sounded. "[Pastors] told me that nothing else they've faced approaches what they've experience in recent years, and that nothing had prepared them for it."

[20] Andrew L. Whitehead and Samuel L. Perry, *Taking America Back for God: Christian Nationalism in the United States* (New York: Oxford University Press, 2020), p. 42. Whitehead and Perry note that "exit polls showed 81 percent of white evangelicals voted for Donald Trump in 2016". However, this has also led to more visibility for evangelical dissenters, who in response "began labelling themselves 'the 19 percent' to declare their opposition to the reactionary politics espoused by others in their faith tradition".

[21] See Rogers Brubaker, "Between Nationalism and Civilizationism: The European Populist Moment in Comparative Perspective", *Ethnic and Racial Studies* (3 March 2017), accessed 1 October 2021. Populist movements in Europe are informed more by what Brubaker names "civilizationism" or "Christianism".

Roughly speaking, at the right, we find Christian nationalism, invoking a vigilante Jesus as its lord; at the left we find Christian social progressivism pursuing justice but unmoored from the just One, Christ, the only prophetic source of true justice and the only check against flawed human executions of it; and in the middle are those calling for us all "to play nice" by returning to civic virtues no longer widely shared. In fact, even amongst Christians, we see these virtues now being boldly denounced with impunity. Of course, these can in no way represent all Christian responses, and by focusing primarily on the contemporary, evangelical Protestant Church, I am leaving out other Christian traditions—most obviously the Catholic and Eastern Orthodox that have rich spiritual resources, and their accompanying lexicons that may afford better ways of framing the issues. I focus only on the American Protestant tradition because, simply, it is the one I know best. Additionally, though it is inevitably reductionist, I focus on only two identity-shaping narratives because of the limits of time and my own expertise, and because these positions do seem representative of the loudest voices in the culture wars. Moreover, my aim is to demonstrate that regardless of one's position in them—though some stances certainly have more pernicious effects than others—each is problematic because it is animated by an unholy ghost longing for an imaginary homeland.

Moreover, common to each of these positions is what I want to call the "myth of purity", whose compelling vision is anchored to achieving some sort of static, final power or, in Rushdie's terms, "fixity". In *The Satanic Verses*, the tragic and ultimately fatal flaw of the protagonist Gibreel Farishta is his inability to reimagine himself in terms other than, as his namesake Gabriel suggests, a fixed, pure identity, unchanging and unchanged by the vicissitudes of a human life which is both noble and selfish, sacred and profane, English and Indian. He has fallen between the barstools of these two cultures and in his inability to be translated by all the new possibilities mongrelization offers, he gradually descends into madness and ultimately suicide. Likewise, this desire for fixity, I suggest, is the fury driving the identity narratives of the Christian right and left. Insofar as they do so, they have the potential to have equally tragic ends.

My vigilante Jesus

In the United States, the conflation of Christian and national identity is as old as Protestant evangelicalism itself.[22] As Frances Fitzgerald's sweeping historical survey, *The Evangelicals: The Struggle to Shape America*, recounts, within the origins of evangelicalism itself in the spiritual revivals that swept English-speaking Europe and America in the eighteenth and nineteenth centuries, was the impulse to define America as a Christian nation.[23] However, sociologists Andrew L. Whitehead and Samuel L. Perry in their recent book, *Taking America Back for God*, point out crucial differences between the Christian nation origins story and Christian nationalism, itself a complex set of attitudes and ideologies. Both those on the political right and left might appeal to the Christian nation origin story to further political reform. For example, and perhaps most famously, Martin Luther King, Jr., whose "Letter from Birmingham Jail" addressed to white clergy in the South, shrewdly reminds them of the aspirational ideals of America's founding fathers expressed in the Declaration of Independence in his argument for civil rights.[24] Furthermore, Christian nationalism is not synonymous with "white evangelical Christians". Though there is overlap, sincere religious commitment, even among white evangelicals, has been shown to have an inverse effect in fostering attitudes antithetical to Christian nationalism

---

[22] This is not meant to suggest all evangelicals are Christian nationalists or that evangelicalism is synonymous with Christian nationalism or with orthodox Christianity. There is a wide range of responses to the "Christian nation" origin narrative among professing Christians in America. Whitehead and Perry's excellent sociological analysis categorises these positions as "Rejecters, Resisters, Accommodators, or Ambassadors". See Whitehead and Perry, *Taking America Back for God*, p. 10.

[23] Frances Fitzgerald, *The Evangelicals: The Struggle to Shape America* (New York: Simon and Schuster, 2017), p. 14.

[24] Martin Luther King, Jr., "Letter from Birmingham Jail", in William Epperson et al. (eds), *Strategies for Reading and Writing* (Dubuque, IA: Kendall/Hunt, 1999), pp. 331–41.

(such as support for environmental stewardship and hospitality toward immigrants).[25]

Christian nationalism, in contrast, is not a particular theological stance but is, according to Whitehead and Perry, a "cultural framework—a collection of myths, traditions, symbols, narratives, and value systems—that idealizes and advocates a fusion of Christianity with American civic life".[26] Central to the ideology are certain attitudes about power, boundaries and social order that invoke religious symbols, scripture and consequentialist logic to defend them.[27] Stoked by fear of the loss of a sacred nation, Christian nationalism's real aim is reconstructing an imaginary homeland through political power. As Whitehead and Perry explain,

> Put simply, Christian nationalism does not encourage high moral standards or value self-sacrifice, peace, mercy, love, justice, and so on. Nor does it necessarily encourage conforming one's political opinions to those that Jesus might have . . . Rather Christian nationalist appeals to "Christian foundations" and "Christian beliefs" were more like code words for a way of life that is "ours" (read: white conservative Christians) by divine right and which "the secularists, the humanists, the atheists, the infidels" want to take away . . . In short, Christian nationalism is all about power.[28]

Retaining (or regaining) power entails reinforcing boundaries between "us" and "them"—illegal immigrants, feminists, secularists, pro-choice proponents, etc. No wonder then that Christian nationalism is often accompanied by parasitic prejudices that feed on fears of cultural corruption and tends also to espouse more traditional views on gender roles and the nuclear family. These too are necessary for cultural order.

---

[25]   Whitehead and Perry, *Taking America Back for God*, pp. 17–20.

[26]   Whitehead and Perry, *Taking America Back for God*, p. 10.

[27]   Whitehead and Perry's book dedicates whole chapters to explaining these three features of Christian nationalism's narrative: power, boundaries and social order.

[28]   Whitehead and Perry, *Taking America Back for God*, p. 86.

As Kristen Kobes Du Mez chronicles in *Jesus and John Wayne*, long before Trump, conservative evangelicals were "drawn to a nostalgic, rugged masculinity", and "the defense [sic] of patriarchy and a growing embrace of militant masculinity would come to define both substance and symbol of evangelical cultural and political values".[29]

The irony, of course, is that even if America were once a homogenous, Christian nation, as Christian nationalism defines it, the impulse driving its agenda is a dangerous nostalgia for a static, fixed identity located somewhere in the legends of the past.[30] Implicit in the drive to recover that identity is an assumption that there is lost land "out there", and that once the legendary homeland has been located, named and manifested, the role of its citizens is to ensure it is never lost again. The stance is therefore inherently fearful, brittle and suspicious of "outside", corrupting influences, so it is inherently hostile to change and competitive. One sees the world not just in terms of "us" *and* "them" but "us" *or* "them". When only one party has the God-sanctioned version of this imaginary homeland, dialogue not only collapses but engaging in it signals weakness and compromise. If the battle for the imaginary homeland pits good against evil, true believers against apostates, dialogue is merely dancing with the devil.

It is worth noting that this competitive posture derives its power from an implicit spatial metaphor in which there is no "room" for different ideologies, theologies, cultures to occupy harmoniously the same social "space". Rather, like fixed objects, they compete for limited cultural real estate.[31] When one's antagonist is viewed as profane or polluting, ousting

---

[29] Kristin Kobes Du Mez, *Jesus and John Wayne: How White Evangelicals Corrupted a Faith and Fractured a Nation* (New York: Liveright, 2020), p. 37.

[30] Donald Trump's 2016 campaign slogan, "Make America Great Again", of course, belies this enchantment with imaginary homelands by presupposing there is "out there" a lost greatness to be reclaimed.

[31] My thinking here is indebted to Sarah Coakley's exploration of gender connotations in kenotic theology, particularly when considering God's freedom and "limitations' in relation to human and creaturely freedom. "Incompatibilist" notions of freedom imagine (quite literally) in spatial terms that the freedom of one being must be limited to make room for the freedom

rather than engaging the offending party becomes a moral necessity to protect, in Miroslav Volf's phrase, the "sacralization of cultural identity".[32]

Of course, this mythical Christian "America" used as the standard by which Christian nationalism measures political and theological orthodoxy is a narrative construct, partly based in truth, partly not. As Rushdie cautions, we all reconstruct our origin myths with "broken mirrors".[33] A failure to recognize this, when coupled with the conviction that God has sanctioned only this one story, leads inevitably and dangerously to "consequentialism, where the ends justify the means. Half-truths, shady practices, and authoritarian measures, if in service to realizing a more "Christian" nation, are deemed necessary to ensure the "right group stays in power".[34] Jesus becomes a vigilante.

Aside from vigilantism's obvious vices of lawlessness, pride and arrogance, at root is impatience. Unable to trust in the slow, painstaking work of love and the ultimate justice of God, it demands power now, even if gaining it requires subverting or circumventing the laws of both heaven and earth. Insisting that room for others (the "other") means less room for me, its competitive, spatial metaphor casts its subscribers into an ungodly game of "Survivor", in which one's own story of an imaginary homeland can endure, pure and fixed, only by pushing other narratives out of the public square.

Christian nationalism, as noted earlier, is not and does not even claim to be "Christian" in any theological sense. But making sense of and responding to it requires clarity about where it has gone wrong in the name of Christ. Impatience is a good place to start. For the way of God's love is the way of patience. As Jürgen Moltmann asserts so beautifully, the

---

of another. These terms, she argues, are inherently competitive, masculine ways of picturing the world. See Sarah Coakley, "Kenosis: Theological Meanings and Gender Connotations", in John Polkinghorne (ed.), *The Work of Love: Creation as Kenosis* (Grand Rapids, MI: Eerdmans, 2001), pp. 192–209, here at pp. 204–6.

[32]   Miroslav Volf, *Exclusion and Embrace: A Theological Exploration of Identity, Otherness, and Reconciliation* (Nashville, TN: Abingdon Press, 2019), p. 27.

[33]   Rushdie, "Imaginary Homelands", pp. 10–11.

[34]   Whitehead and Perry, *Taking America Back for God*, p. 162.

active work of God's Holy Spirit in the world to reconcile all of creation to himself is almighty not because of his power but because of his "almighty suffering patience":[35]

> Through the power of his patience God sustains this world with its contradictions and conflicts. As we know from human history, patience is the most powerful action because it has time, whereas acts of violence never have time and can therefore win only short-term victories. Patience is superior to violence. God does not sustain and rule the world like an autocrat or a dictator, who permits no freedom; he is more like a suffering servant who bears the world with its guilt and its griefs . . .[36]

This is not to say injustice and wrong must go unaddressed. It is to say, however, that vigilantism in the name of the suffering servant, Christ, is not only an anathema but ultimately doomed.

Moreover, on a personal level it also reveals a bewildering blindness to the human condition. We are all mongrels—hybrid hotchpotches of noble and ignoble purposes, of loveliness and sordidness, of generosity and meanness. There are no spiritual (or cultural, for that matter) purebreds. Pluralism, whether we like it or not—with its inherent contradictions and hypocrisies—is in fact the condition of every human soul. God's capacious mercy alone adopted *all* us mongrels and gave us a place at his table. Only the ongoing, sanctifying work of Christ moves a soul inch by inch toward holiness, transforming all its disparate, messy and broken dispositions into a work of amazing grace—a fully human being, *imago Dei*.

---

[35]   Jürgen Moltmann, "God's Kenosis in the Creation and Consummation of the World", in John Polkinghorne (ed.) *The Work of Love*, pp. 137–51, here at p. 149.

[36]   Moltmann, "God's Kenosis", p. 149.

Cancel thy neighbour

If the Christian right is guilty of vigilantism to secure the myth of purity, the Christian left is no less enthralled by the same myth. It differs only in its means of achieving it—moral imperialism enacted through cancel culture.[37] The temptation to excise what one considers ideologically or spiritually unacceptable is not new. The second-century Gnostic Christian, Marcion, when he could not reconcile the God of the Old Testament with the New, simply deleted the seemingly incongruous portions, producing a new and (not surprisingly) reduced canon.[38] In the same way, "cancel culture" attempts to purge its object of its offensive elements by eliminating it.[39] Whatever manifold form it takes—whether tearing down Confederate statues or boycotting Chick-fil-A for its owner's pro-life stance; demanding accountability for sexual predators as in the #MeToo movement, or merely scapegoating an unknown victim for an errant Twitter post—common to all is the effort to punish the guilty for infringing a social code.

But whose code? And derived from where? Even if accountability and reform are the goals, one must ask, accountability to whom and reform in light of what assumed doctrine or perceived good? As Ligaya Mishan

---

[37]   This is not to say that conservative Christians have not also adopted "cancel culture's" tactics. Many would argue it started with them, and now the chickens are just coming home to roost. See for example Jonathan Merritt, "Evangelicals Perfected Cancel Culture. Now it's Coming for Them", in *Religion News* (17 June 2020), accessed 6 June 2021.

[38]   See Bonnie Kristian, "The Old Testament Calls Out Cancel Culture", *Christianity Today*, (6 August 2020), accessed 10 June 2021.

[39]   The term "cancel culture" has manifold definitions and a debated ancestry. See the Pew Research Center's analysis, "Americans and 'Cancel Culture': Where Some See Calls for Accountability, Others See Censorship, Punishment" (19 May 2021), accessed 6 June 2021; See also Ligaya Mishan, "The Long and Tortured History of Cancel Culture", *The New York Times' T-Magazine,* 3 December 2020), accessed 1 October 2021. It is fascinating to note that the title of this exceptionally insightful article in its print version is "The Sacrifice".

notes, "Guilt still derives from communally agreed-upon standards, be they manifest as a religion, ideology, a legal code or just the rudimentary ethics without which no group can survive. The increasing atomization of American society in the twenty-first century has brought about an unmooring from such consensus."[40] Thus, calls (many times rightly so) for social justice nevertheless beg the question—whose definition of "justice"? And according to what moral code or creed? When these questions fail even to be asked, "cancellations offer instead a surrogate, warped-mirror version of the justice system, at once chaotic yet ritualized".[41] Moreover, cancelling bypasses debate and dialogue since it assumes it already has the moral high ground. In doing so, it is just as morally imperialistic, impervious to reason, and dogmatic as its conservative foil, whose alleged intolerance and dogmatism it decries.[42] It often seeks "justice" through speech codes,[43] bowdlerizing history, and demanding others conform

---

[40] Mishan, "The Long and Tortured History", accessed 1 October 2021.

[41] Mishan, "The Long and Tortured History", accessed 1 October 2021.

[42] Interestingly, a "who's who" list of public intellectuals, writers and scholars—including Salman Rushdie—penned recently an open letter published on 7 July 2020, in *Harper's*, calling for the end to cancel culture amongst *the progressive left*: "The free exchange of information and ideas, the lifeblood of a liberal society, is daily becoming more constricted. While we have come to expect this on the radical right, censoriousness is also spreading more widely in our culture: an intolerance of opposing views, a vogue for public shaming and ostracism, and the tendency to dissolve complex policy issues in a blinding moral certainty." In "A Letter on Justice and Open Debate", *Harper's* (7 July 2020), accessed 1 October 2021.

[43] The gender pronoun debate is just one example, as is the now frowned-upon use of the word "normal"– which has been described as the new "n-word". To be clear, I believe charity requires us to call people what *they* prefer to be called, even if we disagree with the ideology giving rise to the speech code. Moreover, languages have always evolved to reflect changing attitudes to the world. However, the point here is that such speech codes arise from some imaginary dream of a desired homeland and operate as hegemonic, totalizing narratives—whether liberal or conservative.

or be cast into outer darkness branded racists, bigots, homophobes, and so on.

Ironically, cancel culture's *telos* is no less an imaginary homeland than its conservative nemesis, the two locked in a death spiral battling for power and purity. Like Janus twins,[44] Christian nationalism looks backward to recover a lost Christian America, while Christian cancel culture strains toward an elusive, Edenic dream of perfect justice in a world purged of racism, bias, oppression, inequity. There is no question these social ills should be vigorously opposed. In question here are the illicit means of achieving them. Like its mimetic rival, cancel culture, too, is marked by a dangerous impatience to purge impurities rather than precipitate, in Martin Luther King, Jr.'s words, a creative tension whose fruit is truthful dialogue.[45] Moreover, when unmoored from any transcendent and shared good, or even any formal intuitional setting, humans become judge, jury and executioner, often screened from any accountability through the anonymity of social media. As Mishan notes, cancel culture is "rudderless, a series of spontaneous disruptions with no sequential logic, lacking any official apparatus to enact or enforce a policy or creed".[46]

To be clear, I am not suggesting cancel culture is synonymous with social justice or with Christian progressivism. However, Christian social justice efforts—including those at my own university—often adopt uncritically the illiberal lexicon and methods of social justice movements untethered from the person and work of Christ. Theologically speaking, any Christian claim to justice must be tempered by humility, since God alone knows all, loves perfectly, and stands outside of time and tribal interests. Furthermore, despite the necessity of addressing injustices, especially those perpetrated by the Church, the *agape* love that gives humans the capacity to move beyond reciprocity, *lex talionis*, and love

---

44   Rushdie also references the Janus image (which he borrows from Tom Nairn) to describe religious nationalism's outlook in "In God We Trust", *Imaginary Homelands*, pp. 376–92, here at p. 384.

45   Martin Luther King, Jr., "Letter from Birmingham Jail", p. 333.

46   Mishan, "The Long and Tortured History", accessed 1 October 2021.

rather than cancel our enemies, flows not from speech codes or diversity training but only from the indwelling presence of the Holy Spirit.[47]

To sum up, both vigilantism and cancel culture within the evangelical church reveal that it has succumbed to an ancient deception. In C. S. Lewis's *The Screwtape Letters*, Screwtape has these words of advice for his protégé, the junior devil Wormwood, as he seeks to derail his human subject's budding faith in the midst of partisan debates:

> Once you have made the World an end, and faith a means, you have almost won your man, and it makes very little difference what kind of world end he is pursuing. Provided that meetings, pamphlets, policies, movements, causes, and crusades, matter more to him than prayers and sacraments and charity, he is ours . . . I can show you a pretty cageful down here.[48]

An eschatological hope

Is this the end of the Church? No, but it is a sobering wake-up call. To suggest a path forward, I want to return to Rushdie's essay, "In God We Trust", his own analysis of the perils of religion becoming a means to a political end. He begins by asserting that our response to the world and our sense of place in it "is essentially *imaginative*: that is, picture-making. We live in our pictures, our ideas. I mean this literally. We first construct pictures of the world and then we step inside the frames".[49] Rushdie observes, "Given the gift of self-consciousness, we can dream versions of ourselves, new selves for old."[50]

---

47 Matthew 5:43–8. Because of the limits of time and space, this inevitably vastly oversimplifies the biblical notion of justice. For an excellent discussion of the ways in which the Christian idea of God's universal justice negotiates culturally embedded notions of justice, see Chapter 5, "Oppression and Justice", in Miroslav Volf's *Exclusion and Embrace*, pp. 175–219.

48 C. S. Lewis, *The Screwtape Letters* (New York: Collier, 1961), p. 35.

49 Rushdie, "In God We Trust", pp. 377–8.

50 Rushdie, "In God We Trust", p. 377.

If this is indeed true, the good news is that we can rethink the stories we live by. To the degree that we in the Christian Church have sought impatiently to bring the righteousness of God through Christian nationalism or the justice of God through "cancelling" our neighbours' offences, we can at least ask, is there another story we should be living? I want to suggest, as I did at the beginning, that rather than being ghosted by an imaginary homeland, we must inhabit, like the exiled writers Rushdie describes, the fertile "in between" spaces of eschatological hope.

What does this entail? For Christians, the cruciform life means reckoning soberly and realistically with evil. It requires shaking off modernity's seductive idealism that asserts "*the world can be healed*". Modernity expects the creation of paradise at the end of history and denies the expulsion from it at the beginning of history. Placed into the fissures of the world in order to bridge the gap that the fissures create, the cross underscores that evil is irremediable. Before the dawn of God's new world, we cannot remove evil "so as to dispense with the cross".[51] No election audit or social media firestorm can realize God's righteousness, peace and joy. Moreover, sin's cruel irony is that our wilful impatience, our moral imperialism employed to rectify perceived wrongs, often has collateral damage far beyond the initial offence. As Fleming Rutledge so powerfully states in her magisterial book, *The Crucifixion*,

> Wishful thinking about the intrinsic goodness of every human being is not enough. Inclusion is not a sufficiently inclusive message, nor does it deliver real justice. There are some things— many things—that must be condemned and set right if we are to proclaim a God of both justice and mercy. Only a Power independent of this world order can overcome the grip of the Enemy of God's purposes for his creation.[52]

The cruciform life also means that we strive not for fixity and existential purity, but instead acknowledge common ground, even with our enemies,

---

[51]   Volf, *Exclusion and Embrace*, p. 18.

[52]   Fleming Rutledge, *The Crucifixion* (Grand Rapids, MI: Eerdmans, 2015), p. 610.

in a universal existential fact: we are all spiritual mongrels in need of grace. To return to Rushdie's linguistic metaphor, embracing the cross means enduring the often-painful process of being "translated" from one sort of being into another. The great good news of the gospel—and, paradoxically, of Rushdie's *The Satanic Verses*—is that translation is how newness comes into the world.[53] Gradually, through the redemptive, transforming work of God's mercy, we move daily closer to being conformed to the image of Christ (Romans 8:29)—and to fulfilling the prophetic vocation of the Church of reconciling all things to God (2 Corinthians 5:19). Thus, we refuse to construct with our shattered mirrors imaginary homelands ghosted anachronistically by fear and loss. Instead, we confess faith in an immanent and transcendent God who calls us to live in the eschatological hope of our one true Homeland, glimpses of which we surely see and are called to make seen, here and now.

---

[53] Rushdie, *The Satanic Verses*, p. 8.

David, George and David: Theologians Artfully Changing Theology

Ann Loades

Times and theology change, and it is sometimes possible to notice both the changes and those responsible for them as they actually happen. The primary focus of this essay is to reflect on the engagement of three theologians, David Brown, George Pattison and David Jasper, with our present-day world. All three of them established their priestly and scholarly careers in England before moving to Scottish universities and the Scottish Episcopal Church. As will become clear, all three have flourished as what would now be called "self-supporting ministers" (i.e., active as ordained Anglicans but with vocations to live in academic contexts). One of the three is Scottish-born. All of them have connections with Durham. These are not incidental facts. By understanding something of where they began their lives as students, teachers and writers of theology, and consequently their hopes and intentions, we begin to open up a wide horizon of what may count as theology, both for their contemporaries and beyond.

DWB and opening up theology

To begin with the most senior: David Brown is a Scot brought up on Islay, though attending a boarding school for his secondary education on the mainland, from where he gained entrance to the University of Edinburgh to read Classics. In Oxford, he was in the first graduating year of Joint Honours in Philosophy and Theology, and moved to Cambridge both for a doctorate in ethics and to train for ordination. Appointed Fellow and Chaplain of Oriel College, Oxford to begin with, in due course he added a university lectureship in Ethics and Philosophical Theology and was much engaged with what now would be identified as "outreach" to both schools and churches. In 1990, he was appointed to a chair in Durham which was attached to a cathedral post. He became a Fellow of the British Academy in 2002 and migrated five years later to become Wardlaw Professor of Theology, Aesthetics and Culture in the University of St Andrews. He was awarded a D.Litt. degree by the University of Edinburgh in 2012, the year in which he was also elected as a Fellow of the Royal Society of Edinburgh. In an important sense, this was "homecoming" after some forty years south of the border. He became President of the Society for the Study of Theology in 2015–16. The years between Oxford and St Andrews, however, were crucial to his being able to develop some of his interests. In retirement, further major publications reveal not merely the changes already made in the intervening years but his arguments for shifts which he commends as essential for theological reflection.[1]

David Brown moved to the University of Durham in 1990 on appointment to another dual-style position, as Van Mildert Professor of Divinity in the University and residentiary Canon of the cathedral. (The Van Mildert professorship is one of the University's foundation chairs, named after the bishop who did so much to establish the institution.) The Department of Theology, though an Anglican foundation, had become increasingly ecumenical during Michael Ramsey's time as Van Mildert Professor (1940–50), and continues to be so. DWB was personally responsible for the establishment of a Chair in "Anglican

---

[1] DWB edited the The International Journal for the Study of the Christian Church: Perspectives on the Church in Scotland 14:2 (2014). He was a member of the Church of England's Doctrine Commission for ten years, and for five on the Doctrine Committee of the Scottish Episcopal Church. He contributed "Theology and Art in Scotland" to David Fergusson and Mark W. Elliott (eds), The History of Scottish Theology 3: The Long Twentieth Century (Oxford: Oxford University Press, 2019), pp. 132–45.

Studies", through obtaining funding for an Ecumenical Lay Canon of the Cathedral. Professor Michael Snape, a Roman Catholic layman, was appointed as the inaugural holder of this position in 2015. The point here is that whilst clearly an Anglican/Episcopalian theologian, for DWB it would be unthinkable not to attend to the width and depth of theology in the twentieth century—as indeed is certainly true of George Pattison and David Jasper. Whilst all three of them have worked largely independently of one another, each of them is sensitive to the creative interplay of traditions.

DWB and the indispensability of the artistic imagination

Without losing his expertise in philosophical theology, DWB addressed himself in Durham to the integration of new resources into some of the courses for which he was responsible. One of these, an introduction to Christian doctrine for first-year students, provided a core sequence of topics via the "Apostles' Creed". Having hunted out the material he needed for what developed into a fine resource of slides, he introduced students to the subject matter through the discussion of full-screen-size "art" work, made possible in lecture theatres with up-to-date equipment. Beyond lectures, study packs of poetry, black and white illustrations, and a wide variety of "prompts" encouraged students to explore all sorts of possibilities on their own initiative. One of the most interesting results was that scriptural texts were given more and more attention as students engaged their imaginations with a range of responses to the clauses of the Creed. One difference for smaller groups in subsequent years of the degree and into "taught" Master's level was that it was possible to engage with music as well. This for him was not just a matter of "illustrating" scripture and doctrine (an initial stage for reflection), but of encouraging students both to see "artists" of many kinds as theologians, and to realize that possibility in and for themselves. Overall, he was preoccupied with "Christian Theology in its Contemporary Setting", "Contemporary Theology" in short. As it turned out, he was laying foundations for his current set of publications!

DWB experimented with his new approach at a series of conferences in New York from 1997 to 2003. Managing simultaneously to sustain his publications in philosophical theology, he made further contacts at discussions of his work at meetings of the American Academy of Religion, then through his supervision of some outstanding candidates for doctorates both in Durham and St Andrews. A massive bibliography (up to 2018) demonstrates his extraordinary interdisciplinary explorations and contribution to theology.[2]

In addition, his commitments in Durham Cathedral, not least to the liturgy, included primary responsibility for some major commissions. Three were for windows, two for great banners in batik (of St Oswald and St Cuthbert), and altars and their furnishings (for St Hild and St Margaret of Scotland). His tribute to the cathedral (and details about these art works) is to be found in the massive book he edited, coordinating a major team of contributors.[3] His own understanding of such a building is to be found in the essay he developed from his Presidential address to the Society for the Study of Theology,[4] reflecting on the New Testament sense of God becoming both "localized" in Christ and "universally present throughout the divine creation", which the cathedral sought to reflect as the Jerusalem Temple once did.

---

[2]   One of the essay collections responding to his work is Christopher R. Brewer (ed.), *Christian Theology and the Transformation of Natural Religion: Essays in Honour of David Brown* (Studies in Philosophical Theology, 64) (Leuven: Peeters, 2018). This volume includes a bibliography 1976–2018. A succinct introduction by the same author is "David W. Brown (1948–)", in Stephen Burns, Bryan Cones and James Tengatenga (eds), *Twentieth-Century Anglican Theologians* (Hoboken, NJ: Wiley-Blackwell, 2023), pp. 185–94.

[3]   David Brown (ed.), *Durham Cathedral: History, Fabric and Culture* (Mellon Centre/New Haven, CT and London: Yale University Press, 2015).

[4]   David Brown, "Let sacred buildings speak: Durham Cathedral and the Jerusalem Temple", *International Journal for the Study of the Christian Church,* 16/2 (2016), pp. 93–107.

DWB—back to Scotland

Of particular importance for his move north, however, were five volumes published with Oxford University Press from 1999 to 2008. The initial stimulus for these was accepting the invitation to deliver the Hensley Henson Lectures in Oxford in 1996, which emerged first as *Tradition and Imagination: Revelation and Change,* and propelled into press the next four, on "discipleship", "place and human experience", "grace and sacrament", through to "metaphor and drama". The whole set of five volumes constitutes a substantial resource for re-engagement with Christian tradition, as the move to St Andrews made clear.

The Institute for Theology, Imagination, and the Arts (ITIA) is now well established (and recently complemented by a new degree in Sacred Music). It came about as the result of the entrepreneurial initiatives of the Revd Professor Trevor Hart of the School of Divinity in the University of St Andrews (another English-born priest-scholar, appointed in 1995), himself contributing to the exploration of new resources for theology most successfully maintained since his move to become Rector of St Andrews, in St Andrews in 2013.[5] In 2010, ITIA was generous enough to host a major three-day international conference on DWB's work, with a focus on each of the five volumes, and his own constructive responses.[6]

---

[5]   Trevor Hart maintains his own website with publications listed at <http://www.trevorahart.com/>, accessed 13 July 2022; and see in particular his major essay, "Protestantism and the Arts", in Darren C. Marks and Alister E. McGrath (eds), *The Blackwell Companion to Protestantism* (Oxford: Blackwell, 2003), pp. 268–86, which connects "human imagining" with the human capacity for hope, memory and desire for the "last things" and God's regeneration of our humanity.

[6]   See Robert MacSwain and Taylor Worley (eds), *Theology, Aesthetics, and Culture. Responses to the Work of David Brown* (Oxford: Oxford University Press, 2012). See further Christopher R. Brewer and Robert MacSwain (eds), *Divine Generosity and Human Creativity: Theology, Symbol, Painting and Architecture* (London and New York: Routledge, 2010). In the light of the two references above, see especially the section, "Meaning in Religious Architecture", pp. 151–203.

Together with new colleagues and a coherent group of graduates attracted to ITIA, DWB was also now blessed with new conversation partners, notably in collaboration with Gavin Hopps (Director of ITIA), for the relationship between theology and music.[7] This material in particular establishes the possibility of analysing and discussing the relationship between music, the "transcendence of self" and becoming alert to "divine presence", in wholly unpredictable modes. That is, musicologists may engage with theology without supposing that only theology understood in a certain way is the sole source of such engagement—a major achievement in the light of the predominance of that understanding, which amounts to considering that the "arts" exist to illuminate what is already known, rather than in their turn to be or become sources of engagement with "divine presence" in quite new ways. This stage of his work also opened up the perspective both of his forthcoming publication on the "reception exegesis" of the four canonical Gospels, and beyond this, to appreciation of the world's major faiths.

These particular publications have been generated under the conditions of the lockdown over the Covid-19 pandemic. Thus he has been provided with yet another opportunity to both pull together and develop a major contribution to what is now known not merely as "reception history", but the even more demanding "reception exegesis" which is revitalizing at least some areas of biblical studies and theology.[8]

---

[7]   They co-authored *The Extravagance of Music* (New York: Palgrave Macmillan, 2018), discussed at a panel meeting of the American Association of Religion, San Diego, 2019. The whole discussion was published in *The International Journal for the Study of the Christian Church* as a special number, 20/1 (2020), and including reflections by Professor Christoph Schwöbel, who had recently joined the School of Divinity from Tübingen, as "Mutual resonance: remarks on the relationship between music and theology", pp. 8–22.

[8]   Two outstanding examples in the series of Wiley-Blackwell Bible Commentaries series (Through the Centuries) are those by John F. A. Sawyer on *Isaiah* (2018), and by Paul M. Joyce and Diana Lipton in their volume on *Lamentations* (2013). These scholars have made the move from "reception history" to "reception exegesis". The commentary on *Lamentations* also marks the significance of such exegesis being undertaken jointly by Christian and Jewish theologians.

In his major new publication (with Eerdmans in 2022) and concentrating on the four canonical Gospels (rather than on any one of them), DWB seeks to erode the contrast between "dogma" and "art as spirituality", and commends the search for meaning in philosophy of religion and biblical studies together by being open to imaginative truths in both visual art and literature.[9] This major book will include approximately one hundred illustrations and a comparable number of poetic and other literary examples. Furthermore, he is studying how one might best approach the variety of the world's major faiths, given that their representatives are nowadays our near and much-valued neighbours. Better understanding of their origins (and of our own) is part of a strategy for fostering greater humility in appreciating one another.

GLP: From Edinburgh to parish scholar

We turn now to a more recent return to Scotland, that of Anglo-Scot George Pattison, recently retired from the 1640 Chair of Divinity at the University of Glasgow. His first degrees were from the University of Edinburgh. He trained for the ordained ministry of the Church of England at what was then Coates Hall, Edinburgh. In its day, this institution was responsible for candidates from both sides of the Scots/English border. As GLP has pointed out, since its closure in 1994 (and, as in the Church of England, its replacement in most dioceses by non-residential and rather different modes of initial "training"), it may well be that the day has passed when priest-scholars in the making will be valued and welcomed.

Be that as it may, as it so happened, in his case, fourteen years in parochial ministry made possible his movement into university and ecclesial engagements as opportunities to do so emerged. Even if that had not been the case, he himself is explicitly clear that he represents and

---

9   David Brown, *Gospel as Work of Art: Imaginative Truth and the Open Text* (Grand Rapids, MI: Eerdmans, 2022) (forthcoming). See also David Brown, "Arts as Theology" in Imogen Atkins and Stephen Garrett (eds), *Companion to Theology and the Arts* (London: Bloomsbury/T. & T. Clark, 2022), forthcoming.

continues an ancient tradition in which there remains an understanding that responsibility for teaching and preaching is to be sustained lifelong by reflection on scripture and Christian tradition. As he has said: "Although this doesn't have to be narrowly academic it has to be serious, critical, and imaginative, and this needs dedicated time."[10] The problem of securing such time and the conditions for reflection can to some extent be solved notwithstanding the demands of parish life, but "training" in areas of "management" and "leadership" in response to diocesan initiatives not only erodes time for study but inevitably affect habits of prayer, meditation, "and the cultivation of a quiet and attentive mind". With sheer determination and a clear focus on its priority and necessity, that older tradition must and can be sustained, but it becomes more and more difficult as someone moves from non-academic to academic life and back again as GLP has done. For the "academic" context now also has additional hazards to negotiate, given pressures towards specialization and short-term results, quantifiable outcomes and practical outcomes, in addition to the importance attributed to "internationalization"—the latter made possible by internet connections as well as travel. GLP has consistently identified places and spaces for "dedicated time", as well as arguing for its priority for others as well as himself. His perspective is shared by both David Brown and David Jasper.

After his ordination training, GLP moved to a curacy in Newcastle-upon-Tyne. From there, he happened to attend a conference on the theological interchange between Germany and England involving members of Durham University's Department of Theology and subsequently registered for a doctorate. He was located by John

---

[10]   See Philip Tonner, <https://philiptonner.com>, accessed 13 July 2022—"Into the Future: An Interview with Professor George Pattison" (which concludes with an online lecture, "George Pattison on Heidegger", an excellent example of his talent for communicating the work of a major thinker with ease and clarity) linked to other online presentations. Pattison's work on Heidegger was of the greatest importance in developing his interest in phenomenology (see notes 16 and 23) indispensable for his Bampton Lectures in 2017, and then the first of three major volumes on "The Philosophy of Christian Life" (see below, note 15).

Habgood (then Bishop of Durham) as priest-in-charge of the parish of Kimblesworth in County Durham. Amongst other enterprises, sponsored marathon running helped to raise money to put central heating in the church, and to his existing language skills he added Danish, essential for his doctoral thesis on Kierkegaard. The latter is the writer to whose work he has returned lifelong, not least as a "conversation partner" with other thinkers, such conversations requiring an enviable breadth and depth of engagement.[11] As it happened, his thesis-writing coincided with that of David Jasper, who submitted his own Durham doctoral thesis on S. T. Coleridge in the same year, 1983.[12]

GLP's move to become Rector of the Badwell Ash group of parishes in Suffolk turned out to be significant for several reasons, one of which was the availability of inter-library loan resources at the Bury St Edmunds Public Library. This made it possible to read, research and prepare material in response to invitations to deliver talks, lectures and broadcasts, and revise these for publication.[13] He was also able to travel to Cambridge for Faculty of Divinity seminars as well as around and about to local theological societies. In Cambridge he established a lifelong friendship with Don Cupitt.[14]

---

[11]   George Pattison, *Kierkegaard's Theory and Critique of Art* (Durham University, 1983); *Kierkegaard: The Aesthetic and the Religious: from the Magic Theatre to the Crucifixion of the Image* (London: Macmillan 1992); *Kierkegaard and the Crisis of Faith: An Introduction to his Thought* (London: SPCK, 1997), together with a string of other publications. GLP is one of the team responsible for the publication of Kierkegaard's *Journals and Notebooks*. At least one more book on Kierkegaard is planned for his retirement.

[12]   The author supervised both Pattison and Jasper as doctoral candidates.

[13]   Two interrelated books resulted: *Art, Modernity and Faith: Towards a Theology of Art* (London: Macmillan 1991; 2nd edn 1998), an indispensable introduction to discussion of the two areas, and a preliminary to *Crucifixions and Resurrections of the Image* (London: SCM Press, 2009).

[14]   See Don Cupitt, *Is Nothing Sacred? The Non-Realist Philosophy of Religion: Selected Essays. Perspectives in Continental Philosophy* (New York: Fordham University Press, 2002).

GLP: Artistic insight forged in parish and university

Of the greatest importance in Badwell Ash, however, was his friendship with the most distinguished art critic, Peter Fuller, whose conversation and publications provided a counterpoint to GLP's explorations. As always, GLP risks engagement with those who with good reason remain unconvinced by a Christian perspective on life.[15] Peter Fuller's tragic death in 1990 marked a year in which GLP moved to the major role of Dean of the Chapel of King's College, Cambridge (from 1991). It was a position with an extraordinary range of responsibilities, quite apart from the stimulus of opportunities to lecture and supervise outstanding doctoral candidates in the Faculty of Divinity.[16] After a decade in Cambridge, GLP enjoyed a two-year breathing space in the University

---

[15] Peter Fuller, *Theoria: Art and the Absence of Grace* (London: Chatto and Windus, 1988). See *Art, Modernity and Faith* and the chapter on Ruskin, "Christian Theoria", pp. 54–77, in which GLP argues against the "redundancy" of God by making his case for allowing "subjective experience to be treated as ontologically significant, as a path on which we may be graced by unsurpassable disclosures of being", (p. 76). On his discussion of Rothko with Peter Fuller, see "After an End: Unsaying Painting", *Crucifixions and Resurrections,* pp. 72–89, and GLP's comment that in encounter with those works, "we learn something about what would be required of us if we were to live with the depths of responsibility and self-commitment that would justify the use of the term 'spiritual'" (p. 89). See also "Anselm Kiefer's 'Palm Sunday'", pp. 107–18, and "Letters from America: Robert Natkin and Friends", pp. 119–28.

[16] Publications which resulted from research leave from King's (spent in Copenhagen) and his time in Aarhus are two interrelated books, *Kierkegaard, Religion and the Nineteenth-Century Crisis of Culture* (Cambridge: Cambridge University Press, 2002), which includes an exceptional section correlating some of the paintings of Manet with Kierkegaard's preoccupations (pp. 182–97) before concluding via Barth to engagement with Dostoevsky and Girard (pp. 198–221), which is extensively rewritten and developed (see note 33); and *Kierkegaard's Upbuilding Discourses: Philosophy, Literature and Theology* (London and New York: Routledge, 2002).

of Aarhus, taking his Durham DD on the eve of becoming Lady Margaret Professor of Divinity in the University of Oxford, and a Canon of Christ Church Cathedral there, from 2004–13. In that latter year, he came back to Scotland, appointed to the 1640 Chair of Divinity in the University of Glasgow, returning to Oxford in 2017 to deliver the Bampton Lectures, with three major volumes published in 2018, 2020 and 2021.[17]

In retrospect, it is clear that during his time in Badwell Ash, GLP was establishing himself as someone who could embrace an extraordinary range of resources, well beyond the limitations of many other theologians, as, for instance, in his preoccupation with the importance of Heidegger.[18] For instance, his view of art "as a unique and irreplaceable interpretation of reality and as such, of great human and religious significance" was integral to his conviction that "there is a radical crisis in contemporary culture" needing to be understood in relation to "the equally radical crisis of contemporary religion and theology". He was thus summoning those who maintained both artistic and theological traditions "to rethink and rework those traditions in a manner appropriate to where we are now".[19] Moreover, this would also require attention to the revelation of "the quality and grace of a beauty which is beyond the duality of beauty and ugliness" in the work of some Buddhist artists which may place us (literally) "in the same space, the same presence, as that which another faith occupies".[20] And there is as it were one rubric which applies throughout his work, which is that "all that is excluded is triviality,

---

[17]   See *A Phenomenology of the Devout life: A Philosophy of Christian Life* (Oxford: Oxford University Press, 2018); *A Rhetorics of the Word* (Oxford: Oxford University Press, 2020); *A Metaphysics of Love: A Philosophy of Life* (Oxford: Oxford University Press, 2021).

[18]   His discussion and analysis of *The Later Heidegger* (Abingdon: Routledge, 2000) is an invaluable introduction to his importance both for possible readers of Heidegger, and for its importance for GLP's own constructive philosophical theology/theological philosophy.

[19]   See the Preface to *Art, Modernity and Faith*, pp. xi–xii.

[20]   "The Theology of Art and the Meeting of Faiths", in *Art, Modernity and Faith*, pp. 155–76, here at p. 158. See also "A Central Asian Pietà", in *Crucifixions and Resurrections*, pp. 142–50.

cynicism and the wanton or careless exercise of the creative gift", which one may add applies as equally to theology as to the arts.[21]

Two books especially focussed on theology and art—including film— the first in 1991, the second in 2009, have as their abiding underlying theme GLP's response to the sense "that life itself, the culture we inhabit, is governed, in a certain way by death", that "it has lost its link to the God who is life and who gives life", by drawing attention to "the God who first begins truly to live when death begins to be undone".[22] He therefore came to argue that philosophy and theology alike needed to rethink death and the possibilities of hope, love, prayer and commitment.[23] So for all the complexities of his engagement with a very wide spectrum of philosophy (and later, phenomenology),[24] he writes as a theologian, articulating his conviction that it is in and through the creative transformation of suffering and contestation of "the history of nothingness that is exemplified in the Passion narrative and encountered in innumerable instances of creative living, that God 'becomes' Creator".[25]

---

[21]   *Crucifixions and Resurrections*, p. 154.

[22]   *Crucifixions and Resurrections*, pp. 41–2.

[23]   George Pattison, "Death" in Nicholas Adams, George Pattison and Graham Ward (eds), *Theology and Modern European Thought* (Oxford: Oxford University Press, 2013), pp. 193–213, his theology developed in his *Eternal God: Saving Time* (Oxford: Oxford University Press, 2015).

[24]   In Tonner: Phenomenology "is a discipline of attentiveness, whether to what is going on in perception, in language, or in e.g., ethical issues. Phenomenology doesn't necessarily tell us what's out there in the world or even what we ourselves are, but it does help us understand how the world shows itself to us and how we experience ourselves in our relation to our world". See the first volume of *A Philosophy of Christian Life*, pp. 43–66.

[25]   *Crucifixions and Resurrections*, p. 58.

GLP: the vision deepened by
Kierkegaard and Dostoevsky

He holds to this belief in the teeth of sustained attention to the horrors of the twentieth century, worldwide, but keeping in mind especially the "destruction on a previously inconceivable scale" of Central and Eastern Europe, whose writers he gives his attention to and brings into theological reflection.[26] Indeed, of the three theologians to whose work we attend in this essay, he is the one who explicitly insists on both the political importance of Christian conviction, and thus the inescapable necessity of the reconstruction of philosophical theology.[27] So in his Cambridge years GLP did not merely teach "philosophy of religion", but also opened this area up to political and cultural life via the question, "How should we best speak in order to help bring about the best life?"[28] For philosophical interpretation of religion is not limited to "aesthetics (seeking an 'image'/'text' which is capable of giving direction and shape to 'religious life'), but it will also attend to the question, 'How would someone who believed this behave?'" Concern for the supreme good for human beings, and how we should be living "in order to give effect to our understanding of that supreme good" should open up questions about political and cultural life, and the inescapable necessity of sensitivity "to the presence of the past in our present decision-making".[29] The "other" world to seek is the world that "through hope, makes this world humanly habitable, the paradise we could have today if we could embrace the doctrine of each being responsible for all", in the struggle between

---

[26] *Crucifixions and Resurrections*, p. 101.

[27] A powerful statement of his argument is the essay by GLP, "The Desert is in the Words we Speak", in Andrew Hass (ed.), *Sacred Modes of Being in a Postsecular World* (Cambridge: Cambridge University Press, 2021), pp. 205–22, connected to "Political Calling in an Age of Technology", in the second volume arising from the Bampton Lectures, *A Rhetorics of the Word*, pp. 41–70.

[28] George Pattison, *A Short Course in the Philosophy of Religion* (London: SCM Press, 2001), p. 141.

[29] *A Short Course in the Philosophy of Religion*, p. 20.

experienced evil and hope.[30] Theology, therefore, "should have deep roots in human beings' actual attempts at living the religious life, their searching for salvation, their efforts at praise".[31]

No one attentive to the history of continental Europe should find it surprising that GLP continues to engage not only with Kierkegaard (irrespective of whether Anglo-USA "analytic" philosophers of religion deemed him worthy of their attention), but with anyone whose life and writing would shed light on how he discerned the integration of hope with living in certain ways in sometimes appalling circumstances.[32] Many of these writers are mentioned in his earliest publications, simply awaiting further attention.[33] For instance, it was indisputably necessary that much of his attention was given to Dostoevsky and his world, well before an initial visit to Russia itself in 1998, and through the rest of his career.[34]

---

[30]   *A Short Course in the Philosophy of Religion*, pp. 202–3.

[31]   *A Short Course in the Philosophy of Religion*, p. 137. On certain key words, and on "Alleluia" in particular, see GLP's "Language and the Revelation of Silence: Reflections on Mystical Theology", in Ann Vind, Iben Damgard, Iben, Kirsten Busch Nielsen and Sven Rune Havsteen (eds), *In-visibility: Reflections upon Visibility and Transcendence in Theology, Philosophy and the Arts* (Göttingen: Vandenhoeck and Ruprecht, 2020), pp. 65–84. This relates to some of the material in his Bampton Lectures.

[32]   See George Pattison's blog, Confessions of a Devout European: <https://confessionsofadevouteuropean.wordpress.com/>, accessed 17 October 2022.

[33]   For example, "Into the Abyss", on Paul Tillich in *Art, Modernity and Faith*, pp. 100–17, and Berdyaev in "From Creation to Re-Creation", in *Crucifixions and Resurrections*, pp. 57–9, and GLP's re-engagement with Berdyaev in "Berdyaev and Christian Existentialism", in Caryl Emerson, George Pattison and Randall A. Poole (eds), *The Oxford Handbook of Russian Religious Thought* (Oxford: Oxford University Press, 2020) (online). His attention to Jewish tradition is also noteworthy.

[34]   In *Art, Modernity and Faith* he had written on "Icons of Glory", pp. 118–33, a "mode of presence" of the saint depicted. Attention to links between "art" and the characters in some of Dostoevsky's novels appear in a variety of contexts. See "'Human, all-too Human?' Anastasia Filippovna's 'Portrait of Christ'", in the online journal *Eurozine*, 15 December 2021, <https://www.

Kierkegaard and Dostoevsky taken separately at the very least enable their readers to resist the limitations of "nothingness", and together open up "eschatology" and the possibilities of hope. Thus they summon their readers to a "free faith" which is "necessarily difficult, responsible and profoundly moral".[35] The personal and political importance of acquiring a conscience "by wanting to have it" is explored in an important essay on "Unavowed Knowledge". This returns to Dostoevsky by way of two examples of what was at some level the choice to fail to know and to think as represented by Speer and Eichmann.[36]

---

eurozine.com/human-all-too-human/>, accessed 13 July 2022 ; "Abject Wisdom: Reflections on the Religious Meaning of Dostoevsky's heroines", in Natalie K. Watson and Stephen Burns (eds), *Exchanges of Grace: Essays in Honour of Ann Loades* (London: SCM Press, 2008), pp. 46–54; a Guest Lecture recorded on 14 October 2020 at a conference in Vienna in 2020 is published as "The Problem of Religious Art in Modernity—uses and abuses of the Icon in Russia" and viewable at <https://www.youtube.com/watch?v=9NUeY6QjihQ&list=PLjrO4-ISuhVh6f1q1bifJc0u-gzufmlJH&index=1>, accessed 13 July 2022. One exceptionally demanding and important essay is "Freedom's Dangerous Dialogue: Reading Kierkegaard and Dostoevsky Together", which develops his earlier discussion of René Girard, rare among theologians, in George Pattison and Diane Oening Thompson (eds), *Dostoevsky and the Christian Tradition* (Cambridge: Cambridge University Press, 2001), pp. 237–56, here at pp. 241–5. The editors jointly contribute an "Introduction: Reading Dostoevsky Religiously", pp. 1–28. See also Paul Gifford, *Towards Reconciliation: Understanding Violence and the Sacred after René Girard* (Cambridge: James Clarke & Co., 2020). See also GLP, "Dostoevsky", in Caryl Emersonet al. (eds), *The Oxford Handbook of Russian Religious Thought*, "Suffering, Redemption, The Bible, Christ, the Russian Idea, and his Reception in Twentieth-Century Religious Thought"; and <https://conversationswithdostoevsky.com/>, accessed 13 July 2022.

35 "Freedom's Dangerous Dialogue", p. 253.
36 George Pattison, "Unavowed Knowledge", in his selected essays, *Kierkegaard and the Quest for Unambiguous Life: Between Romanticism and Modernism* (Oxford: Oxford Scholarship online, 2013). We might compare Mary Miller, *Jane Haining: A Life of Love and Courage* (Edinburgh: Birlin, 2019) on the life

GLP's Bampton lectures prompted his three volumes on *A Philosophy of Christian Life*. Each volume has a particular focus, of which it is only possible here to suggest some of the contents which may provide some initiation into his own effort of understanding. The first volume is concerned with "the desire to orientate one's life in relation to God", (desire, aspiration), drawing on "the devout life" tradition as, for example, in the writings of de Sales and Fénelon.[37] The second volume is concerned with articulating what that orientation means, in terms of vocation, a "call from God", which includes both "Prophetic Calling: At the Burning Bush" and an extraordinary meditation on the Prologue of the Fourth Gospel.[38] The third volume is focussed on what the previous two have revealed about "the character of reality", that is, about "love". Its introductory material recalls the two former volumes, and how GLP has established that what God calls us to is a relationship in which we are in turn able to call upon him, with "the devout person vowing or promising themselves to the relationship that is established by the call", and thence to the possibility of mutual naming.[39] In this volume, there are also some refreshing "voices" such as those of Edwin Muir, and Dante in the penultimate chapter, "In the End, Love".[40]

---

of a Scot from Dunscore who went to Budapest to a school which educated both Jewish and Christian girls whom she would not abandon. She returned there in the worst of times, was imprisoned, and sent to Auschwitz, where she died in 1944. Films of Sophie Scholl, her brother and friends, and of Franz Jägerstätter, make the point about the cost of such knowledge.

[37] Part I, 2, 67–85 and beyond. The root of his interest in these writers lay in a suggestion of his "director" when an ordinand.

[38] Part II, 71–99, 131–47, and the links to the diary of a Lutheran pastor, Ulrich Fentzloff, from 1991–2016.

[39] Part III, 1–2.

[40] Part III, 100–107, and ideally prompting attention to his exploration of a monograph from just a few years earlier, *"The Heart Could Never Speak". Existentialism and Faith in a Poem of Edwin Muir* (Eugene, OR: Cascade, 2013).

A third "radical conservative"

DJ's career has been equally extraordinary, since he identified the possibility that he could establish a new interdisciplinary "track" in the UK to become of significance in both "academy" and "church". In this he has succeeded to an extent he may have hoped for but could hardly have guaranteed, though he is far from being uncritical about what he has established. He continues to write on a range of subjects representing his wide interests and addressed to a variety of audiences. His writings on church matters often have relevance to the Scottish Episcopal Church, but not to the exclusion of a wider ecclesiastical landscape.

To begin with, DJ was most fortunate that at school he came to love poetry in particular and literature more generally (including "classics" in Greek and Latin), all of which led to graduation in English in Cambridge (1972). Following a year in India serving with the Church Missionary [now Mission] Society, he moved to St Stephen's House in Oxford for his second initial degree in Theology (1975), completing his first stage of training for ordination in the Church of England with a Certificate in Theology the following year. During his first curacy in Buckingham, he was attached to Keble College, Oxford, writing a BD thesis on "The Reconstruction of Belief in the late Victorian Novel" (awarded in 1980). He also undertook some tutoring in the nascent University of Buckingham. His interest in the Victorian era has remained with him, and it looks as if he could have settled for a career primarily engaged with mostly nineteenth-century literature.[41]

---

[41]   e.g. David Jasper (ed.), *The Selected Works of Margaret Oliphant: Part II, vol. 8, Writings on Biography* (London: Pickering and Chatto, 2012); "The Poetry of the Oxford Movement: Theology in Literature", in *The International Journal for the Study of the Christian Church*, 12/3–4 (2012), pp. 1–14; on the importance of Newman, see *Literature and Theology as a Grammar of Assent* (London: Routledge, 2016); "Church and State in the Nineteenth Century and the Revival of Thomas Becket", *International Journal for the Study of the Christian Church*, 20/3–4 (2020), pp. 251–63.

Developments in Durham

From his first curacy, he moved north in 1979 to become Chaplain and College Officer at Hatfield College, University of Durham, and curate at a church just across the River Wear. As it so happened, 1979–80 marked the beginning of a difficult time of transition within the Church of England, and his engagement with those changes seems to have had a long-term impact on his own theological focus and development. For it was in this period that the Church of England was actively engaged in liturgical revision to which DJ's father, R. C. D. Jasper, was committed while on the staff of King's College, London and Westminster Abbey, continuing the work as Dean of York (1975–84).[42] With its origins in the 1960s, this programme would conclude with the publication of the *Alternative Service Book* (ASB) in 1980.

The ASB became "alternative" to the Book of Common Prayer, primarily because of the vigorous attention the matter of such wholesale change received from an unexpected source. A Liturgical Commission had been set up in 1955, its members primarily historians of liturgy. A new General Synod had also emerged, its bishops and other members of the Synod supposing themselves to be competent to receive and approve the texts proposed. As the Revd Professor Bryan Spinks has explained, the procedures involved virtually guaranteed the wrecking of the "liturgical prose" written by writers (outwith Synod or the Commission) with a gift for the "poetic" quality liturgy requires.[43] DJ's initial response to the commitment of his father to the ASB led to a joint publication, *Language and the Worship of the Church*.[44] He has consistently maintained that

---

[42]   He and liturgist Paul Bradshaw jointly edited *A Companion to the Alternative Service Book* (London: SPCK, 1986). The ASB was to be replaced by *Common Worship* (London: Church House Publishing 2000–6).

[43]   Bryan Spinks, "A Response to The Language of Liturgy: A Ritual Poetics", *Scottish Episcopal Institute Journal* 3/2 (2019), pp. 21–5. The book discussed was DJ's *The Language of Liturgy: A Ritual Poetics* (London: SCM Press, 2018).

[44]   R. C. D. Jasper and David Jasper, *Language and the Worship of the Church* (London/New York: Palgrave Macmillan, 1990), to *The Language of Liturgy*

liturgy can and must be "expansive", whilst no one should underestimate the difficulties of writing liturgy, as he has argued throughout his career.

His appointment at Hatfield carried with it the possibility of a Research Fellowship, and, as a member of the University staff, to register for a PhD. It was at this point that he made the acquaintance of GLP, then based in his Kimblesworth parish. DJ's thesis resulted in his first monograph on S. T. Coleridge, followed by a string of publications which established him as an expert on Coleridge and the latter's importance for the languages of theology and liturgy.[45] Subsequent monographs in rapid succession and published simultaneously in the USA gave him standing in the Departments of Theology and English in the University, the latter of particular importance for his professional future as a full-time member of academic staff.

Launching his Centre

From his base in Hatfield College, in 1980 he launched a Conference on Literature and Religion, international in its scope not least in the course of its first five meetings, DJ himself editing five volumes of the Conference Proceedings. He recalls with great gratitude the presence of some of the distinguished participants, not least Peter Walker, Bishop of Ely (his ordaining bishop), an expert on W. H. Auden, and the one bishop ever to have given him unequivocal support for his explorations of theology and literature.[46]

---

as above, almost twenty years later, by which time he had become a member of the Scottish Episcopal Church Liturgy Committee.

[45] David Jasper, *Coleridge as Poet and Religious Thinker: Inspiration and Revelation* (London: Macmillan, 1985; Allison Park, PA: Pickwick Publications, 1985), quickly followed by *The New Testament and the Literary Imagination* (London: Macmillan, 1987; Atlantic Highlands, NJ: Humanities Press, 1987). It is evident from his bibliography that his work on Coleridge was especially appreciated in France.

[46] Some of his recollections of those early conferences are incorporated into a major essay, "The Study of Literature and Theology" in Andrew Hass, David

By 1986, he had founded the Centre for the Study of Literature and Theology. Then in 1987 he established Oxford University Press's best-selling new journal, *Literature and Theology*, to which he added in 1989 a new book series, *Studies in Literature and Religion*, published by Macmillan, himself writing the first introductory volume (subsequently co-edited with Professor Elisabeth Jay).

In the midst of these ventures, in 1988 he changed colleges, to become Principal of St Chad's College, an Anglican institution integrated into Durham University, bringing to the college the prestige of what he was establishing as a new interdisciplinary area.[47] He was, in time, to identify what he discerned as lying at the core of his concerns, that is, "the articulation of the relationship between the individual and wider forces at play, the subtle continuances of religious traditions in ever changing circumstances, and perhaps a sense of the eternal ever present in the matter of the day".[48] Never to be forgotten was his appreciation of the work of Ulrich Simon. Simon, a German Jew, became a Christian priest and, at the close of the Second World War, was appointed to a post in King's College, London, where he became Professor of Christian Literature (1972–80). Books of his published in 1987 and 1989 (the last of which DJ edited) inescapably reminded his readers of the depths of evil

---

Jasper and Elizabeth Jay (eds), *The Oxford Handbook of English Literature and Theology* (Oxford: Oxford University Press, 2009) (online).

[47] See his reflections in "Disciplined Interdisciplinarity", July 2021 in *Textual Matters* <https://czasopisma.uni.lodz.pl/textmatters/libraryFiles/downloadPublic/622>, accessed 13 July 2022, drawing on his recollections of a friend from Poland, one of his contacts in mainland Europe, each is to work at interdisciplinarity in their own respective contexts.

[48] David Jasper, "A Study of Literature and Religion: a British Perspective", *Religion and Literature* 41/2 (2009), pp. 119–23, here at p. 121; and "Interdisciplinarity in Impossible Times: Studying Religion through Literature and the Arts", in Heather Walton (ed.), *Literature and Theology: New Interdisciplinary Spaces* (London: Ashgate, 2011), pp. 5–18. A comprehensive account of the development of the whole field, including DJ's contribution, is Eric Ziolkowski *Religion and Literature: History and Method* (Leiden: Brill, 2019), pp. 77–9.

in human affairs that seem almost beyond the language of any Christian consolation.[49] To the problem of language about such evil DJ himself returned thirty years later when he turned his attention to the work of Geoffrey Hill's profoundly disquieting poetry. As he was to comment, whereas the fashion in modern theology and modern liturgical writing is for simplicity of language and therefore of thought, rather, the true poet shows us that "We are, or we should be, working hard, suffering to understand".[50]

From Durham to Glasgow

Clearly DJ needed a full-time "academic job", and most fortunately one turned out to be on offer at the University of Glasgow, to which Professor Stephen Prickett had been appointed in English (1990–2000), joining there Robert Carroll, a member of the academic staff since 1968, and made Professor of Hebrew and Semitic Studies in 1991. Professor Prickett, with his own formidable expertise in the interplay between Christianity and Literature (well established in the USA), recognized what DJ had to offer in this interdisciplinary area in the UK. Thus in 1991 DJ was appointed as Senior Lecturer and Director of the Centre for the Study of Literature and Theology, which developed into the Centre for the Study of Literature, Theology and the Arts, given the development

---

[49]   Ulrich Simon, *Atonement: From Holocaust to Paradise* (Cambridge: James Clarke & Co., 1987); *Pity and Terror* (London: Macmillan, 1989). See also David Jasper, "Retrieving a Theological Sense of Being Human", *Literature and Theology* 29/2 (2015), pp. 125–37; "A Critical Spirit and the Will to Believe: Habits of Mind in Literature and Theology", *Scottish Episcopal Institute Journal* 1/1 (2017), pp. 6–19, here at p. 1, a development from *Literature and Theology as a Grammar of Assent* (London: Routledge, 2016).

[50]   See David Jasper, *What a World Art Thou. Reflections on Four Poets and Religion* (Glasgow: Scottish Episcopal Church, 2018), p. 48. These lectures were expanded as, *Heaven in Ordinary*. See also "Between Literature and Liturgy: a Pragmatics of Worship", *Anglican Theological Review*, 73/4 (1991), pp. 375–87.

of a good relationship with the then Glasgow School of Art.[51] DJ's own lecture (the first Annual Lecture of the Scottish Episcopal Institute) on "The Role of the Arts in the Church of Tomorrow" is available to view as well as to read, an example of his well-established commitment to the Scottish Episcopal Church. It is very much in the spirit of Ulrich Simon that DJ argues that "Christian theology, rooted in the apostolic tradition and history, *begins* in dark questioning and the searing revelations of poetry and art", poetry being the very origin of religious thinking and formation.[52]

It is noteworthy that during his time in Glasgow, Professors Prickett and Carroll seized the opportunity to provide an admirable introduction for The Authorized King James Version of the Bible (The World's Classics, 1997), arguing in their Preface (v–vi) that one reason for the Bible's continuing attraction to a wide range of readers (to painters, philosophers, poets, playwrights, songwriters and writers of all description) was the amazing transformative dynamism of the text itself. "If in the beginning was the word, then continually has that word been in the world transforming it and being transformed by that world through other words and continually shall it be in transformed worlds and words to come." DJ clearly had found his own academic niche and a base from which he could contribute his own perspectives in constructive and helpful ways.[53] One gem of his writing from his first decade in Glasgow (unsurprisingly a liturgical text)

---

[51]   DJ has been a firm supporter of artists in various media. See, e.g., "The Spiritual in Contemporary Art", in Rina Arya (ed.), *Contemplations of the Spiritual in Art* (Bern: Peter Lang, 2013), pp. 231–45.

[52]   See *Scottish Episcopal Institute Journal* (online) 1/4 (2027), pp. 3–19. Compare his proposal for how "being religious" merges out of and is constituted by "the mystery of narrative and story" in "Narrative Ways of Being Religious" in Frank Burch Brown (ed.), *The Oxford Handbook of Religion and the Arts,* (Oxford: Oxford University Press, 2014), pp. 130–45, here at p. 141.

[53]   See e.g., David Jasper, "Literary Readings of the Bible", in John Barton (ed.), *The Cambridge Companion to Biblical Interpretation* (Cambridge: Cambridge University Press, 1998), pp. 21–34; "The Bible in Literature", in John Rogerson (ed.), *The Oxford Illustrated History of the Bible* (Oxford: Oxford University Press, 2001), pp. 278–91.

is on the twenty-third psalm, and its shift from "the shadow of death" to divine rescue—a good place to begin in reading his work.[54]

The interplay of English and Theology

DJ's academic progress has included major contributions to a number of institutions, for he not only attended conferences such as the gatherings at the American Academy of Religion, and lectured in the USA and Australia, but also established a network of connections far and wide in Europe, as well as a range of Erasmus programme links throughout the EU. One result was the supervision of a stream of postgraduates from across the world. Having seen the importance of engaging with the "management" of universities, he also took his turn as Dean of Divinity and Head of Theology and Religious Studies at Glasgow, a stint which in 2002 he happily concluded with the award of his Oxford DD. He was subsequently made a Fellow of the Royal Society of Edinburgh (2006), and a year later an Honorary Doctor of Theology of the University of Uppsala.

DJ could never have expected that by the present millennium his international reputation would be such that he would be invited to distinguished professorships in China at Renmin University, Huazhong University, Wuhan, and Hong Kong, co-sponsoring the "Beijing–Scottish Seminar", and on the Executive Committee of the World Conference on Sinology. A raft of publications in English and Chinese (translations provided by Chinese colleagues) have followed, important not least for impinging on the consciousness of those of us who have minimal understanding of the life of Christian communities in China.[55] Thus, as Professor Yang Huilin (Renmin University) has commented, "It would

---

[54]   David Jasper, "The Twenty-Third Psalm in English Literature", *Religion and Literature* 30/1 (1998), pp. 1–11.

[55]   On two theologians see Chen Yongtao, "T. C. Chao (1888–1979)" and Philip Wickeri, "K. H. Ting (1915–2014)" in Stephen Burns et al. (eds), *Twentieth Century Anglican Theologians: Evelyn Underhill to Esther Mombo* (London: Wiley-Blackwell, 2021), pp. 22–33 and 91–101. See the list of publications in this volume for further material representative of DJ's engagement with China.

be difficult to find another person who has contributed more to stimulate and cultivate the interdisciplinary studies of theology and literature in China over the last two decades".[56]

One might well ask, "What else?" DJ in a sense anticipated GLP in writing three interconnected volumes, already extensively discussed, in a collection of essays on DJ's "Sacred Trilogy".[57] As Andrew Hass, editor of that collection, points out, in these volumes theology is being reworked, provoked by DJ's attempt to advance what "the sacred" might mean in today's world.[58] As DJ himself explains, the first volume draws on his earlier engagement with the arts; the second and third in consequence embrace human embodiment and community; and all remains unfinished. For the crucial connection that needs to be made is between the sense of the sacred and the practice of the liturgy, suspended between language and silence in darkness.[59] We note here only that whilst DJ has made possible attention to the texts of Scripture (awaiting their rediscovery in present-day ecclesial groups), he has given his critique and exploration to a wide range of conversations on "embodiment", engaging with "silence in darkness". It is necessary to read and re-read his work on the Eucharist. This is not because he makes the common mistake of reducing "liturgy" to one "sacrament"—far from it—but because almost uniquely among theologians he has engaged with "embodiment" and its appalling vulnerability, and yet finds hope in "divine presence".[60] He

56 Yang Huilin, "The Interdisciplinary Nature of Literature and Theology" in Hass (ed.) *Sacred Modes of Being*, pp. 137–63.

57 See Hass, *Sacred Modes of Being*; David Jasper, *The Sacred Desert*; *The Sacred Body*; *The Sacred Community*.

58 See Church and The Academy February 2022 Andrew Hass, *Sacred Modes of Being in a Postsecular World* (Online seminar paper delivered to the Church and Academy group coordinated by David Jasper, February 2022) <https://www.youtube.com/watch?v=DRuG0ZCy_Zk>, accessed 13 July 2022.

59 See DJ's "Afterword" in Hass, *Sacred Modes of Being*, pp. 223–33, here at p. 226.

60 See "The Eucharistic Body in Art and Literature", in Watson and Burns, *Exchanges of Grace*, pp. 213–23; "Literature and the Eucharistic Body of Christ" in Brewer, *Christian Theology and the Transformation of Natural Religion*, pp. 129–44.

might, indeed, endorse Altizer's concluding words in the essay collection in response to his trilogy, on the "absolute death" that makes possible "resurrection itself".[61]

No doubt he will continue to develop that connection, not least as his readers will read and re-read that trilogy and make their responses to it. As with DWB and GLP, there is, as ever, so much to learn from his engagement with his understanding of Christian tradition in all its complexities. Finally at this point in his progress we note that his commitment to the SEC has been unequivocal, not least having been a member of the SEC's Liturgy Committee, as well as serving two stints as Convenor of its Doctrine Committee, and as Canon Theologian of St Mary's Cathedral, Glasgow.[62] In the immediate future one major task lies ahead, for he is co-editing with Professor Jeremy Smith *The Lay Folks' Mass Book*, an example of an "expansive" liturgy if ever there was one. For the title of the book was the name given to a poem (likely from the fourteenth century) by Canon Simmons, Rector of Dalton Holme near Beverley. The LFMB guides a layperson through the Latin Mass and provides prayers in English. The last edition of this "poem" was published in 1879, so engagement with a new edition has turned his attention once again to the nineteenth century.[63] We have no reason to suppose, any more than with the other two theologians we have discussed, that this will be the last we will hear from him!

---

[61]   Hass, *Sacred Modes of Being*, p. 134.

[62]   DJ has been Convenor of the Doctrine Committee of the Faith and Order Board of the SEC, 2008–13; 2017–20, contributor and general editor of the first eight volumes of the Grosvenor Essays of that Doctrine Committee (2004–12), co-editor of two collections of essays (see list of publications), priest-in-charge of St Andrew's, Uddingston and St Cuthbert's, Cambuslang, Diocese of Glasgow and Galloway.

[63]   With Jeremy Smith, "*The Lay Folks' Mass Book* and Thomas Frederick Simmons: Medievalism and the Tractarians", *Journal of Ecclesiastical History,* 70/4 (2019), pp. 1–20; David Jasper, "Thomas Frederick Simmons: A Forgotten Victorian Clergyman", *Scottish Episcopal Institute Journal* 5/3 (2021), pp. 133–46.

A brief reflective conclusion

The three theologians discussed in this essay are all products of the Church of England, but have spent part of their careers in Scotland, and it is there that they are now retired. All three have seen theology as an imaginative exercise in which attention to the contribution of the arts is inescapable. The balance, though, has been different. If of the three Brown has developed attention to the visual, and Pattison has sought the most European vision, Jasper has contributed most to furthering understanding of the relationship between religion and English literature. It is to him that we must turn for real insight into a diversity of the poets, including the liturgical poets. While he has always rooted such reflections in the practice of the liturgy, he has always embraced the task of analysing just how the success of liturgy depends upon the "poetic" and has never regarded such a task as completed. It is, therefore, with a great sense of something learnt that I have written this essay in his honour.

Ups and Downs of Nineteenth-Century Theology: Issues Theological, Literary and Poetic

Trevor Hart

The story of theology in the modern age, it has been suggested, may helpfully be traced by paying attention to a series of shifts in emphasis from one pole to the other of a seeming paradox within the doctrine of God; namely, between what theologians are wont to call God's transcendence with respect to the world on the one hand, and God's radical immanence or presence to the world on the other.

So, for instance, Stanley Grenz and Roger Olsen adopt this dialectic device in their careful chronicling of theology in the twentieth century.[1] Articulated typically in terms of the spatial metaphors embedded inescapably in religious language—and perhaps misled by a failure to grasp the essentially poetic logic of such language—the religious and theological truths at stake, they suggest, are often misconstrued as matched in a sort of zero-sum game. God must either properly be pictured as "up there", "high above" the created cosmos, or else be identified "down here" with us, "in" the midst of the world and sharing fully in its processes and events. In the nature of the case, absent due sensitivity to the way metaphor works, paying Paul is bound to involve robbing Peter ("up" and "down" being literal and logical opposites) and initiatives laying stress

---

[1]   Stanley J. Grenz and Roger E. Olsen, *Twentieth-Century Theology: God and the World in a Transitional Age* (Downers Grove, IL: InterVarsity Press, 1992).

on the radical transcendence of God tend, sooner or later, to provoke a vigorous swing back in the other direction in order to safeguard the concerns bound up with the affirming of God's immanence. Rather than resulting either in equilibrium (except of a very unstable and provisional sort) or the heroic achievement of an Hegelian "higher synthesis", the story is instead one of wearying ebb and flow, retreat and advance, exile and restoration, with no significant theological ground ever really being made.

Almost exactly one hundred years earlier, looking back across the decades of the nineteenth century to its roots in the late eighteenth, the liberal Anglo-Catholic theologian Aubrey Moore (1848–90) traced more or less the same dialectic. The story of theology in this era, too, he suggested, flip-flopped identifiably between insistence upon a remote transcendence, the more extreme forms of which threatened to banish God altogether from the cosmos, and radical versions of immanence which tended instead to reduce God to the dimensions afforded by the cosmos itself, either containable by or identifiable with it in whole or in part.[2] The Bible on the other hand, Moore observed, appears remarkably unconcerned by any such antagonism or contest, and is able to move easily from picturing God as exalted over all things in the highest heaven to finding God intimately and closely involved in the minutiae of natural processes, historical events and the fabric of individual lives.

It might be suggested by some, no doubt, that this is due to a degree of intellectual naivety or lack of sophistication on the part of biblical authors and the religious cultures they represent. Perhaps. Or, perhaps the shoe is on the other foot, and theirs was a culture with an intuitive grasp of the essentially imaginative and poetic nature of our patterns of speech and thought about God, happy to permit metaphors (up and down, here and there, inside and outside) to conflict and cross-fertilize creatively as useful fictions when the truth of an apprehension seemed to require it. In any event, unworried by such dialectical categories as "transcendence" and "immanence", the biblical texts resound with images intended to

---

[2]   "The Christian Doctrine of God", in Charles Gore (ed.), *Lux Mundi: A Series of Studies in the Religion of the Incarnation*, 9th edn (London: John Murray, 1889), pp. 57–109.

convey God's radical *otherness from* the world God has created, while yet (and at the same time) managing to portray God as radically *present to and involved in* the world. Indeed, if we would follow biblical intuitions, then we would perhaps have to say that it is precisely *because* God as Creator is radically other than his creature that God is so close to it and to us—closer to us even, we might say, than we are to ourselves. If spatial metaphor connotes anything, then we are bound to say that, far from being remote from us this God, having created "all things, visible and invisible", now "sustains in being all that is" not by some exercise of divine fiat across unimaginable distance, but by holding the cosmos and each of us in his loving embrace from first to last, and, as George MacDonald notes in one of his *Unspoken Sermons*, can never withdraw from us without us ceasing to be.[3] Far from compromising or being secured only despite God's "transcendence" or unbridgeable "otherness" from the world, in other words, on this account God's closeness and involvement look very different, being in effect a function, mode or expression of it.

Moore's essay, taking in a wide historical sweep, suggests that this biblical apprehension of God as uniquely present to all created times and places precisely because, as Creator, God transcends them and grants them their being, finds its first intellectually robust articulation with the careful formulation of the Christian doctrine of God as trinity during the fourth century. For here, the Greek notion of "Logos" as the overarching rational unity in which the world coheres, already appropriated by the Gospel of John and by some early Christian theologians such as Clement of Alexandria, is now formally drawn into the scope of the language used in liturgy and theology to identify God's presence and activity, fusing the creaturely and the divine by identifying the orderliness and meaning of the former with something that exists as *a distinct mode of God's own being*—the divine Logos or Word, who was in the beginning and by and through whom all things were made, and who holds or binds all things together in himself. Logos, in other words, is something God and God's

---

[3]   George MacDonald, *Unspoken Sermons* (Whitehorn, CA: Johannsen, 1997), p. 31. For a reliable account of MacDonald's wider theology see Kerry Dearborn, *Baptized Imagination: The Theology of George MacDonald* (Aldershot: Ashgate, 2006).

creation have in common; but this is not the whole story about God who, as Father, remains distinct from his Logos or Word, and transcendent with respect to the creaturely sphere. By its failure to acknowledge such a distinction in God, Moore notes, Unitarianism (a dissenting theological tradition far more prominent in the nineteenth century than since) is incapable of affirming the radical immanence of God without constant risk of collapsing into pantheism, its whole God, as it were, being sucked down into the order and "logic" of the processes of nature and history without effective remainder.[4]

It is at this point that Moore's account of the matter goes awry, taking a theological turn which provides a convenient foil to the thought of two of his near contemporaries, F. D. Maurice (1805–72) and the aforementioned George MacDonald (1824–1905). Maurice is chiefly remembered now as an Anglican theologian, having held chairs both in Divinity at King's College, London, and Moral Philosophy at Cambridge. It should also be recalled, though, that he had previously been instrumental, together with his mentor and friend A. J. Scott, in establishing the emergent academic discipline of English Literature, having been only the second appointee to one of the first chairs in that subject (also at King's College) as early as 1840[5] when, as literary historian Franklin E. Court observes, Matthew Arnold was still only fourteen years old and the recognition of English Literature as a worthy academic subject by the University of Cambridge thirty-eight long years away yet.[6] For his part, MacDonald is usually classified miscellaneously as an author, poet and preacher, all of which he undoubtedly was; but he, too, as a close friend, confidant

---

[4]   Gore, *Lux Mundi*, p. 102.

[5]   He moved to the Chair of Divinity in 1846. Scott was appointed Professor of English Literature and Language at the relatively juvenile University College London (founded in 1828) in 1848.

[6]   Literary historian Franklin E. Court refers to Scott and Maurice as primary movers in the birth and shaping of the new discipline and "academic precursors of modern literary studies". Franklin E. Court, *Institutionalizing English Literature: The Culture and Politics of Literary Study, 1750–1900* (Stanford: Stanford University Press, 1992), p. 122. On Arnold and Cambridge see *ibid*, pp. 117, 138.

and intellectual disciple of both Scott and Maurice, duly found his main source of gainful employment in the teaching of English Literature and in literary criticism, including eight years as Professor of English Literature at Bedford College for Women[7] from 1859 to 1867, and as an itinerant lecturer in this *avant garde* discipline to audiences ranging from the "working men" attending educational institutes established by the spirit of Christian Socialism in London and Manchester, to the well-heeled Anglican undergraduates in the lecture halls of King's College on the Strand.[8] Since A. J. Scott was himself both ordained and a considerable theologian (another intellectual emigré from north of the border cast out by his refusal to subscribe to certain austere Calvinist dogmas officially endorsed by his national church), it is worth noting in passing that the roots of English Literature and literary criticism are entangled from the outset with theology, though not yet of the sort that is later to be found at particularly low ebb on the sands of Dover Beach. It is to the theology of these pioneers in that fruitful interdisciplinary relationship that we now return.

The vulnerability of Aubrey Moore's reading of the classic trinitarian tradition is that it effectively *identifies* the distinction between the Father and the Son or Logos in God with that other distinction between God's transcendence and God's immanence or presence in the world (whether in creation or, subsequently, incarnation), a view which is, stated thus, rather more Hegelian than Christian. While the patristic writers certainly held that God's Word was closely bound up with God's *relationes ad extra*

---

[7]   Established in 1849 by Elizabeth Jesser Reid to provide education for women identifiable as religious "dissenters" whether by virtue of birth or personal conviction. Scott, a Presbyterian Scot from Greenock, had himself held this position a decade earlier.

[8]   The elision of this larger part of MacDonald's intellectual contribution in popular portrayals of the man and his work is both striking and unfortunate. It is overturned in the unrivalled but as yet largely unpublished scholarship of Kirstin Jeffrey Johnson, just some of which is to be found in her doctoral dissertation: '*Rooted in all its Story, More is Meant than Meets the Ear*. A Study of the Relational and Revelational Nature of George MacDonald's Mythopoeic Art'. (University of St Andrews, 2010.)

(that is to say, God's relatedness to the created order) from the beginning, they also insisted that the distinctions identifiable *within* God between Father, Son or Word, and Spirit *pre-exist* the act of creation; thus, while there is clearly a positive relationship between the "logos" or ratio of the world and the Word or Logos in God, the two are not simply identical, as though God's going out of himself to create *is* the point at which the divine Logos assumes a distinct existence or *hypostasis*. The Logos is already present, immanent in God, and there should be no suggestion that God's investment of creation with order and meaning and value lays bare its substance, let alone exhausts it. On the contrary, it is out of its inexhaustible fullness that creation is born, a point which MacDonald makes provocatively by referring us not to the Logos but instead to the *imagination* of God.[9] The relationship, he suggests, is one analogous to the way in which an artist or poet brings to expression something born in their imagination, granting it form and order as well as mere concrete existence. And although the order must first in some sense have been in the poet's own mind's eye, it does not exhaust the possibilities of the creative impulse, and, once made, has its own integrity and freedom over against it. It is precisely the grace or gift of *existence* (and otherness from itself) which the poetic imagination bestows upon it. The analogy has its distinct limits, of course, which is why MacDonald typically eschews the use of the language of "creating" in connection with any human acts of *poesis*, reserving that term for the incomparable aspects of the divine circumstance.[10] But the analogy holds good at this point at least: the orderliness of creation is a natural expression of the divine artist's capacity first to imagine and then to fashion it, and thus is a gift or grace bestowed upon the world together with its existence. But the divine Logos himself wholly transcends this particular "cosmos", rather than being bound up—let alone confined—within it.

Another feature of MacDonald's own characteristic way of referring to God's action in calling a world to exist alongside himself is his insistence that God does not, as the tradition has it, create *ex nihilo* ("out of

---

9   George MacDonald, *A Dish of Orts* (Whitehorn, CA: Johanssen, 1996), p. 3.

10   MacDonald, *Orts*, 2, 20. See also *Sermons*, pp. 418–19.

nothing") but "out of God's nature",[11] as the "flowing forth of his heart",[12] language which at first blush suggests some Neoplatonic emanation that holds the world itself to be divine, born or summoned forth out of divine "stuff". But this does not appear to be what MacDonald intends at all. On the contrary, he is ever mindful, he tells us, of the "unsurpassable gulf which distinguishes . . . all that is God's from all that is man's", part of which is precisely the fact that, whereas every human artist begins with something already given to him or her, in a vital sense the world is indeed called or summoned forth to exist by God and alongside God where once there was nothing except God himself.[13] MacDonald is mindful too that it is the very purpose of God in creation and redemption to bestow "divine life" as a gift upon creatures who are themselves finite and free, and must choose to receive it.[14] His worry about the formula *ex nihilo*, though, is its possible suggestion of divine caprice, as though God might not have created at all, as though creating were not, as we might say, something that "comes naturally" to God. Nothing could be further from the truth than this, MacDonald insists. "The being of God is love", he writes in a contracted syllogism, "therefore creation".[15] Again, therefore, creation is to be understood not merely as the work of God's hands, but "as the flowing forth of his love of us, making us blessed in the union of his heart and ours". And, underpinning this, MacDonald himself resorts to Trinitarian categories, not now appealing to the language of the Logos, but to the more mainstream biblical and credal language of Father and Son, whose mutual love for one another in the Spirit is the music of eternity, a relational fullness which nonetheless always tends to overflow, and would always have others share in its joy. "Speaking after our poor human fashions of thought—the only fashions possible to us—", he writes, "I imagine that God has never been contented to be alone even with the Son of his love . . . but that he has from the first willed

---

[11]   MacDonald, *Sermons*, p. 424.

[12]   MacDonald, *Orts*, p. 247.

[13]   MacDonald, *Orts*, pp. 2, 3.

[14]   MacDonald, *Sermons*, p. 301.

[15]   MacDonald, *Sermons*, p. 299.

and labored to give existence to other creatures who should be blessed with his blessedness."[16]

Here, then, is the final reason for resisting any theological scheme which would apportion and limit immanence to the peculiar remit of the second person of the trinity in order supposedly to preserve the transcendence of the first (a zero-sum approach which is needless to the extent that biblical patterns are permitted to shape our imagining of the circumstance, and more akin to the impulses of Arianism than those of what duly became trinitarian orthodoxy).[17] For MacDonald and for Maurice (by whom MacDonald was undoubtedly influenced in this respect), *salvation*, the partaking in divine life for which we were created and to which God now calls us, consists in our sharing in the eternal relation or bond of love between Father and Son; and this not in any abstract way, but very concretely—in the down-to-earth realities of our life in the world, in discovering that the God and Father of Jesus is our Father too, in realizing that at the heart and root of *all* things is a divine reality the most fitting analogy for which is a human parent's goodness and love for a child; and in relating to God as Father from moment to moment as Jesus himself did, driven by nothing more than

---

[16]   MacDonald, *Sermons*, p. 299.

[17]   Scholarly readings of Arianism tend nowadays to present its founder not so much as a theological radical driven by adherence to philosophical rather than theological convictions, but instead as a theological conservative whose arguments were grounded in what was at times a rather arthritic exegesis of biblical texts. Nonetheless, the habits of exegesis most likely to have formed Arius were those associated with the tradition of the Catechetical School in Alexandria, heavily influenced in its turn by the religious philosophy of Plotinus, whose unswerving emphasis on the radical transcendence of The One is brought to bear on the biblical text in ways comparable to the "Hellenic Judaism" of Philo. The impulse of Arian theology, in other words, was almost certainly not, as typically supposed, a concern to diminish the status of the Son of God, but instead to secure the transcendence of the Father, of whom Jesus himself had said, "The Father is greater than I" (John 14:28). For a judicious account see Rowan Williams, *Arius: Heresy and Tradition* (London: Darton, Longman and Todd, 1987).

a desire to obey him and so to be made ever more fully like him. To know God as Father, to know the Father to be closer to us than we are even to ourselves and to be holding us even (perhaps most especially) when we walk through life's darkest and most painful experiences, this, for MacDonald and for Maurice, is of the essence of eternal life itself. But it is just this that Unitarianism and Moore's neo-Arianism alike are unable to permit. Each in its way projects the divine Father into a remote transcendence, leaving him far removed from any creaturely concerns and experience rather than embracing these and drawing them into the very life of God itself, making them unequivocally God's own in the flesh and blood of the Son who is *homoousios* with the Father (shares fully in the "being" of God) eternally. While from one perspective, therefore, the incarnation might indeed look like a "going out" of God to become "not God", as Karl Barth puts it provocatively,[18] the insistence of Christological orthodoxy is that it must also be acknowledged as a radical "drawing in" of what is indeed not God (the creature) nevertheless to share in its proper creaturely fashion in the dynamics of that same life and love in which God's being eternally consists. The point of the distinction between Father and Son in God, therefore, Maurice and MacDonald held, was not that the Father was transcendent and the Son immanent, but simply that the Father is not the Son and the Son not the Father, the relation between them being that love or communion in which their shared "being" eternally consists.

F. D. Maurice was in fact raised as a Unitarian, eventually receiving baptism in the Church of England in his twenty-sixth year and to the great distress of his father—a Unitarian minister who had already seen his wife and daughters make the same ecclesiastical transition. Michael Maurice was of good dissenting stock, a man with liberal principles, a strong conviction in love and justice as the key attributes of the God in whom he believed, and an equal aversion to the doctrines of Evangelicalism which, he held, compromised precisely those qualities in its teaching about God and the heart of God's dealings with humankind. Frederick Denison clearly soaked up the characterization of God as loving and just

---

[18]   Karl Barth, *The Göttingen Dogmatics: Instruction in Christian Religion*, vol. 1 (Edinburgh: T. & T. Clark, 1991), p. 136.

from first to last, and it shaped his later theology from top to bottom. But the Unitarian God he found rather too abstract, too remote from the world and its messy complexities ever to be the pulse of a living faith. As his biographer Florence Higham writes,

> [Maurice] had always believed in a God of Love in theory, but . . . gradually he came to feel that only if men could contemplate God in a human form and could believe that His Spirit was still potent to remove from the human heart the selfishness that shut him out, only then would God become real and truly significant. So, he professed faith in God the creator, God manifest in Christ, God guiding men by the light of his Holy Spirit.[19]

Maurice wanted a God whose love was active in the world, active in the lives of men and women, available to all who would avail themselves of it, and powerful in its impact. And, under the impact of the mature Coleridge (who, courtesy of his own personal struggles with sin and brokenness, had finally exchanged his earlier dalliances with the pantheistic leanings of German Idealism for a more orthodox trinitarianism[20]) and the writings of another Scot, Thomas Erskine of Linlathen (1788–1870) (close friend of A. J. Scott and, duly, of both Maurice and MacDonald),[21] he gradually found himself, as Higham puts it, "in a new atmosphere, as if . . . he had emerged from a dark tunnel into a land diffused with the light of God's presence".[22]

It was precisely this, an apprehension of God's immediacy and God's threefold invitation to the human creature to commune with himself,

---

[19] Florence Higham, *Frederick Denison Maurice* (London: SCM Press Ltd, 1947), p. 27.

[20] See further Trevor Hart, "Who am I: Coleridge, Imagination and the God of *Biographia Literaria*" in *The Coleridge Bulletin*, New Series 38 (2011), pp. 53–66.

[21] For a valuable account see Don Horrocks, *Laws of the Spiritual Order: Innovation and Reconstruction in the Soteriology of Thomas Erskine of Linlathen* (Milton Keynes: Paternoster, 2004).

[22] Higham, *Maurice*, p. 30.

that Maurice found in the trinitarian faith of Anglican orthodoxy, a faith which increasingly burned itself into his heart, rather than simply lodging inertly in his head as the sort of arithmetical conundrum to which regular rehearsal of the so-called "Athanasian Creed" at Mattins and Evensong threatened to reduce it. In the terms eventually coined by his direct contemporary John Henry Newman (1801–90), what Maurice sought and found here was an account of the God of the gospel to which he could grant "real" rather than merely "notional" assent.[23] The desire for actual communion with God, to know God "not in a vague, loose sense, but actually to know Him as a friend" was, he suggested to his father in a letter dated February 1832, what the human heart craved most deeply, even when that craving was, as it often was even in himself, obscure to itself and overlaid by sin. It was, at root, the craving of our very human creatureliness, that *for which* we were made, and it was in satisfying this same demand of the heart (the "real test" of any doctrine of God, Maurice insisted) that he discovered the truth of trinitarianism.[24] God was no longer remote, but close at hand; no longer one aloof from the trials of existence in the world, but one who had borne them fully himself, and revealed himself most fully precisely in the manner of his doing so; the world no longer a disenchanted place, but the theatre of God's glory and God's action in drawing people back to himself and, in the Johannine language which Maurice himself so loved, giving them "power to become children of God" (John 1:12).

A similar emphasis on the reality and immediacy of God to the receptive soul is to be found in MacDonald's writing, not least in what is sometimes referred to as his "sacramentalism", under which heading I think we might include two distinct sorts of things. First there is his love of Nature, dating back to his early years spent in the Scottish countryside, and nurtured by his love for poetry, especially that of the Romantics with their grasp of Nature as haunted by the presence of God himself. In his

---

[23] John Henry Newman, *An Essay in Aid of a Grammar of Assent* (London: Longmans Green, 1870).

[24] Frederick Maurice (ed.), *The Life of Frederick Denison Maurice Chiefly Told in His Own Letters*, vol. 1 (London: Macmillan, 1884), p. 133.

essay, "A Sketch of Individual Development",[25] MacDonald presents a sense of wonder, curiosity, mystery in the face of Nature as a normal part of human development, before exposure to the ideology so often attendant upon the teaching of the natural sciences squeezes that sense of wonder out of us, leaving in Nature's place only quantitative analysis and a law-regulated mechanism cold in its indifference to humankind.[26] MacDonald was no unduly enchanted opponent of the right of natural science to demand a hearing for its discovery of the regular patterns and processes of the material world. He had himself trained as a chemist, and held (again, as did both Scott and Maurice) that all genuine truth must be God's truth, and therefore to be welcomed wherever it was to be found. But precisely as someone with a hands-on knowledge of science's dealings with the world at its coal face, MacDonald was more aware, too, than many of his Christian peers, of those proper limits within which science could respectfully claim any authority, and utterly impatient of the imperialistic tendencies (still with us, alas) which would grant it unquestioning deference well outside those proper bounds. "Madam Science," he insists, shows no antagonism whatever "to Lady Poetry; but the atmosphere and plan on which alone they can meet as friends who understand each other, is the mind and heart of the sage, not of the boy".[27]

In any case, having achieved what I suppose today might be called a "secondary naivety" or post-critical perspective in this regard, for MacDonald as for some of his poetic forebears, Nature was without doubt "charged with the grandeur of God"[28], a "place full of a presence" as Margaret Elginbrod describes it in the opening pages of MacDonald's first novel. Indeed, she tells Hugh Sutherland (who, while she has been contemplating the pulsing depth of the fir wood, has instead been quarrying its surfaces in a much more instrumental manner for images with which to supply his own verse, being ironically oblivious to that which would transfigure his poetry into liturgy), "I canna richtly say ma

---

[25]   MacDonald, *Orts*, pp. 43–76. The essay dates from 1880.

[26]   MacDonald, *Orts*, pp. 51–2.

[27]   MacDonald, *Orts*, p. 51.

[28]   From the poem, "God's Grandeur", by Gerard Manley Hopkins.

prayers in ony ither place."[29] Nature was a place which might provoke a response not just to its own beauty, but to God himself, where one might "read the word of God in his own handwriting; or rather . . . pore upon that expression of the face of God, which, however little a man may think of it, yet sinks so deeply into his nature, and moulds it towards its own likeness".[30] These are strong statements, and clearly testify to MacDonald's sense that God might give his beauty, goodness and holiness to be known (and does give them to be known) sometimes more fully, directly and clearly through a soul's immersion in the unalloyed encounter with nature than in the constipated, tortured and (he believed) all too often disloyal mis-characterizations of God to be heard raining down from pulpits across the land.

MacDonald, like Erskine, Scott and Maurice before him, anguished over the theological schemes into which, he believed, Scripture had been tortured and forced in the churches, all but obliterating the true character of the God portrayed in it, and leading to all manner of pastoral and spiritual malformations. His response, like theirs, was certainly not to set Scripture aside, but to immerse himself in it ever more thoroughly, seeking an interpretation of it which was consonant in its particulars with an overarching characterization of God as a loving father determined to deliver his sons and daughters from their sins so that they might enjoy life in all its fullness. But MacDonald felt no need to limit God's unwavering pursuit of his creatures to the church's handling of its scriptural inheritance. According to Erskine, the "spiritual order" as he called it was shot through the material order like leaven in the lump, and the "spiritual eye, and ear, and heart . . . might see, and hear, and love God in everything—in every object of nature, in every event of time, in every duty, every difficulty, every sorrow, every joy".[31] I see no reason to suppose that, if pressed, MacDonald would or could have challenged the broad catholicity of this vision; but more than his friends (and perhaps it

---

[29]   George MacDonald, *David Elginbrod* (London: Hurst & Blackett Ltd, 1863), pp. 33–4.

[30]   MacDonald, *Elginbrod*, p. 40.

[31]   William Hanna (ed.), *Letters of Thomas Erskine of Linlathen From 1800 Till 1840* (Edinburgh: David Douglas, 1877), p. 74.

was his own poetic gift which influenced him here) MacDonald followed
the Romantics in finding God more fully present and more likely to be
apprehended (and with sanctifying effect) in, with and under the glories
of Nature (both pastoral and sublime) than anywhere elsewhere in the
world.

MacDonald himself refers to this conviction as he finds it palpable
in Wordsworth's poetry, for instance, as "Christian Pantheism".[32] The
description is deliberately playful and provocative; but while it may
send someone seeking a PhD topic back excitedly with shibboleths
to discern the colour of Wordsworth's orthodoxy, we should be in no
doubt about MacDonald's own. He was *not* advocating pantheism (the
identification of God with nature, and thus the deifying of nature). The
conviction that God is close to creation rather than far removed from it
is, as we have already seen, an ordinary observation of biblical faith, no
matter how shocking it might have been to those still emerging from the
Deism of the eighteenth century. For the apostle Paul, the more shocking
realization was that God himself, in the person of the Spirit of Christ,
dwells *in* us, tabernacling in each of us, just as the divine Son tabernacles
in our flesh as the man Jesus, thereby making it his own. In fact, for
Erskine, and Maurice and MacDonald in his wake, the incarnation was
a moment which changed history for good; for by uniting himself with
our humanity, they held, Christ, the eternal Son of the Father, had united
himself to every human being in such a way that his own life (the life of
God taking appropriate creaturely form) might flow from him into them
as the sap flows through the vine, with transfiguring, sanctifying effect.
This was the ancient claim of many of the church fathers in their wrestling
with Scripture, sometimes sniffily rejected by more modern theologians
on the basis that it seems to presuppose a metaphysic borrowed from
Platonism or some other philosophical system long past its sell-by date.

Two things may be said about this: first, the suggestion that because
Plato (or whomever among the intellectual giants of history) offered
something to the world, any theological ideas contingent on it should
be treated with inherent suspicion is not one MacDonald or his friends

---

[32]   See MacDonald, *Elginbrod*, p. 34. C.f. the essay "Wordsworth's Poetry", in
      MacDonald, *Orts*, pp. 244–63.

would have had much time for as such. Each of them, as I have said, held that truth, whatever its source, if it commends itself to the human heart, conscience and intellect, should be welcomed and reckoned with. But in any case, we risk mistaking the intellectual scaffolding for the substance of the building (to borrow one of MacDonald's own favourite metaphors) if, without further ado, we identify the idea of God uniting himself to humankind with redemptive effect as an obvious product of Platonism. It's not. It finds expression in all sorts of biblical categories and institutions ranging across both testaments, and is presented by some of its patristic advocates as little more than an inference of the claim that in Christ, the Creator of the world himself (in whom we live and move and have our being) has made himself one of us, and is intimately related to each of us no longer as our Creator alone, but now as our brother, one with whom we share (as the Reformer John Calvin puts it) a "fraternal alliance" by virtue of having creaturely "flesh" in common.[33] Such a claim, insisting as it does that what God now shares with us is not limited to a spiritual participation in the realm of nonmaterial universals or Forms (the *kosmos noetos*) but extends all the way down to the messy exigencies of particular flesh and blood lives lived, is one any self-respecting Platonist will be inclined to baulk at rather than encourage, let alone endorse.[34]

To return, though, from this fleeting digression: MacDonald's discovery of God close at hand in nature, finding the face of God impressed upon nature, is not Pantheism in any textbook meaning of that word. It is simply the sensibility of the Psalms, which acknowledges God's presence to be found even in the depths of *Sheol* and ascribes to the hills

---

[33] The incarnation itself, Calvin argues in his commentary on Psalm 22, establishes a "true fellowship of the flesh" by virtue of which all humans possess an *ius fraternae coniunctionis* with Christ, although "the true enjoyment thereof belongs to genuine believers alone". John Calvin, *Commentary on the Book of Psalms*, translated from the original Latin and collated with the author's French version by the Rev. James Anderson, vol. 1 (Edinburgh: Calvin Translation Society, 1845), p. 379; c.f. *Corpus Reformatorum* 31:231.

[34] See further, Trevor Hart, *In Him Was Life: The Person and Work of Christ* (Waco, TX: Baylor University Press, 2019), pp. 55–115.

and the trees their own peculiar liturgical calling and capacity to sound forth God's praise—an image on which MacDonald offers a delightful riff in his description of "a noisy stream, that obstinately refused to keep Scotch Sabbath, praising the Lord after its own fashion".[35]

Where MacDonald's "sacramentalism" is concerned, the other thing to mention briefly, perhaps, is his related (but I think distinct) suggestion that God has made the world to be the sort of place where there are direct correspondences between things we find to be true in the material order, and the realities of our inner lives (our minds, our hearts, our imaginations) such that the one provides a natural language in terms of which to speak of the other.[36] I say this is a distinct suggestion from MacDonald's claims about Nature, because the relevant "spiritual" realities which he has in mind, while hardly divorced from the reality of God (since nothing creaturely *is* finally divorceable from the reality of God) are themselves purely and properly creaturely realities—thoughts, feelings, mental actions, apprehensions of beauty, and so on. Our humanity, he understands, immerses us awkwardly in two distinct dimensions of reality at once. Our bodies key us into a world of material objects and processes; but there is another aspect to us which we know will not be reduced to or confined by materiality alone—the soul, mind, spirit, imagination or whatever else we may choose to call it, and the order of meanings, values, persons and other things unavailable to any empirical science for inspection, dissection or classification. The circumstance is a challenging one, MacDonald suggests, not least because as citizens of both dimensions we are called upon to hold them together rather than allowing them to drift apart, and constantly to interpret each in terms belonging rightly to the other. Among other things, he notes, this means that our language is originally and inexorably *metaphorical,* driven as we are to borrow terms used first to denote physical conditions, actions, relations and the like now to suggest non-material states, actions and relations. Thus, the act of paying attention (Latin *attentio*) to something is a "stretching towards" it so as to "grasp" its importance more fully; an

---

[35] MacDonald, *Elginbrod*, p. 36.

[36] See his essay, "The Imagination: Its Functions and its Culture", in MacDonald, *Orts*.

argument "goes back and forth" in its consideration of an issue "from all sorts of different angles"; our heart is "chilled" by some piece of bad news; and so on and so forth.

The constitution of our "species being" itself, in other words, makes *poetic* ventures inevitable. This observation itself was not new, and MacDonald borrows it openly from Carlyle. He does with it, though, what Carlyle does not; namely, grounds linguistics or poetics within an unashamedly *theological* vision of creation, and of the human creature in particular. Such connections or correspondences, MacDonald insists, are neither accidental nor arbitrary, but are part of the fabric which holds reality together as a single coherent whole. The material forms that resonate naturally with immaterial things, that is to say, lie already to hand, put there by God for our eventual discovery and enjoyment in use. The simplest bodily gesture expressive of an inner state thus lies on the same plane (albeit at a different point on it) as the most lofty instance of poetry. What is common to both is that command of metaphor to which Aristotle refers as, in its most exalted mode, the mark of genius.[37] It is the eye for detecting identity in difference, oblique yet profound correspondences most of which still remain hidden, but which, when we grasp them and tease them out, strike us at once as exuding that "air of rightness" of which Ricoeur speaks in his own discussion of metaphor,[38] distinguishing them at once from the merely fanciful or clumsily conventional, and granting us revelatory glimpses of the mesh around which the world is woven.

Characteristically, but at odds with the wider habit of his own century, MacDonald demurs on theological grounds from all easy talk of genius or of the "creative" power of the poetic imagination. Only God truly creates, he insists, and the distinction between God's artistry and ours is one we must keep clearly in view. Again, no sooner do we reckon with themes such as presence and sacramentality than we find ourselves hard up against the utter difference and incomparability of the God who is

---

[37]   Aristotle, *Poetics* 1459a.

[38]   Paul Ricoeur, *The Rule of Metaphor: Multidisciplinary Studies of the Creation of Meaning in Language* (Toronto: Toronto University Press, 1977), p. 239.

constantly present and close to the world he has made.[39] In a sense, he avers, we are not even poets or "makers" but merely *trouvères*, "finders" engaged in a constant heuristic play, stumbling across and uncovering a deeper connectivity forged in the creation of the world itself, that it might be a habitation fit for the flourishing of human beings, those most imaginative of creatures.[40] This is how MacDonald understood it—a world crying out for imaginative response, because already laden with a surplus or excess of symbolic significance. A world, furthermore, teeming with further meaning as yet to be discovered or given birth. For here, again, in the sphere of imaginative response, MacDonald recognized, there is a paradoxical interplay between the heuristic and the creative,[41] even our most daring trespasses beyond what the world already has to offer frequently feeling as though the new creative thought or vision itself is one in some sense already "out there", placing us under obligation, revealing itself to us, waiting to be uncovered or given voice, rather than sheerly summoned into being by the artistic imagination.[42]

And in some sense, of course, it is always thus. No artist or writer or composer ever begins *de novo*, but draws more or less consciously on fragments, samples of experience which he then reconfigures into

---

[39]   Thus "We must not forget ... that between creator and poet lies the one unpassable gulf which distinguishes ... all that is God's from all that is man's; ... It is better (therefore) to keep the word creation for that calling out of nothing which is the imagination of God." MacDonald, *Orts*, pp. 2–3.

[40]   MacDonald, *Orts*, p. 8.

[41]   "The man who cannot invent will never discover." MacDonald, *Orts*, p. 13.

[42]   See, e.g., MacDonald, *Orts*, p. 24. MacDonald addresses directly the then current (and today still common) speculation that would push the relevant creative mechanism into the shadows of the unconscious (individual or corporate). He sees no reason to deny this, but every reason to offer a solidly theological account of the matter: "From that unknown region we grant they come, but not by its own blind working ... God sits in that chamber of our being in which the candle of consciousness goes out in darkness, and sends forth from thence wonderful gifts into the light of that understanding which is His candle. Our hope lies in no most perfect mechanism even of the spirit, but in the wisdom wherein we live and move and have our being" (pp. 24–5).

something new. But MacDonald insists upon a theological and religious rather than a merely sociological or psychological account of the matter. God, he suggests, has hidden things—meanings, imaginative possibilities, works and worlds of art—in the depths of the world that he has made. And even in our most creative ventures, therefore, we are in truth "following and finding out" what God has already imagined and given to the world as part of its developmental potential,[43] and in poetry as well as in science (albeit often in a different mode) the chief role of imagination is "to inquire into what God has made".[44]

All this is sometimes referred to as MacDonald's Platonism, and Stephen Prickett (erstwhile President of the George MacDonald Society) has referred suggestively to him as a "temperamental Platonist".[45] At the end of the day, though, I'm not sure about the helpfulness of the category, or the need to resort to it in order to account for this aspect of MacDonald's thought. As already indicated, I have no necessary aversion to Platonism as a source of helpful philosophical tools, and no particular desire to absolve MacDonald from his entanglements with the thought of one of the world's greatest philosophical minds. But the eschewal of materialistic naturalism is not yet Platonism, and acknowledgment that creation consists in things both "visible and invisible" (as the creed has it), and thoughtful recognition of ourselves as creatures with a foot in both those categories, compels intelligent theological reflection about how those two dimensions might be related to one another. Such reflection has been conducted in recent years, for example, by philosopher Nicholas Wolterstorff, whose discussion of "cross-modal correspondences" in human experience touches upon the very same phenomenon,[46] and something similar lies at the heart of Iain McGilchrist's recent work on the impact of the bi-hemispheric structure of the human brain in

---

[43] MacDonald, *Orts*, pp. 41–2.

[44] MacDonald, *Orts*, p. 2.

[45] Stephen Prickett, *Victorian Fantasy* (Waco, TX: Baylor University Press, 2005), p. 170.

[46] See, e.g., Nicholas Wolterstorff, *Art in Action: Toward a Christian Aesthetic* (Carlisle: Solway, 1997), pp. 96–121.

structuring our distinctly human ways of experiencing the world.[47] Neither are Platonists of any sort that I can easily identify; but both, significantly, while offering their accounts solely from within the remit and scope of their respective disciplines, do so from a perspective more than sympathetic to the sorts of theological claims MacDonald makes.

One final note of caution where MacDonald's sacramentalism is concerned: while he holds that material realities of all sorts, but especially our experiences of Nature, can be the means in, with and under which God may engage us, and offer himself for our apprehension and engagement in turn, he by no means sees this as an automatic or even a probable occurrence in every case. In his first venture into the form of the novel, as we have already seen, Margaret Elginbrod's rapture in the fir wood at dawn is matched by Hugh Sutherland's relative indifference, the wonder of the holy place leaving him virtually unscathed, for the time being at least.[48] Worse than this, far from being sacramental, translucent with respect to the spiritual order, the things of this world (even the things of nature) can become opaque, occluding our vision rather than enabling it, and, as we seek to grasp them for their own sake, drag us down into a material tyranny from which we must be delivered. So, MacDonald writes, "No man who has not the Father so as to be eternally content in him alone, can possess a sunset or a field of grass or a mine of gold or the love of a fellow creature according to its nature—as God would have him possess it—in the eternal way of inheriting, having and holding. He who has God, has all things, after the fashion in which he who made them has them."[49] The spiritual condition of the one who encounters (or is encountered by) the objects and events of this world is just as relevant to the epiphanic nature of the encounter as whatever presence we may suppose is there to be apprehended. Theologically, for MacDonald and for Maurice (for whom, Florence Higham suggests, "*every* activity of life was sacramental"[50]) it was

---

[47]   Iain McGilchrist, *The Master and his Emissary: The Divided Brain and the Making of the Western World* (New Haven and London: Yale University Press, 2009).

[48]   MacDonald, *Elginbrod*, pp. 33–4. See n. 29 above.

[49]   MacDonald, *Sermons*, p. 201.

[50]   Higham, *Maurice*, p. 115.

always and at best a matter of the God who is *with* us, close to us, seeking
to draw us to himself in, with and under the whole of the creaturely world
in which, by body and soul, we are immersed, calling out and soliciting
resonance from the God who is in us, the Christ who, by virtue of the
incarnation, is now joined to us and present by his Spirit in the depths
of our innermost being. But that resonance may be and all too often is
drowned out by the cacophony of sin and the curving in of the self upon
itself (and away from God and from truth) in which sin consists.

"There is a light within you, close to you," Maurice urges his readers.
"Do you know it? Are you coming to it? Are you desiring that it should
penetrate you through and through? Oh, turn to it! . . . It will reveal
yourself to you! It will reveal the world to you! . . . When I say Repent: I
say, Turn and confess His presence. You have always had it with you. You
have been unmindful of it."[51] "The spirit of God," writes MacDonald, "lies
all about a man like a mighty sea, ready to rush in at the smallest chink
in the walls that shut him out from his own",[52] seeking opportunities to
strengthen what is good, and to burn out what is evil. For, organic and
oceanic metaphors aside, redemption is a matter of the heart and the
will; and, if God's purpose is that his creatures should share in his own
life and joy, become partakers in the divine nature, then what this means
humanly is the conformity of heart, mind and will to the Father's own.
"Because we are come out of the divine nature," MacDonald writes, " . . .
we must choose to be divine, to be of God, to be one with God, loving
and living as he loves and lives, and so be partakers of the divine nature,
or we perish".[53] The "unsurpassable gulf" between creator and creature,
the intimate presence of creator to creation, and the radical participation
into which the one is invited and drawn by the other prove, at the last,
to be matters grasped more in terms of the moral than the metaphysical;
and they are manifest nowhere more completely than in the realm of the
human imagination, which lives and moves and has its being entirely as
the creative offspring of God's own.

---

[51]   Maurice, *Essays*, p. 101.

[52]   George MacDonald, *Robert Falconer* (London: Hurst & Blackett Ltd, 1868),
p. 181.

[53]   MacDonald, *Sermons*, p. 424.

Truth or Meaning: Revelation in the Desert—Redel's Sermon on Exodus 19

Hannah Altorf

By means of introduction

David Jasper's *The Sacred Desert* commences with an image that lingers in the imagination. It is from the author's notes on his own solitary retreat in the desert of Texas. He writes:

> I had forgotten what real darkness was like. At first it was frightening. I have a flashlight, and I was afraid I might not be able to find the little path which could lead me back to my door. I could see, literally, nothing ... And the silence. I think of my remark to my friend before I set out last week that "there is nothing there". No sound of traffic ... or airplanes or trains or music or voices. It is silent, and yet there is sound everywhere. I suppose I must call it natural sound, and it is frightening.[1]

It is unlikely that someone as steeped in hermeneutics as Jasper would start his book with just any image. The note speaks of the author's courage to go into a place that challenges one's senses. It brings the reader outside their normal surroundings of light and enlightenment and away from more familiar ways of making sense. It brings them closer to liminal

---

[1] David Jasper, *The Sacred Desert: Religion, Literature, Art, and Culture* (Oxford: Blackwell, 2004), p. v.

experience. As Jasper writes, "The desert tests people up to and beyond their limits."[2] It is a place of "disorientation".[3]

The desert has been the meeting place of humans with God, as it is for instance in Exodus 19. The Israelites arrive at Sinai and Moses climbs the mountain. The text describes a pivotal moment in the exodus story and yet, on closer reading, it raises more questions than it answers. It turns out to be impossible to keep track of Moses' ascents and descents or to say with any certainty who was with Moses on the mountain. The text seems to embody the disorientation of the liminal experience it depicts.

The Documentary Hypothesis has dealt with these textual problems by flooding the desert with light.[4] It argues that Torah was not written by Moses, as tradition holds.[5] Rather, the text is an amalgam of different authors put together by an editor. These authors have been identified by their distinguishing characteristics. One author is called J, for their use of the tetragrammaton, the four-letter Hebrew word, for the name of God. Another author is E, named after their use of Elohim for God. P is the priestly source, who is mostly concerned with priestly matters. D the author of Deuteronomy and R is the redactor or editor of it all. The challenge for consecutive generations of scholars has been to attribute

---

[2]   Jasper, *The Sacred Desert*, p. 16.

[3]   Jasper, *The Sacred Desert*, p. 18.

[4]   For two current examples of such scholarship see Wolfgang Oswald, *The Book of Exodus* (Boston: Brill, 2014) and Heun Kyu Joo, *The God of Compassion at Mount Sinai—A Literary and Theological Interpretation of the Tangled Mix of Law and Narrative in the Sinai Pericope (Exodus 19:1–24:11)* (doctoral dissertation submitted to St Michael's College, Toronto, 2016), <https:// tspace.library.utoronto.ca/bitstream/1807/75521/1/Joo%20Heun%20 Kyu%20201611%20PhD%20thesis.pdf>, accessed 13 July 2022.

[5]   Traditionally Torah is believed to have been written by Moses. This belief dates from the second temple period, but it was already questioned in Late Antiquity. (See Jeffrey H. Tigay, "The Documentary Hypothesis, Empirical Models and Holistic Interpretation", in Jun Ikeda et al. (eds), *Modernity and Interpretations of Ancient Texts. The Collapse and Remaking of Traditions. IIAS Reports* (Kyoto: International Institute of Advanced Studies, Kizugawa-City, Kyoto, 2012), pp. 116–43, here at p. 116.)

sections, sentences and even parts of sentences to these authors and thus to divide the text as neatly as possible.

Yet to do so has proven to be an almost impossible task. Agreement among even a selection of only three scholars can be as low as 16 per cent.[6] Perhaps it was only a matter of time before an altogether different response was created, one which Jasper calls "a masterpiece of post-modern irony".[7] J may have started life as a mere answer to a problem, yet she (indeed *she*) was given flesh and blood by the American literary critic Harold Bloom. In collaboration with translator David Rosenberg, Bloom imagines that J was a woman attached to the court of David and Solomon.[8] In later work, Bloom identified J with Bathsheba, wife of king David.[9]

Thus, a path is made through the desert. While for some, any speculation on authorship may be a step too far, for others, this does not go far enough. For as diverse as their methodologies are, the Documentary Hypothesis and Bloom's "masterpiece of post-modern irony" share methodology. Their concern is with what has been written. The same is true too of many feminist reimaginations of women in the Bible, which create beings out of even the most fleeting references.[10] Yet, where does this leave the voices of the women who are not mentioned at all, though we have to assume that they too once spoke? What methodology brings them out of the darkness?

The text below offers a reply to such queries by giving voice to one of them.

---

[6]   Wolfgang Oswald provides a short overview of three such readings of this text and calculates that they do not agree much. Only about 16 per cent they assign to the same author. (Oswald, *The Book of Exodus,* pp. 175–8.)

[7]   David Jasper, *Literature and Theology as a Grammar of Ascent* (London: Routledge, 2016), p. 171.

[8]   *The Book of J,* translated from the Hebrew by David Rosenberg, interpreted by Harold Bloom (New York: Grove Weidenfeld, 1990).

[9]   Harold Bloom, *The Western Canon: The Books and School of the Ages* (New York: Harcourt Brace & Company, 1994), pp. 4–5.

[10] See for instance Ellen Frankel, *The Five Books of Miriam: A Woman's Commentary on the Torah* (New York: HarperCollins, 1998), as well as feminist work discussed below.

Translator's introduction

Moses' life was shaped by women: by the two midwives, Shiphrah and Puah, who told the king of Egypt that Hebrew women give birth so quickly, that it is impossible for any midwife to abide by his ruling to kill all the boys born from Hebrew women; by his mother Jochebed, who kept him hidden for three months and then heroically managed to save his life by putting him in a basket; by his sister Miriam, who ran alongside the river as the basket floated towards Pharaoh's daughter and talked her into adopting him, and who was a co-leader through the desert; by Pharaoh's daughter Bithiah, who raised the little boy as her own; and by Zipporah, his wife, who miraculously saved him—or their son, the story is ambiguous.[11]

Apart from Shiphrah and Puah, the women are not named in the story of Moses' early survival. Instead, their names have to be deduced from other texts. Even less is known about the next generation of women, the women whom Moses nurtured—rather than those who nurtured and supported him. There is no mention of Moses' daughters in Tanach. Biblical sources only mention two of his sons, Gershom and Eliezer (Exodus 2:21–2, 18:3–4, 1 Chronicles 23:14–15). Indeed, commentators have noted that after their initial and crucial role, women hardly feature in what follows.[12]

This is where the sermon below comes in. It is understood to be by Redel, Moses' daughter, who was named after her maternal grandfather (Exodus

---

[11] These stories are found in Exodus 1, 2, and 4 (Zipporah). Miriam is named as a leader alongside Moses and Aaron in Micah 6:4.

[12] These early chapters have received ample discussion in feminist research looking for "positive portrayals of women in the Bible" (J. Cheryl Exum, "Second Thoughts about Secondary Characters: Women in Exodus 1.8–2.10", in Athalya Brenner (ed.), *A Feminist Companion to Exodus to Deuteronomy* (Sheffield: Sheffield Academic Press, 1994), pp. 75–87, here at p. 76), but as Exum argues, even though this portrayal is positive and the women are powerful, they are portrayed as "using their power in the service of patriarchy" (p. 82). Exum's article expresses the concern that is also prominent later in Redel's sermon: " . . . even though men and women share in the making of history, symbolic production has been controlled by men" ("Second Thoughts", p. 79).

2:16–21).[13] *Redel's sermon offers new understanding of the generation of women that went into the land with Joshua.*

Below is a first translation of the sermon, with critical notes and references by the editor. The editor would like to encourage sharing this text with communities, be it as sermon or study session or both. It is recommended that Exodus 19 is read alongside.

And Redel spoke these words saying:

We just heard my cousin Achsah sing the story of the events of thirty years ago.[14] How we left Rephidim and came to Sinai. How my father went up to the mountain and how he was back again and I remember crying out with everyone else: "Everything that the LORD has spoken we shall do" (Exodus 19:8).

And yet.

I also don't remember it like this.

The story that my cousin sang to us is both familiar and strange. I grew dizzy keeping up with the many times my father went up and down the mountain. I lost count. Did he go up as many times as he went down? Did he come down that very first time, did he speak to us and then go up again?[15] I am certain my sons and daughter were there with me, but how can that be, as I myself was only a child? And yet, I see it so vividly, my little girl standing next to me and how loud and proud she too said, "Everything that the LORD has spoken we shall do."[16]

---

[13] Reuel is one of the names by which Moses' father-in-law was known. See Exodus 2:18 when Moses first meets his daughters. Reuel is probably better known as Jethro, the name used for Moses' father-in-law in Exodus 3:1 and again in Exodus 18.

[14] Achsah is Miriam's daughter. Again, her name has to be deduced from other verses. (Joshua 15:13–19; Judges 1:10–15, see Jill Hammer, with Shir Yaakov Feit, *The Omer Calendar of Biblical Women* (2012), p. 54.)

[15] These difficulties become clear on close and critical reading of the text. As explained at the start, the Documentary Hypothesis has tried to solve them by assuming the text has multiple authors.

[16] Compare here Deuteronomy 29:14–15: "I am making this covenant . . . not only with you who stand here with us today before the Lord our God, but also

"Everything that the LORD has spoken we shall do."
But what *did* God say? Achsah sang to us:

> You yourselves saw what I did to Egypt, and I bore you on the
> wings of eagles and I brought you to Me. And now, if you will
> truly heed My voice and keep My covenant, you will become for
> Me a treasure among all the peoples, for Mine is all the earth.
> And as for you, you will become for Me a kingdom of priests and
> a holy nation (Exodus 19:4–6a).

I don't remember it like this.

I don't remember agreeing to a covenant without knowing what was
in it.[17] Was I simply overwhelmed and still felt like flying through the air?
Perhaps a kingdom of priests sounded good. After all, I am from the tribe
of Levi, the granddaughter of a priest and the daughter of a priestess.[18]

I don't remember it like this.

I almost stopped Achsah in her singing, because it didn't make sense.
The whole story of us camping at Sinai, the anxious preparations, the
two tables, and everything else. It seemed just a mash-up of stories and
I wanted to know the *real* story. I want to know what truly *happened.*

---

with those who are not here with us today." C.f. here too the discussion on
this passage in the Midrash Tamchumah Yitro 11 and Shevuot 39a, where it is
argued that future generations and future converts were also standing at the
foot of the mount and are included in the covenant. For all biblical quotations, I
am using the translation by Robert Alter, *The Hebrew Bible: Volume 1: The Five
Books of Moses, Torah* (New York, London: W. W. Norton & Company, 2019).

[17]   Contemporary sources suggest Redel may not fully appreciate how treaties
were made. There were different stages in the agreement. (See for instance
Dominik Markl, "God's Covenant with Humanity and Israel", in John Barton
(ed.), *The Hebrew Bible: A Critical Companion* (Princeton: Princeton
University Press), pp. 313–37.)

[18]   Her grandfather Yithro, or Reuel, was a priest. His daughter, Zipporah,
Redel's mother, is often thought to be a priestess because of her decisive act
to circumcise their son that saves either the son or Moses. (See Exodus 4:26.
The text is ambiguous as to who is saved.)

I remember seeing my cousin J writing it all down. And J—like our grandmother Jochebed after whom she is named—has a clear head. Surely, she would not have been swayed by emotions, until she had it all written down—even in that impossible moment when we heard God speak.[19] J is good. My father often uses what she has written for his official account.[20]

Am I making too much of this?

Someone explained to me just now that the story does not follow any logical order because that makes it more lively. And then another one told me what I was confused by were mere asides.[21]

But others are using a clever argument that this cannot be J's text, because she would never use the word "Elohim" to speak about God. She only uses "Adonai". My brother Eliezer, on the other hand, does use the word "Elohim", so some think that he wrote it. Other are saying that Levi, one of the priests, has written parts of this account too and I don't know who put it all together.

I want you to stop those arguments for now, because it is all getting rather loud and silly. And some of you make me uncomfortable. I wonder

---

[19] See too Oswald, *The Book of Exodus*, p. 178 on what he calls "not self-evident" encounters with God.

[20] The discussion that follows resembles that of the Documentary Hypothesis, which is the hypothesis that the Bible was written by different authors, whose writings were later put together by a redactor or by redactors. (See also the introduction.) According to the Documentary Hypothesis J was one of the authors. Others are E, P and D. Yet, according to the Documentary Hypothesis, J was not a contemporary of Moses, as this sermon suggests. Bloom has argued that J was a woman at Salomon's court—again, not a contemporary of Moses (*The Book of J*, p. 9).

[21] In current scholarship, these are called *synchronic* readings. These readings consider the text in its final form, in contrast to *diachronic* readings which look for the way a text was developed. The first synchronic reading mentioned by Redel can, for instance, be ascribed to Cornelis Houtman, the second one to Gregory Chirichigno and Joe Sprinkle. (See Oswald, *The Book of Exodus*, pp. 173–4.)

what is exactly at stake for you. Why are you so keen to argue that it was not Moses, but J or Eliezer or Levi or whoever who wrote this?[22]

You may be right that this is not what J wrote down. Something happened to it when it was copied and copied again and then retold and then written down once more. I am not certain we can find out exactly who wrote what and when, let alone what happened that day. It seems part of that knowledge is lost—and lost forever.

Is this simply bad luck? I suspect some of the copiers had their reasons for suggesting that God only spoke to Moses, or that God spoke to Moses and Aaron (and was not Miriam at their side?) or to the elders. And I don't want to listen to their version any longer. I want to remember it as if we were all listening to God and not as if we only heard it from the elders who heard it from Moses. No.[23]

Perhaps all that Achsah sang about, what I mentioned at the start, about being borne on the wings of eagles and the kingdom of priests, that was all added later. That would at least do away with *some* of those times my father went up and down the mountain.[24] And it would also not be until he came down the mountain for the final time that we said, "All the words that the LORD has spoken we shall do" (Exodus 24:3). We never said it at the start. All that happened in the beginning was: Moses went up to the mountain (Exodus 19:2b–3a) and then came down and spoke to the people and told them to prepare (Exodus 19:14–15).

Even so, why was the part about the wings and the kingdom of priests added?[25]

---

[22] One contemporary reason for Redel's feeling of discomfort could be the suggestion that the Documentary Hypothesis is tainted because of the anti-Semitism of Julius Wellhausen, one of its main advocates. (See Alan T. Levenson, "Was the Documentary Hypothesis Tainted by Wellhausen's Antisemitism?" TheTorah.com, 2021, <https://thetorah.com/article/was-the-documentary-hypothesis-tainted-by-wellhausens-antisemitism>, accessed 13 July 2022. cp. *The Book of J*, p. 21.)

[23] See here too Oswald, *The Book of Exodus*, pp. 178 ff.

[24] This account allies with what Oswald calls the "Exodus-Mountain-of-God-Narrative" (*The Book of Exodus*, p. 182).

[25] See Oswald, *The Book of Exodus*, for an explanation.

It is easy to see that Levi and his friends added parts and why. It is all those scenes where Aaron is suddenly very important and when we the people are nowhere near the mountain top. I don't like those very much and I was happy to see that someone else added another scene that brought us closer to the event again. We do not speak, but at least we get to see Moses talk to God.[26]

I can see that these ideas are making some of you uneasy. I heard someone whisper that if this story is such a mess, perhaps we should stop telling it altogether.

You are right to feel uneasy and I am not going to make you feel better just now. That needs a much longer conversation and I promise you that we shall have that. For now, I think we should endure, perhaps even nurse the unease. I want to add even more trouble.

Because, so far we have looked at the text that is there, but what about everything that has been left out? What about all that has not even been written down, for whatever reason?

I mean, it is obvious that there have been attempts to write us, the women, out of this story. When my father Moses tells the people to prepare, for instance, he only speaks to men when he says:

Do not go near a woman (Exodus 19:15).

Did he then say to the women: do not go near a man? Were his words to women not recorded? (And don't say that women do not need to be told and that they can stay secluded and at home, because they are naturally more religious. Don't. Don't.)

And then, there was the part where the women danced and sang. I am certain we did, because my aunt Miriam was there, the prophetess, and she loves to dance. She will always dance. Even when we had just crossed the sea and there were bodies of Egyptians lying all around us, she sang and danced and then we—I think we were drunk with fear and

---

[26]   See Oswald, *The Book of Exodus*, for an extensive analysis of the different layers mentioned here.

with relief—we all danced. And then Moses took over. Or was it the other way around?[27]

But when Achsah sang there was nothing about dancing on the mountain.

I am reminded of a story my great aunt Dikla once told me. (She is the one married to great uncle Ari, who married out. Actually, depending how you look at it, so did both my parents.) The story of Yehudit, the sister of Gavriel. A sad story because Yehudit was a very talented poet, at least as talented as Gavriel. But she was a girl and so her parents gave her no space and she died very young and was buried somewhere at the crossroads, but nobody knows where anymore. My great aunt assured me the story was true, but I had never heard of this Yehudit before.[28]

It would be so awful if that were to happen to Achsah or to J or to me. That no one would have heard of us. So, what about those stories that have disappeared? How do we know about them? And how skewed is our vision when we only argue about what *is*?

When I think back to what Achsah sang, I am now glad that there are different stories, even when my father going up and down makes me dizzy. So anyone who tells about what happened on that mountain should include me and my daughter. We were there. Just like Miriam and Moses and the elders we stood there, and just like them, we shouted. I think we shouted the loudest.

I know that my sisters will not forget me. They will refuse to believe that for centuries all we did was bake bread and darn socks, until in some magical moment thousands of years from now, women will not only find

---

[27] On this song at the sea and who was first, see Exodus 15, Phyllis Trible, "Bringing Miriam out of the Shadows", in Brenner (ed.), *Feminist Companion*, pp. 166–86, here at pp. 169–73.

[28] This story resembles the famous story of Shakespeare's sister Judith in Chapter 3 of Virginia Woolf's *A Room of One's Own*. Woolf imagines a sister as gifted as Shakespeare, who would not be allowed to develop her talents. She was not given the same schooling, nor could she try her luck in London's theatres, and she ends tragically killing herself and "now lies buried at some crossroads where the omnibuses now stop outside the Elephant and Castle" (Virginia Woolf, *A Room of One's Own* (New York: Harcourt, 1957)).

their voice, but as by some miracle they will be utterly fluent. That too is just a story. We do not stay silent until we are given permission or a script to read. You may not know when they are our words, but we speak all the time.[29] All the time.

What is the evidence of my sisters, you ask. What is the evidence for any of this, I reply. After all we are speaking about that most elusive of events, an encounter with God. What happened? What truly happened?[30]

You think that none of it happened?

Editor's note

The fragment ends here as the sermon moves into conversation. Several different voices can be distilled from the sermon above, but it is likely that further research will reveal even more.[31]

---

[29] Compare Exum, "Second Thoughts", p. 79, quoted in note 12.

[30] Compare Bloom: "What happens to representation when altogether incommensurable realities juxtapose and clash? How can Abraham haggle with Yahweh? How is Jacob able to wrestle a nameless one among the Elohim to a standstill . . . ?" (*The Book of J*, pp. 25–6).

[31] I would like to thank Dr Sandra Jacobs, Dr Deborah-Kahn Harris and Sherry Ashworth for their comments on earlier versions of this text.

On the Power of Writing

Jeremy J. Smith

The functions of writing

We have long known that language in its broadest sense—the ability to communicate information or feelings—is not restricted to human beings. Blackbirds, whales, bees, dogs—or indeed Ludwig Wittgenstein's lion—all have things to say to each other, even if their conception of the world is so different that we humans find it hard if not impossible to understand them. However, there do seem to be some distinctive things that humans can do with language. We can lie; we can use metaphor; and we can write.

The last of these three activities may be presumed to be the most recent development in human evolution. There are indications of symbolic ("proto-writing") systems from the early Neolithic period; however, most authorities agree that the earliest forms of writing in the generally understood sense are in the script known as cuneiform, which was impressed on clay tablets using a wedge-shaped stylus. Cuneiform was first deployed in Mesopotamia, from around 3000 BCE, in Archaic Sumerian, primarily it seems for documentary purposes relating to local administration; civilization, it seems, begins with accounts, transactions and taxes.[1] Writing systems can communicate over time and space, whereas until the end of the nineteenth century, with the rise of new technologies such as sound-recording, speech could not (save through the uncertain processes of memory). In societies where record-keeping

---

[1] See further Geoffrey Sampson, *Writing Systems* (Redwood City, CA: Stanford University Press, 1985), pp. 46–61.

was important, therefore, writing had distinct functional advantages. It is no coincidence that when William the Conqueror wanted to "modernize" his new English kingdom in the years after 1066, he commanded the creation of Domesday Book, a way of recording information about land ownership, in written form (and indeed in Latin, the unchanging language because "dead") that would last until the Day of Judgement.[2]

But these workaday origins and aspects, although of course remaining, should not obscure the fact that writing came, in time, to develop more extended functions. Cuneiform lasted a long time, and the cuneiform/ clay tablet library of the great Assyrian ruler Ashurbanipal (669–?631 BCE) contained not only substantial quantities of documentary texts but also literary (*The Epic of Gilgamesh*), magical, ritual and academic texts, and—an offshoot of the last—records of oracular queries, and of interpretative divinations undertaken by the empire's scholars and priests. It is no coincidence that Ashurbanipal liked to be depicted on bas-reliefs, even when wrestling with lions, with a stylus in his belt to indicate his learned credentials. Ritual statements, carefully set out according to standardized formats, were also inscribed over the fearsome bas-reliefs of lions and mythical beasts that the Assyrian monarchs placed at the gates of their cities.[3] Ancient Mesopotamia was a place where public texts had special properties, and it is thus perhaps unsurprising that it was the setting, in the biblical book of Daniel, for the famed "writing on the wall" that so disconcerted Belshazzar:

> Immediately the fingers of a human hand appeared and began writing on the plaster of the wall of the royal palace, next to the lampstand. The king was watching the hand as it wrote. Then

---

[2]   For discussion of the functions of the Domesday Book—interestingly, a work that was only partially successful in performing the functions for which it was intended, largely because of cultural conservatism—see Michael Clanchy, *From Memory to Written Record*, 3rd edn (Oxford: Blackwell, 2012).

[3]   For details and discussion of the artifacts associated with Ashurbanipal, see the essays collected in Gareth Brereton (ed.), *I am Ashurbanipal King of the world, King of Assyria* (London: Thames and Hudson/The British Museum, 2018).

the king's face turned pale, and his thoughts terrified him. His
limbs gave way, and his knees knocked together (Daniel 5:5–6).

A characteristic practice of the rulers of Nineveh, followed by both
Ashurbanipal and his father Esarhaddon, was to bury, in the foundations
of their city, clay "prisms" on the sides of which were recorded key events
in their rule; and such customs have continued. Graves are of course
obvious locations, even when belief systems do not necessarily support
the value of grave-goods; the Stonyhurst Gospel of St John (now London,
British Library, MS Additional 89000) was deposited with St Cuthbert
when the saint died in 698, only to be retrieved 400 years later when the
saint's body was translated to a splendid shrine in Durham Cathedral.
Placing a copy of the Bible in the foundations of churches, for instance,
has a long pedigree, which could be extended to other locations; a Texas
builder was reported, in 2005, to have developed the habit of placing an
open Bible in the concrete floors of every house he constructed.[4] And,
more sinisterly, in 1934 two copies of Hitler's *Mein Kampf* were deposited
in a copper capsule underneath a Nazi leadership-training centre in what
is now Zlocieniec in Poland, to be unearthed by archaeologists in 2016.[5]

The socio-cultural functions involved in the placement of all such
texts, whether buried in the ground or ritually repeated at the gates of
cities, suggest that writing has more purposes than the straightforward
transmission of information: their "truth" is a complex business. Were
such texts for the edification or entertainment of contemporaries, or
of posterity (as in the modern custom of burying "time capsules")? Or
do they have some other performative function, underpinning flagging
ideologies or some worshipful activity, in which texts have iconic power
based on other qualities than legibility? In this essay, two texts from the
past, both with a religious focus, are shown to have iconic power that
can, with historical imagination, be recuperated.

---

[4]   See https://www.chron.com/news/houston-texas/article/Home-builder-
       puts-Bible-in-slab-of-every-house-1513676.php, accessed 13 July 2022.

[5]   See <https://www.warhistoryonline.com/featured/nazi-era-time-capsule-
       opened-archaeologist-perfectly-preserved-copies-mein-kampf-included.
       html>, accessed 13 July 2022.

A visit to the Ruthwell Cross

To illustrate some of these complexities involved in such matters we might, for instance, take one of the oldest "literary" artefacts in present-day Scotland: the runic writing on the great stone cross at Ruthwell, Dumfriesshire, which is usually dated to the beginning of the eighth century CE. The cross used to stand on the open hillside overlooking the Solway Firth, until it was torn down and broken up during the iconoclasm that raged in southern Scotland in the century after the Reformation. Subsequently it was rescued, re-erected and "restored" by an early-nineteenth-century enterprising antiquarian Church of Scotland minister, the Revd Henry Duncan, who had it re-erected and placed safely within the village's kirk, where it is now housed in an especially-built apse.

Originally the cross, which is over five metres high, was visible to mariners, and a sign to them that they were approaching the powerful Anglian kingdom of Northumbria, whose founding figure, King Oswald, had erected a cross before his victory in 633/4 over the pagans, at "Heavenfield" beside Hadrian's Wall (usually identified with a spot near Hexham in present-day Northumberland). Crosses were ever since that date especially venerated by the Northumbrian rulers, and came to be their hegemonic symbol of choice, expressed through their collection of relics of the True Cross, and through display on their coins. It is notable how many of these crosses—not just the Ruthwell Cross overlooking the Solway—are liminal; other examples include the Bewcastle Cross in Cumbria, where Northumbria abutted on older British cultures, or a group of crosses in Derbyshire, on the border with Mercia. Such crosses almost certainly had several functions, not least as memorials, as a location for preaching, or as the focus of cultic attention within monastic settings,[6] but they were also boundary symbols, at least in part the equivalent of a customs barrier or a border post.[7]

Even though it is now located indoors, having in previous centuries been scoured by the weather of what was possibly its original bright colouring, the cross retains its numinous power.[8] Its complex decorative sequence includes a stylized figural representation of Mary Magdalene washing Christ's feet, and vine-scrolls "inhabited" by birds and fantastic beasts, and decorated with bunches of grapes; vine-scrolls have traditionally been eucharistic symbols. Scenes of John the Baptist and Saints Paul and Anthony in the desert support the argument that the cross had monastic associations, for all three were considered to be founders of monasticism.[9] However, the monument is perhaps best known nowadays for its inscriptions, both in Latin, in roman letters, and in Old English, the latter in the Germanic writing system known as runes.

The Latin texts gloss the images carved on the stone. Thus the image of Mary Magdalene is accompanied by a description derived from Luke 7:37–8: "[She] brought an alabaster jar of ointment. She stood behind

---

[6]   See Fred Orton, "Northumbrian identity in the eighth century: the Ruthwell and Bewcastle monuments; style, classification, class, and the form of ideology", *Journal of Medieval and Early Modern Studies* 34 (2004), pp. 95–145, and Catherine Karkov, "Ruthwell Cross", in Geoff Rector, Helen Fulton, Jacqueline Fay, Robert Rouse and Sian Echard (eds), *The Encyclopedia of Medieval Literature in Britain* (Oxford: Blackwell, 2017) (online publication) for some interesting suggestions.

[7]   There has been a small debate as to whether the Ruthwell monument was actually a cross, or rather an obelisk; the present-day crossbeam is a reconstructed element dating from the nineteenth century, since only a small fragment of the presumed original crossbeam survives. This fragment is now kept in a metal holder on the side of the pit in the apse in which the cross has been sunk (to allow for its decoration to be inspected more closely). However, most scholars agree that the monument, like others, was a cross.

[8]   See Raymond I. Page, *An Introduction to English Runes* (Woodbridge: Boydell, 1999), p. 155.

[9]   See Michael Swanton (ed.), 1978. *The Dream of the Rood* (Manchester: University Press, 1978), p. 15.

him at his feet, weeping, and began to bathe his feet with her tears and to dry them with her hair ... ".[10] Other texts indicate the theological sophistication of the sculptural sequence; thus the image of Christ in Judgment, his feet trampling beasts set below him, is accompanied by a paraphrase of Psalm 91:13, viz. "Jesus Christ, judge of righteousness: beasts and dragons recognized in the desert the saviour of the world."[11]

The Old English text on the Ruthwell Cross is rather different, and seems to be distinct from the decorative scheme—to such an extent that some scholars have even suggested that it is a later imposition: a view not yet widely accepted.[12] Whatever its date, it appears to be a version of—or a quotation from—the poem now known as *The Dream of the Rood*: an identification first made by the Victorian scholar John Mitchell Kemble in 1844. The full version of *The Dream* survives in an eleventh-century manuscript now in Vercelli, Italy, where, it seems, a passing pilgrim left it en route for Rome, on the eve of the Norman Conquest, for a reason no longer accessible: Vercelli, Biblioteca Capitolare, MS CXVII, better-known as the Vercelli Book.[13] This manuscript was written in Late West Saxon, the variety of Old English deployed in Wessex, in the south-west of England, whereas the runic inscription on the Ruthwell Cross is in

---

[10] The Latin reads as follows: + ATTUL[IT ALABA]STRUM UNGUENTI & STANS RETRO SECUS PEDES · EIUS LACRIMIS · COEPIT RIGARE · PEDES EIUS · & CAPILLIS · CAPITIS SUI TERGEBAT.

[11] + IHS XPS IUDEX · AEQUITATIS · BESTIAE · ET · DRACONES · COGNOVERUNT · IN · DES · ERTO · SALVATOREM · MUNDI ·. Psalm 91:13 reads as follows, in the King James Version: "Thou shalt tread upon the lion and adder: the young lion and the dragon shalt thou trample under feet." Contemporary exegesis held that this passage prefigured Christ's rejecting temptation in the wilderness (see, e.g., Luke 4): something very apposite for the monastic profession (see Swanton, *The Dream of the Rood*, p. 14).

[12] See Page, *Introduction to English Runes*, Patrick Connor, "'The Ruthwell monument runic poem in a tenth-century context", *Review of English Studies*, new series 99 (2008), pp. 25–51, and Jeremy J. Smith, *Transforming Early English* (Cambridge: Cambridge University Press, 2020), p. 79.

[13] Kenneth Sisam, "Marginalia in the Vercelli book", in *Studies in the History of Old English Literature* (Oxford: Clarendon Press, 1953), pp. 108–19.

the Old Northumbrian dialect, a usage current in southern Scotland and northern England.

The Vercelli version of the poem, drawing inspiration from the "riddle" tradition that is such a feature of much Old English verse, is a dream vision. The Dreamer, not otherwise identified, is presented with a vision of a Cross, "a wondrous tree rising into the air surrounded by light", which appears paradoxically as an instrument of torture and a jewel-embellished object of splendour. The Cross then speaks: it describes how, once a tree, it was cut down "by strong enemies" on the edge of a wood, and then "commanded" to execute criminals. The Cross then narrates the Good Friday story, transmuted into a Germanic heroic epic. In an ironic reversal of the "arming of the hero" trope, "the young hero, who was almighty God, stripped himself" (*ongyrede hine þa geong hæleð, þæt wæs God ælmihtig*). He then "ascended" onto the Cross, which "trembled" when the "warrior embraced" it. The Cross participated with Christ in being "insulted" through "wounds of malice"; it struggled with the Germanic trope traditionally called the "heroic dilemma", whereby it was "commanded" to stand upright, even though as a tree it owed loyalty to God and could have "felled" the enemies. "All creation wept, they lamented a king's fall; Christ was on the Cross" (*Crist wæs on rode*). Christ's followers—referred to as *fuse* "eager (ones)" and *hilderincas* "warriors"—lifted down the corpse of the "prince" (*æðeling*), stood round it "while he rested there for a time, weary after the great battle", and then placed it in a tomb that "they carved from bright stone". After singing a lament, these followers departed, but the Cross, along with its fellow trees, was again cut down, a "terrible fate", and cast into a deep pit. Later however the Lord's "thanes" (*þegnas*) retrieved the Cross, and "dressed" (*gyredon*) it with gold and silver; the Cross has been thus transformed, and is now a symbol of Christ's triumph, a "victory-tree" (*sigebeam*). The Cross commands the Dreamer to describe the vision, relating it to Christ's ascent to heaven and how through the Cross humanity is to be redeemed. The Dreamer then awakes and meditates on what he has seen.

The Ruthwell version is much shorter, and fragmentary because of weathering, and of the actions of the seventeenth-century iconoclasts. The framing dream vision is omitted, as is the meditation, but the central epic Good Friday sequence is in part reproduced; the heroic aspect of the text is thus especially emphasized. The runic text begins with the stripping sequence, albeit abbreviated (conventionally transliterated, in the Old Northumbrian dialect, as *[ond]geredæ hinæ ĝod almeʒttig* "God almighty stripped himself"); the Cross is described as raising the "powerful king, lord of heavens", but (in accordance with the heroic dilemma) "daring not to bend", and thus sharing in the insult; "Christ was on the Cross" (*krist wæs on rodi*). The arrival of the "eager ones" (*fusæ*) is referred to, followed by the deposition.

The Ruthwell poem, because of its physical location, could be construed with the benefit of hindsight to be one of the earliest pieces of "Scottish literature"—even if the notion of Scotland, at the time of the cross's creation, was some way in the future.[14] But it is hard to accept this text as part of a continuous literary tradition, not least because the runic inscription on the Cross has been described as "maddeningly hard to read".[15] To illustrate the layout, here is how the line *[ond]geredæ hinæ ĝod almeʒttig* appears on the Ruthwell monument (a transliteration into roman letters appears alongside):

[. . .]ᚷᛖᚱᛖ	[. . .]gere
ᛞᚫ	dæ
ᚻᛁ	hi
ᚾᚫ	næ
ᚸᚩ	ĝo
ᛞᚪ	da
ᛚᛗ	lm
ᛖᛇ	eʒ
ᛏᛏᛁ	tti
ᚷ	g

Elizabeth Okasha's comments on the inscription are in this context worth citing in full:

14 See Thomas Clancy and Gilbert Markus (eds), *The Triumph Tree: Scotland's Earliest Poetry* AD *550–1350* (Edinburgh: Canongate, 1998).

15 Page, *Introduction to English Runes*, p. 147.

I am ... of the opinion, that it is highly unlikely that anyone in eighth-century England could stand in front of the Ruthwell cross, read its texts and understand them. Firstly, there is the physical problem of reading letters some five centimetres in height located up to four meters above one's head. Secondly, it would be necessary to be literate both in Old English and in Latin. Thirdly, one would have to be able to read both roman and runic script. Fourthly, the texts are not well organized for easy reading. The Latin texts are set partly horizontally and partly sideways to the reader; the Old English texts in runes read horizontally but are placed in such narrow bands that each line of text contains a maximum of four letters and one word can therefore be spread over up to three lines. It may be that in rural Northumbria in the eighth century there were people capable of reading the Ruthwell cross texts in spite of all these difficulties, but it does not seem very likely. To me it seems clear that the commissioner of the cross and the drafter of the texts had other motives in mind than the conveying of information to a reading public.[16]

Indeed, Okasha's statement understates the difficulty; *almeʒttig* "almighty" is spread over no fewer than five lines, and the first letter of the word is preceded by the last letter of *ĝod*. Reading a text with any degree of fluency, whether working with a logographic writing system such as that used for Chinese, or with a broadly phonographic system like runic or roman lettering, requires the identification of words; but the Ruthwell inscription seems to go out of its way to make such identification hard. Indeed, it has recently been argued that the deployment of the Ruthwell runes may actually be motivated "not by a desire to *maximise* readability but by a desire to *obstruct* readability".[17]

---

[16]   Elizabeth Okasha, "Literacy in Anglo-Saxon England: the evidence from inscriptions", in *Medieval Europe 1992: Art and Symbolism*, vol. 7 (pre-printed conference papers, University of York, 1992), pp. 87–8.

[17]   Yin Liu, "Stating the obvious in runes", in Matti Peikola, Aleksi Makilahde, Hanna Salmi, Mari-Liisa Varila and Janne Skaffari (eds), *Verbal and Visual*

The inscription represents, in sum, a puzzle: a code whose key is hard to find. Indeed, there has for a long time been a curious problem with the runes: how did they function? Were they "simply" a writing system, or were they something more, i.e., did they have some kind of magical significance? This tension between the "practical" and the "magical" has bedevilled runic studies since the runes were first studied by early modern antiquarians in the seventeenth and eighteenth centuries, and persists until the present day. The runic writing system has moreover had a special, often dubious, twentieth- and twenty-first-century afterlife, not least in far-right aesthetics derived from Nazi ideology: an afterlife that many scholars have valiantly (and very understandably) striven to discredit, but which the uses of the term *rūn* in Old English writings nevertheless somewhat—it must be admitted—encourage. We might briefly contemplate the range of meanings covered by the following citations, with present-day English glosses, from the Old English epic poem *Beowulf*:

- *beadurūn* "battle-counsel, hostile speech" (501)
- *helrūnan* "those skilled in the mysteries of hell", i.e. "demons" (163)
- *rūn* "(secret) consultation" (172)
- *rūnstafas* "runic letters" (1695)
- *rūnwita* "confidant, trusted adviser" (1325)

The semantic fields covered by these lexemes strongly suggest that the word *rūn* was associated with a special skill, mystery or puzzle, and there is persistent evidence amongst pagan Germanic peoples that the runes were considered to have esoteric properties. A somewhat cryptic stanza in the Old Norse eddic poem *Hávamál*, for instance, has been taken to indicate that the god Odin, having been hanged on the world-ash tree Yggdrasil for nine days, was then able to interpret the runes.[18]

Communication in Early English Texts (Turnhout: Brepols, 2017), pp. 125–39, here at p. 139. My italics.

[18] See, however, Rolf Bremmer, "Hermes-Mercury and Woden-Odin as inventors of alphabets: a neglected parallel", in Alfred Bammesberger (ed.),

Such narratives and usages have led many folk since the eighteenth century at least to consider runes as somehow magical, an association that has been stubbornly retained in present-day popular culture, encouraged by (e.g.) the fantasy writings of J. R. R. Tolkien. In this context, the runic text on the Ruthwell Cross might be explained as something arcane: legible only to an adept elite, *rūnwitan*, skilled in the mystery of *rūnstafas*. For such readers, the power of the Ruthwell poem might be presumed to lie in its bringing together of its content—a focused description of Christ's heroism, presented in the idiom of Germanic epic—and its medium, the runic script. One of the images on the Cross is of Christ healing the man born blind, as related in John 9. The panel is juxtaposed with that containing Mary Magdalene; Bede considered the episodes to be linked, representing "the divine power to illuminate a believing soul, mankind having been blinded by the sin of Eve".[19] The runic code might, then, offer a comparable hermeneutic opportunity.

The issue of legibility raised by Okasha, however, remains, and it is possible, even likely, that the runes were carved primarily with a rather distinct function: as an act of praise akin to prayer. The primary intended audience for the Ruthwell text, in such circumstances, would be God. A set of Germanic symbols, originally pagan, has thus been transmuted into Christian signifiers, for divine apprehension.

Evoking the past

Written texts, then, can have semiotic functions that stretch well beyond the simple transmission of information. As all linguists know, languages are not just means for sharing factual information; they also express emotions and power relationships, and have performative functions. And the modes of writing too have meaning; scripts and typefaces carry with them socio-cultural connotations. Decoding the "true" meaning of texts is never really straightforward.

Old English Runes and their Continental Background (Heidelberg: Winter, 1991), pp. 409–19.

[19]   Swanton, *The Dream of the Rood*, p. 17.

Numerous examples demonstrate this characteristic of writing systems. Italic script, for instance, developed at the end of the fifteenth century as a signifier of humanist associations; James VI of Scotland wrote in italics to flag his humanist credentials, unlike Elizabeth I of England, who used the older secretary script. At around the same time "roman" font was developed, as a classicizing and "Renaissance" gesture, by the great Venetian printers, who based the font's design on inscriptions and handwriting surviving from Roman antiquity. Humble scripts and typefaces therefore can develop ideological associations, and for a second example of a "meaningful" writing system we might examine a text dating from some 800 years after the Ruthwell Cross, albeit one that has roots in Old English culture.

In late 1566, the evangelical London printer John Day (1521/2–84) published an edition of a prose homily by Ælfric of Eynsham (c.950–c.1010), viz. *A testimonie of antiquitie, shewing the auncient faith in the Church of England touching the sacrament of the body and bloude of the Lord here publikely preached, and also receaued in the Saxons tyme, aboue 600. yeares agoe*: the first ever printed edition of a work in Old English. Day—as the title suggests—was a committed evangelical who was the leading printer of his time, patronized by magnates such as Elizabeth I's favourite Robert Dudley, later Earl of Leicester. Career highlights were the *English Metrical Psalter* of Thomas Sternhold and John Hopkins, and John Foxe's *Acts and Monuments*, better known as the *Book of Martyrs*: editions of Foxe's text appeared in 1563, 1570 and 1576. The commitment involved in the latter was by contemporary standards astonishing: the first edition consisted of some 1800 pages presented in a mixture of typefaces, accompanied by complex paratextual devices, including some quite remarkable woodcuts.[20] Day was thus "one of the London book-trade's most innovative and adept members", according to the *Oxford Dictionary of National Biography*, and the obvious choice to produce *A testimonie*, given its high profile; the work was, it is now known, edited by

---

[20] Two of the most famous woodcuts depict Archbishop Thomas Cranmer's martyrdom; see further Diarmaid MacCulloch, *Thomas Cranmer* (New Haven, CT: Yale University Press, 1996), pp. 602–3.

John Joscelyn (1529–1603), Latin secretary to Matthew Parker, Elizabeth I's Archbishop of Canterbury.[21]

A *testimonie* formed part of Parker's programme in support of the "Elizabethan settlement", justified by appealing to historical—and of course English—precedents. The book was an edition of Ælfric's Easter homily *In die Sancto pasce*, dating originally from the end of the tenth century, drawn primarily from a manuscript in Parker's own library (now Cambridge, Corpus Christi College, MS 198). Joscelyn makes explicit the reason for the publication:

> Great contention hath nowe been of longe tyme about the moste comfortable sacrament of the body & bloud of Christ our Sauiour: in the inquisition and determination wherof many be charged and condemned of heresye, and reproued as bringers vp of new doctrine ... But that though mayest knowe (good Christian reader) how this is aduouched more boldly then truly, in especiall of some certayne men which be more ready to maintaine their old iudgement, then of humilitie to submitte them selues vnto a truth: here is set forth vnto thee a testimonye of verye auncient tyme, wherin is plainly shewed what was the iudgment of the learned men in this matter, in the dayes of the Saxons before the conquest.[22]

A *testimonie* was, according to the Preface, evidence that the Roman Catholic belief in the "real presence" in the Eucharist (i.e. transubstantiation)—which the newly formed Church of England considered "repugnant to the plain words of Scripture"—was a later imposition. Ælfric said nothing about transubstantiation, since the doctrine was actually not fully articulated until the Lateran Council of 1215; his homily was therefore taken as evidence that the doctrine

---

[21] John Joscelyn (ed.), *A testimonie of antiquitie, shewing the auncient faith in the Church of England touching the sacrament of the body and bloude of the Lord here publikely preached, and also receaued in the Saxons tyme, aboue 600. yeares agoe* (London: Day, 1566).

[22] Joscelyn, *A testimonie*, sig. A.ii r-v

was "farced" (Joscelyn's term) by the later papacy. The edition of the Old English text was also a major scholarly achievement. Not only had Joscelyn had to teach himself Old English, using manuscripts of Ælfric's Latin grammar as a crib to "reverse-engineer" understanding, but in addition he had had to trawl through many bulky manuscripts to find a text that spoke to a particular ideological agenda.

A testimonie was, however, not only an important work for sixteenth-century theological debate; it was also technically challenging. Day deployed not only roman and italic typefaces, and a variety of ornaments, but also tried—in a rather peculiar act of "counterfeiting"[23]—to reflect Anglo-Saxon script typographically.

Pre-Conquest English scribes generally used Caroline minuscule for copying Latin and a slightly different (albeit derived) script for copying Old English, viz. Anglo-Saxon square minuscule. The two scripts differed in their forms for the letters *a, d, e, f, g, h, r* and *s*, and writing in Old English also required three extra letters: þ "thorn", ƿ "wynn", and ð "eth". When Day printed *A testimonie*, those letters common to the Caroline and Old English scripts were reproduced in roman fonts, but he arranged—presumably instructed by Joscelyn—for special letters to be cut, probably by the Huguenot craftsman Pierre Haultin, to reflect the *distinctiones* used for copying Old English.[24]

---

[23] The term was Parker's. The word *counterfeit* seems to have had a connotation of fraudulence since its first recorded appearance in the English language at the end of the thirteenth century, but relevant other, non-pejorative, meanings "to imitate, copy" and "to represent/reproduce" seem to have been current from the 1360s to the middle of the seventeenth century. See OED *counterfeit*, v., meanings 8 and 9, and *counterfeit*, adj. and n., meanings A.4, A.9, B.3. Parker assembled a substantial body of craftsmen "within my house" of "drawers and cutters, painters, limners, writers and bookbinders", all tasked with working intensively on his manuscript collection. See Malcolm B. Parkes, "Archaizing hands in English manuscripts", in J. P. Carley and C. G. C. Tite (eds), *Books and Collectors 1200–1700: Essays presented to Andrew Watson* (London: British Library, 1997), pp. 101–41, here at p. 123, and references there cited.

[24] Peter Lucas, *From Author to Audience: John Capgrave and Medieval Publication* (Dublin, University College Dublin Press, 1997), pp. 165–6.

Although he did not reproduce the (lack of) word division in his Old English exemplar, Day nevertheless attempted to carry over Old English habits of punctuation. He therefore deployed the "humanist'" semi-colon to reflect the characteristic *punctus versus* found in eleventh-century manuscripts, even though the significance of the two marks was very different, and the *punctus* where the comma mark would be expected.[25] The opening of the text appeared therefore as follows (the Early Modern English translation, supplied in italics in the original, appears beneath):[26]

> Men ða leoꝼoꞃtan . ᵹelome eoꝑ iꞅ ᵹeꞃæd ymbe uꞃeꞅ hælendeꞃ æꞃiꞅte . hu he on ðiꞅum andꝥeaꝥdum dæᵹe æꝼteꝥ hiꞅ ðrowunᵹe mihtiᵹlice of deaþe aꝥaꞅ ;

> *Men beloued, it hath bene often sayd vnto you aboute our Sauiours*
> *resurrection, how he on this present day after hys suffering, mightily*
> *rose from death.*

---

[25] The semi-colon was designed primarily—as it is now—to link two clauses (*cola*) equiparatively; the punctus versus found in late pre-Conquest manuscripts marked the completion of a *periodus*, and is thus comparable with the present-day full-stop. By Day's time, comma marks flagged the shorter units known as *commata*, which the earlier scribes generally distinguished—if at all—by the simple punctus. For an authoritative discussion of the deployment of such marks, see Malcolm B. Parkes, *Pause and Effect: A History of Punctuation in the West* (London: Scolar, 1992).

[26] The Old English quotation here is presented in the computer-compatible font known as *Junicode*, developed by the modern scholar Peter Baker; the typeface's name derives from Franciscus Junius (1591–1677), who had commissioned a special font, *Pica Saxon*, based on that used by Day. Pica Saxon, in various slightly modified forms, was regularly used for the printing of Old English texts during the eighteenth and early nineteenth centuries. Perhaps ironically given its reformist origins, it was the font of choice for the traditionalist "non-juring" scholars known as the "Oxford Saxonists" (see further Smith, *Transforming Early English*, Chapter 2).

Day was clearly proud of this technical tour de force and provided a list of the special "Saxon Caracters" [*sic*] at the end of the book, as a handy point of reference. However, given the obvious fact that the Anglo-Saxons did not have the required technology, Day's enterprise was profoundly anachronistic, and it is worth pondering on what the printer—presumably under the direction of Joscelyn, whose annotations of the Corpus manuscript show that he collated the printed book with its exemplar—was trying to achieve with this mode of presentation.[27]

Clearly, there was no intention to deceive the reader. The answer must be that the development of such a typeface was "emblematic of the past", thus evoking a particularly English and "auncient" identity.[28] Parker, Joscelyn and indeed Day—all of whom formed a "community of practice" collaborating in a common ideological endeavour—were asserting their links with the pre-Conquest past, thereby incorporating Ælfric into a perceived evangelical narrative.[29] In such a situation, a challenge to legibility was accepted—and of course made easier by the provision of a parallel-text translation.[30]

And there are comparable practices to be found in present-day cultures, such as the Israeli adoption of Hebrew lettering. Traditional Hebrew lettering generally—save in word-final position—lacks "ascenders" and "descenders" of the kind that distinguish roman <b> and <p>. Moreover, many groups of Hebrew letters are very similar in shape, consisting of a

---

[27] For an image of the Corpus MS, showing Joscelyn's annotations, see Smith, *Transforming Early English*, p. 244.

[28] Parkes, "Archaizing hands in English manuscripts", p. 123.

[29] Emily Butler, "Recollecting Alfredian English in the sixteenth century" *Neophilologus* 98 (2014), 145–59, here at p. 154 and *passim*.

[30] Despite its undoubted scholarship, there is some evidence that the edition of the Old English work was regarded as in some sense decorative. The translation of *A testimonie* was regularly reprinted in the seventeenth century as a polemical text, but the Old English version was very often omitted, e.g., in William Guild's edition of 1624, printed by the Aberdeen printer Edward Raban. See further Smith, *Transforming Early English*, pp. 59–60.

horizontal stroke at the top and a vertical at the right.[31] As a consequence
of this characteristic of the writing system, problems for initial literacy
have been identified, and innovative type-founders are now producing
new fonts that distinguish letters more clearly; there is also some
evidence that handwritten forms of Hebrew are becoming more cursive,
allowing for the development of extra distinguishing flourishes. However,
as Geoffrey Sampson has pointed out, the adoption of Hebrew script
and fonts "by the founders of a highly-developed nation, all of whom
were familiar with other forms of writing, must be explained in terms of
emotional considerations to do with history and religion".[32]

Cracking the code

The two case studies from the history of English discussed in this short
paper have demonstrated that writing systems are much more than a
simple mode of transmission to be mapped onto speech. Numerous
further examples could have been adduced, ranging from Egyptian
hieroglyphs to the Inca quipu, both of which are known to have had
ritual as well as more humble recording functions.

Recent research into writing systems is increasingly aware of this
characteristic. In an important paper, Mark Sebba has argued that
writing systems "function as markers of difference and belonging, and
[are] involved in the creation of identities at different levels of social
organization".[33] Sebba points out that, in present-day societies, scripts
and typefaces "are particularly powerful identity markers, as they often
have associations with particular secular and—especially—religious

---

[31] See Dina Feitelson, "The relationship between systems of writing and the
     teaching of reading", in Marion Jenkinson (ed.), *Reading Instruction: an
     International Forum* (Newark, NJ: International Reading Association, 1967),
     pp. 191–9.

[32] Sampson, *Writing Systems*, p. 98.

[33] Mark Sebba, "Sociolinguistic approaches to writing systems research", *Writing
     Systems Research* I (2009), pp. 35–49, here at p. 36.

cultures, and this may evoke strong positive or negative reactions".[34] Writing systems in sum have iconic power: "The power of language as icon must never be underestimated. Like it or not, the Urdu script means Muslim, the Devanagari script means Hindu . . . ".[35] And this iconicity can extend to small details of spelling, or even diacritic marks; for instance, the adoption of the umlaut mark in the name of the heavy-metal band *Motörhead*, combined with the use of "Germanic" *Fraktur* typeface, is clearly an index of a particular musical culture with connotations, albeit obscure, of social threat, no doubt derived in part from historical associations.

An important axiom commonly encountered in several disciplines is the *uniformitarian hypothesis*, which was first formulated in the writings of the great eighteenth-century Scottish Enlightenment geologist James Hutton (1726–97); and the notion has commonly been employed in historical linguistics. It may be observed that present-day natural languages function in ways which can in principle be described systematically, and presumably they did so in the past: human beings are after all still human beings. To quote Suzanne Romaine, "The linguistic forces which operate today and are observable around us are not unlike those which have operated in the past. Sociolinguistically speaking, this means that there is no reason for claiming that language did not vary in the same patterned ways in the past as it has been observed to do today."[36] For historical linguists the uniformitarian hypothesis has proven exceptionally fruitful, allowing the development of plausible explanations of numerous past phenomena.

Yet the uniformitarian hypothesis does not of course require the imposition of present-day social or belief structures onto the very different patterns of the past. It demands that we acknowledge the role of society in explaining behaviour; it does not demand that we consider

---

[34]   Sebba, "Sociolinguistic Approaches", p. 39.

[35]   Robert D. King, *Nehru and the Language Politics of India* (Delhi: Oxford University Press, 1998), p. 84.

[36]   Suzanne Romaine, *Socio-Historical Linguistics* (Cambridge: Cambridge University Press, 1982), pp. 122–3; see also Tim William Machan, *English in the Middle Ages* (Oxford: Oxford University Press, 2003), p. 12.

that the behavioural codes of the past—linguistic or otherwise—are unchanged. A primary challenge for any researcher into past cultures is cracking those codes, allowing our ancestors to speak (or at least write) to us. This essay, in a small way, has tried to demonstrate that, unlike with contemporary lions, we can make at least some sense of how past humans perceived their world.

14

Liturgy and the Buried Giant

John Reuben Davies

> Theology—whether Jewish or Christian—is embedded in the
> past and the command to remember, or to forget.
>
> *David Jasper*[1]

I begin with an Arthurian romance about the enigma or contradictions
of memory: Kazuo Ishiguro's novel, *The Buried Giant* (London: Faber
and Faber, 2015). Set in the pseudohistorical sub-Roman Britain born in
the imagination of Geoffrey of Monmouth (Bishop of St Asaph, 1152–5),
the novel confronts us with questions of peace and justice. For the sake
of peace, should the violence of the past be forgotten? For the sake of
justice, are past wrongs worth remembering?[2]

At the level of societies, Ishiguro shows us how the historical
perspective afforded by memory inspires abiding enmities and continual
rounds of violence and retribution. But the dilemma continues at the
personal level too. Memory is on the one hand the main ingredient of
friendship and marriage. Memory nourishes and deepens all human

---

[1] Foreword to Alana M. Vincent, *Making Memory: Jewish and Christian
Explorations in Monument, Narrative, and Liturgy* (Eugene, OR: Pickwick,
2013), p. ix.

[2] For a reading of *The Buried Giant* against Geoffrey of Monmouth's *History
of the Kings of Britain*, see Jonathan Brent, "Violence, memory, and history:
Geoffrey of Monmouth and Kazuo Ishiguro's *The Buried Giant*", *Cambridge
Journal of Postcolonial Literary Inquiry* 8/3 (2021), pp. 323–44, here at pp.
323–4.

relationships. But memory is also the source of the anger and emotional pain that can tear those relationships apart.

Memory, then, is fundamental to human nature, but it also fuels many acts of inhumanity. Memory in other words is both a blessing and a curse.

Ishiguro's tale takes us into a world in which people lack long-term memories. They can carry on their everyday business. They can form organized communities with laws and conventions; yet they do not know why they live as they do. There is no past. Communal memory does not persist much beyond the present moment. But the protagonists of this tale, Axl and Beatrice, an elderly couple from among the Old Britons, have an inkling that there is something beyond their present experience.

The lack of memory in this pseudohistorical land is caused by a mist that now and again lifts to give Axl and Beatrice a glimpse of their past life. They realize they had a son and set out to find him. Their journey takes the form of an Arthurian quest, a search and pursuit for lost memories. Can memory of their life together bind Axl and Beatrice's marital union more closely and securely than their day-to-day habitual affection for each other? Can memory fashion an indissoluble bond impervious to death?

The power of memory returns to Axl and Beatrice during the journey. They piece together lost fragments. But their marriage now carries forgotten burdens of betrayal, distrust, loneliness and disappointment. Although they gain in self-understanding, their regained memories create a distance between them. They are changed into individuals, each with a different story and a separate destiny. Uncovered pasts, unredeemed memory, a failure to live in truth, leave them—and all of us—facing loneliness and isolation.

The story of Axl and Beatrice is the heart of the larger allegory on the theme of memory. In this realm, where Arthurian legend continues to inform our knowledge of fifth-century Britain, King Arthur himself is no longer with us. We nevertheless reacquaint ourselves with Arthur's nephew, Sir Gawain, now an elderly man dressed in rusty chainmail. Britons and Saxons coexist peacefully. But this peace depends on the same fog of forgetfulness that hung over Axl and Beatrice. This oblivion-inducing mist proceeds from the breath of "a dragon of great fierceness" called Querig, who is "hidden in difficult terrain", and makes the Saxons forget about the massacre of their kin at the hands of Arthur and the Britons.[3]

Sir Gawain had promised King Arthur that he would protect the dragon to maintain the mist of forgetfulness. A Saxon warrior called Master Wistan, who can pass for a Briton, challenges Sir Gawain to a duel and kills him. Wistan then slays Querig the dragon, the mist dissipates, and the people's memories begin to come back. "The giant, once well buried." declares Master Wistan, "now stirs."[4]

As the mist disperses, Axl, Beatrice and their travelling companions remember a time of bloodshed and death when the Britons at King Arthur's command rid the land of Saxon settlers. The slaying of the dragon intimates a return of the old animosities between the two peoples and the advent of a new war. The Saxon armies, "swollen by anger and thirst for vengeance", will massacre Britons in return for the slaughter of their own people until, like the Amalekites, their remembrance will be blotted out from under heaven: "Country by country, this will become a new land, a Saxon land, with no more trace" of the Britons' presence.[5]

Memory, liturgy and righteousness

For the ancient Jewish people, the community's formative events were remembered—told and retold—through the liturgy. This retelling and remembering was intended to draw out a fitting response. Worship and way of life were formed through the collective memory of God's saving acts. This formation of worship and way of life through the celebration of a rememorative liturgy was perpetuated in Christianity and remains the case for Christians today.

Since the time of the Exodus, the annual Passover liturgy allowed succeeding generations to re-live in ritual form the original deliverance from the bondage in Egypt. The liturgy handed on a belief in- an

---

3   Kazuo Ishiguro, *The Buried Giant* (London Faber and Faber, 2015), p. 69.

4   Ishiguro, *The Buried Giant*, p. 324.

5   Ishiguro, *The Buried Giant*, p. 324. For the reference to the Amalekites, see Vincent, *Making Memory*, pp. 11–31.

experience of—the saving power of the Lord who "brought us out of
Egypt with a mighty hand and an outstretched arm" (Deuteronomy
26:8). The celebration of the Passover maintained the identity of God's
chosen people "throughout the generations" (Exodus 12:14, 42).

Because of God's true faithfulness, Isaiah and Jeremiah could point
to the Exodus from Egypt as an archetype, and an assurance, of the
deliverance from Babylonian captivity for which they were hoping.[6]
Then, for Christians, the suffering, death and resurrection of Jesus at
the time of the Jewish Passover, on the paschal night, brought about a
deliverance with significance for the whole of creation. Among the early
Christians, the paschal sense of expectancy was continued at Easter time
and was again maintained "from generation to generation", but now as
an awaiting of Jesus Christ's coming again in glory.

The Paschal mystery—the passion, death and resurrection of Christ—
celebrated rememoratively during the Triduum of Maundy Thursday,
Good Friday and the Easter Vigil, is the source of all Christian liturgy.
Through the liturgy, the Paschal mystery comes to meet us in our lives.
Indeed, the whole of Jesus's life was paschal mystery. All faithful Christian
life is paschal mystery. All salvation is embedded in that union of life
and liturgy.[7]

The celebration of liturgical rites is nevertheless only one element of
the Christian life, the truly liturgical life. In Israel of the eighth century
BCE, Hosea proclaimed his prophecy from the LORD: "I desire steadfast
love and not sacrifice, the knowledge of God rather than burnt-offerings"
(Hosea 6:6). The Lord Jesus himself invokes the first half of that verse
in Matthew's Gospel, and prefaces it with the instruction, "Go and learn
what this means" (Matthew 9:13).

Hosea's message contrasts two ideas of religion. One is about
discharging religious obligations through the machinery of sacrifice and
offering—the celebration of liturgical rites. The other speaks of loyal love
with deep roots. This second idea of deep-rooted and steadfast love calls
for the establishment of justice and righteousness in everyday living.

---

[6]   Isaiah 43:15–21; 48:20–1; 51:9–11; Jeremiah 23:7.

[7]   Lizette Larson-Miller, *Sacramentality Renewed: Contemporary Conversations
       in Sacramental Theology* (Collegeville, MN: Liturgical Press, 2016), p. 71.

On the one hand, Hosea, with Isaiah, Amos and Micah—the other prophets of the eighth century BCE—calls for religion to be brought out of the sanctuaries and into the streets. Yet none of the prophets advocates doing away with the sacrifices and offerings or the abolition of liturgical rites. Indeed, Isaiah's inaugural vision takes place in the temple, during a liturgical celebration. In their call for the renewal of religion, they advocate a form of worship that remembers God's acts of blessing and delivering. They appeal for a religion which expresses the response expected from a people who have experienced God's grace and saving acts.[8]

Communities of memory

In this way, the Christian can perhaps begin to grasp the redemptive potential of communal memory. Memory has power to make whole and restore rather than wound and destroy. But how do we remember well?

Remembering well is Miroslav Volf's concern in *The End of Memory*.[9] Volf proposes that, when filtered through the lens of the sacred memories—the Exodus and the Paschal Mystery—damaging, destructive, wounding memories can ultimately heal. The re-presentation of salvation history can work towards the redemption of recurring memories of injury, insult and injustice.[10]

Remembering is also a communal activity.[11] We remember as members of communities. The handing on of memories involves

<hr/>

[8] Hosea 2:8; 11:1; Amos 2:9–11; Micah 6:4.

[9] This is Miroslav Volf's fundamental question in *The End of Memory: Remembering Rightly in a Violent World* (2nd edn, Grand Rapids, MI/ Cambridge, UK: W. B. Eerdmans, 2021).

[10] Volf, *The End of Memory*, pp. 124–9; Miroslav Volf, "Memory, eschatology, eucharist", *Liturgy* 22:1 (2007), pp. 27–38, esp. pp. 36–8.

[11] See Volf, *The End of Memory*, p. 126, referring to the work of Maurice Halbwachs, *La Mémoire collective* (Paris: Presses universitaires de France, 1950). On communal memory more generally, the fundamental work is Paul Ricoeur, *Memory, History, Forgetting*, transl. by Kathleen Blamey and David Pellauer (Chicago, IL: University of Chicago Press, 2004).

mutual recognition. That mutual recognition then results in an act of acknowledgement and confirmation—an act of witness. And in Ishiguro's work (as Yugin Teo observes) we view this acknowledgment as both private and public; something that is "passed down through the generations and haunts the collective consciousness".[12]

To remember wrongs suffered through the lens of sacred memory, through liturgical *anamnesis* of the Paschal Mystery, Christians must be members of a sacred community. Churches are communities that live by means of the liturgical remembrance and making present of the Paschal Mystery. Through the liturgy they acknowledge and bear witness to the communal sacred memory. Without the language and actions of liturgy, the Christian memory of who we are and who we should become would fade away.

Peter Atkins reminds us of a frequently quoted saying of Milan Hübl, a Czech academic historian, as represented by Milan Kundera in his novel, *The Book of Laughter and Forgetting* (1979), a work written against the background of a Czechoslovakia that had "vanished from the world" as a result of "Russification" in the Soviet era:[13]

> "You begin to liquidate a people," Hübl said, "by taking away its memory. You destroy its books, its culture, its history. And then others write other books for it, give another culture to it, invent another history for it. Then the people slowly begins to forget what it is and what it was. The world at large forgets it still faster.[14]

---

[12]   Yugin Teo, *Kazuo Ishiguro and Memory* (Basingstoke: Palgrave Macmillan, 2014), p. 78.

[13]   See Peter Atkins, *Memory and Liturgy: The Place of Memory in the Composition and Practice of Liturgy* (Aldershot: Ashgate, 2004), p. 24. Milan Kundera's references to "Russification" and the vanishing of Czechoslovakia are cited in Nina Pelikan Straus, "Erasing history and deconstructing the text: Milan Kundera's *The Book of Laughter*", *Critique* 28/2 (1987), pp. 69–85, here at p. 69.

[14]   Milan Kundera, *The Book of Laughter and Forgetting*, transl. by Aaron Asher (London: Faber and Faber, 2000), p. 218.

Indeed, Kundera then makes an allusive response to Hübl: "Is it true that the people will be unable to survive crossing the desert of organized forgetting?"[15]

Churches, then, are communities that can offer the memory of the Paschal Mystery as a lens for memories of wrongs suffered. But do churches always offer this lens of sacred memory? They certainly remember the passion, death and resurrection of Christ in the celebration of the Eucharist. But how can we incorporate remembering of wrongs suffered into the celebration of the Eucharist?

Volf points out a potential difficulty. The memory of the Passion can become twisted when it is about what God has done for us, without any consequence of how we should remember wrongs suffered. We then remember wrongs suffered only to seek comfort or lend religious legitimacy to whatever uses we want to put these memories to.

> No wonder that we sometimes find thirst for revenge celebrating its victory under the mantle of a religiously sanctioned struggle for faith, for protection, for nation, for our way of life—and all of that in the name of Christ who died on the cross![16]

---

[15] *Ibid.*

[16] Volf, "Memory", p. 36. At the time of writing, this point has an immediacy in the savage conflict playing out in Ukraine, where the armed forces of the Russian Federation are bombarding Ukrainian cities, reducing them to rubble, and slaughtering civilians in the process. The Russian invasion of a sovereign state is underpinned in part by a nationalist religious narrative and the explicit support of the Patriarch of Moscow.

Memory and reconciliation

Léon van Ommen has extended our knowledge of how the experience of liturgy can form communities of reconciliation.[17] How its members experience the liturgy, says van Ommen, is fundamental to the formation of the community: "The liturgical dialogue between God and people is not only influenced by the experience of community, but the dialogue itself shapes the community".[18]

In *The Buried Giant*, the return of memory heralds the return of war. When historical memory fuels enmity between communities, the sharing of living space or individual friendships are no remedy. We have already met the Saxon warrior, Master Wistan, who grew up with Britons, learned their tongue, adopted their customs, and befriended Axl and Beatrice. Wistan, despite his upbringing among the Britons and his friendship with Axl and Beatrice, wants his young Saxon companion, Edwin, to swear that he will maintain an undying hatred for the Britons.

Miroslav Volf warns us that there are Christian communities which hold on to resentments or let them fester. In the spring of 2022, Volf's prophetic warning and the consequences of resentment were made real in eastern Ukraine. When a Church, an ecclesial hierarchy, a nation's rulers, nurse in the communal bosom the offences committed against them, favouring communal or national memories and traditions above the Paschal Mystery, rather than allowing them to be redefined by it, remembering through the lens of the liturgy leads down a false path. When there is a fixation on memories of wrong, on seeking the

---

[17]   Armand Léon van Ommen, "Worship, truth, and reconciliation: a liturgical spirituality of peace-making", *Liturgy* 34:1 (2019), pp. 58–66; Armand Léon van Ommen, *Suffering in Worship: Anglican Liturgy in Relation to Stories of Suffering People* (London: Routledge, 2017); Léon van Ommen, "Liturgy and pastoral care: pastoral worship and priestly counseling", *Studia Liturgica* 46/1–2 (2017), pp. 208–21; Léon van Ommen, "Anglican Liturgy and Community: The influence of the experience of community on the experience of liturgy as a challenge for liturgical renewal and formation", *Studia Liturgica* 45:2 (2015), pp. 221–34.

[18]   van Ommen, 'The influence of the experience of community', p. 234.

punishment of evildoers and driving them away from our presence, we create a distorted remembrance of salvation history, and the process of remembering becomes an abomination.

The case of Russian Orthodox hierarchy in Moscow seems obvious. But within the Scottish Episcopal Church (the perspective from which this essay has been written), there is need for awareness and caution in church life and liturgical practice too. The SEC is a province of the Anglican Communion that not only has its origins in the social, political, cultural, intellectual and religious developments of the sixteenth century, but was also wrought in the political and religious conflicts of the seventeenth and eighteenth centuries. And these conflicts have left scars.

For other countries, the seminal theological thinkers and leaders of reform movements, and others who suffered and died for professing insights and convictions contrary to those upheld by religious and political rulers, are commemorated in the liturgical calendar. The Liturgy Committee of the SEC has recognized, however, that identifying such figures in the historical SEC is a potentially divisive process, and one which could also lead down a false path.

The church which emerged from the shadow of the Penal Laws during the eighteenth century encompassed communities which had remained faithful to the reformed episcopal polity through the vicissitudes of the preceding centuries, as well as more recent immigrants to Scotland, whose heritage lay in the established churches of England and Ireland.

The Faith and Order Board of the SEC therefore resolved not to propose the inclusion of named individuals in the liturgical calendar, but rather that two group commemorations be created, and to remember Scottish Saints and Martyrs of the Reformation Period, and the other Members of the Church who suffered under the Penal Laws. The character and emphasis of these proposed commemorations is somewhat different. Commemoration of the Scottish Saints and Martyrs of the Reformation period acknowledges the suffering inflicted by whoever was in power at any time. This includes at times suffering inflicted by senior clerics and lay aristocracy of what became the SEC upon the less powerful with contrary theological convictions. John Ogilvie, arrested and imprisoned under the orders of Archbishop Spottiswood in 1614, and eventually hanged and eviscerated, is one of the more obvious examples.

The Commemoration of the Members of the Church who suffered under the Penal Laws is specific to what became the SEC, and recognizes that men, women and children, most of whose names are not known, remained faithful to the church at considerable cost, in the face of constant discrimination and intermittent violence.

For the Commemoration of Scottish Saints and Martyrs of the Reformation Period, the Faith and Order Board proposed that the commemoration be kept on 19 January, during the Week of Prayer for Christian Unity. This recognizes the lasting divisions in the Church which resulted from the Reformation, and that, whatever role those who suffered may have played in these, the SEC and other Christian denominations in Scotland today are committed to overcoming these, working together for the gospel, and seeking collective healing and mutual forgiveness. This purpose is emphasized in the Collect and reflected in the lectionary identified for the proposed commemoration.

The Commemoration of Members of the Church who suffered under the Penal Laws has been proposed as a commemoration to be kept on 15 June, the date in 1792 on which the repeal of the Penal Laws took effect. This acknowledges the legacy of discrimination and repression, as well as the new beginning made possible by the repealing of the Penal Laws, by which congregations of diverse history, membership and political sympathies were united in what became the SEC. This is again reflected in the Collect and readings.

In the wider Anglican Communion, the International Anglican Liturgical Consultation (IALC) has been addressing the role of liturgy in reconciliation. The meetings of IALC in 2013, 2015 and 2017 recognized that the journey towards reconciliation requires space, time and patience and should include ritual moments and symbolic enactments. The Anglican Church of Canada, meanwhile, has developed a "Reconciliation Toolkit" which includes liturgical resources.[19]

Most recently, in April and May 2022, the Archbishop of Canterbury was due to meet with Anglican Indigenous people and Indigenous leaders in Prince Albert, Saskatchewan; Six Nations Reserve near Brantford,

---

[19]   Anglican Church of Canada, *Reconciliation Toolkit: Worship*, online at <https://www.anglican.ca/tr/reconciliation-toolkit/>, accessed 14 July 2022.

Ontario; and Toronto, Ontario. This visit is part of a particular focus of his primacy on the work of reconciliation. A statement from General Synod Communications recognized that:

> Anglican history in Canada is entwined with the Church of England, British explorers, colonists and Crown representatives. Their presence in treaty negotiations and subsequent partnership with the government are part of the legacy of colonialism that contributed to residential schools and to abuse and cultural deprivation. A significant purpose behind Archbishop Justin's visit is to recognize and repent of where those relationships have done damage rather than good, particularly with Indigenous peoples.
>
> During his visit the Archbishop will meet and listen to residential school survivors; visit Indigenous reserves; and share in the work of reconciliation to which the Anglican Church of Canada is committed.[20]

To remember in a reconciling way, says Volf, one must "observe the community struggle, and sometimes fail, to embody those same practices". Above all, he says, we need Christ—who comes through the community in faith—to dwell within us and live his life through us. A community of sacred memory mediates Christ as reconciler and embodies reconciling remembering. This practice of sacred memory therefore mediates and embodies reconciliation both to those who suffer wrong and to those who commit it.

At their best, communities of sacred memory are the schools of right remembering—remembering that is truthful and just, that heals individuals without injuring others, remembering that motivates struggles for justice and the grace-filled work of reconciliation.

For van Ommen, attention to the pastoral needs of the people who form the gathered, worshipping community allows the liturgy, its ritual

---

[20] General Synod Communications, "Visit of the Archbishop of Canterbury to Canada", 10 February 2022, online at <https://www.anglican.ca/news/visit-of-the-archbishop-of-canterbury-to-canada/30038462/>, accessed 14 July 2022.

and ceremonial, its words and actions, "to (re)gain their significance for the spiritual well-being of the participants".[21] He also points to the liturgy as a kind of binding agent in pastoral care. For if we pay attention to ritual and liturgy in pastoral care, we remind people that they are part of a community, part of a story. They share in "the grand narrative" of God and humankind.[22]

Part of this narrative of God and humankind involves lament, for lament must come before healing, forgiveness and reconciliation. Léon van Ommen's insights have opened a wider space for liturgical lament in the official rites of the Scottish Episcopal Church. And in 2022, the Scottish Episcopal College of Bishops authorized new material for times of lament, including a special Eucharistic Prayer.[23]

Dangerous memory

We have seen how Ishiguro's *Buried Giant* warns us about the dangers of memory. And this "dangerous memory" is Bruce Morrill's starting point in his quest for a mechanism to connect liturgical theology and political theology.

The interaction of liturgical and political theology allows us to learn what is meant by Hosea's prophetic utterance, "I desire steadfast love and not sacrifice".[24]

---

[21]   van Ommen, "Liturgy and pastoral care", p. 221.

[22]   van Ommen, "Liturgy and pastoral care", p. 221.

[23]   David Jasper contributed to the development of these experimental texts as a member of the Liturgy Committee from 2015 to 2019.

[24]   *Anamnesis as Dangerous Memory: Political and Liturgical Theology in Dialogue* (Collegeville, MN: Pueblo/Liturgical Press, 2000). A theology of "dangerous memory" was elaborated by Johann Baptist Metz, *Faith in History and Society: Toward a Practical Fundamental Theology*, transl. by David Smith (London: Burns & Oates, 1980); and "Communicating a dangerous memory", in Fred Lawrence (ed.), *Communicating a Dangerous Memory: Soundings in Political Theology*, Supplementary Issue of the Lonergan Workshop Journal 6 (Atlanta, GA.: Scholars Press, 1987), pp. 37–53.

The first observation is that liturgy, and liturgical theology, is not about externals in themselves—rites and rituals, candles and copes—but the "ancient traditional practices of the Church's liturgy" are nevertheless its foundation and context. One of the liturgy's fundamental purposes is to transform all who participate in it. The liturgy is "a charge for all to witness to God's redemptive will for the world".[25]

Political theology, meanwhile, is not about ideology or tactics. Christianity keeps the memory of the crucified, risen, ascended Lord alive, and this memory is the interpretative key for unlocking the gospel. It opens "the modern manacles of privatized religion and institutional power structures".[26] The memory of Jesus Christ is a "dangerous memory of freedom"—a memory dangerous for "the social systems of our technological civilization".[27]

In this theology of the "dangerous memory", first described by Johann Baptist Metz, the gospel scandalizes and interrupts the banality and boredom of bourgeois religion; it waits to ambush comfortable Sunday piety. When we remember suffering in solidarity with Jesus—and this is the "dangerous memory"—the present is called into question. A moment of renewal interrupts the everyday.[28] This is perhaps part of what David Jasper is also saying when he writes that memory "can be counter-cultural, standing over against a diminished and diminishing world and in spite of all".[29]

Metz pointed to theology's mission in late modernity. Theology today must rise above "the level of a pure assertion that is suspected of ideology" and be able to "define and call upon a *praxis* [a conscious, willed action based in faith] in which Christians can break through the complex social,

---

25 Morrill, *Anamnesis*, p. 75. Here, Morrill draws on the works of Alexander Schmemann, as summarized, for example, in David W. Fagerberg, *What is Liturgical Theology? A Study in Methodology* (Collegeville, MN.: Liturgical Press, 1992), pp. 143–79.

26 Morrill, *Anamnesis*, p. 30.

27 Morrill, *Anamnesis*, p. 31; quoting Metz, *Faith in History*, p. 109.

28 Morrill, *Anamnesis*, p. 53

29 David Jasper, *Literature and Theology as a Grammar of Assent* (London: Routledge, 2016), p. 105.

historical, and psychological conditions governing history and society".[30] Theology must therefore have nothing to do with the idolatry of ideology.

Morrill's answer points to the need for a Christian way of living out our faith "in mystical and political imitation". He uses Alexander Schmemann's liturgical theology as he observes that "each liturgical celebration is an experience of the redeemed order of creation".[31] Through the liturgy, God intends humankind to know God. Liturgy is the special place for remembrance and embodies the pattern of activity through which God's remembrance of creation and of humankind happens. In turn, liturgy is where our remembrance of God takes place.[32]

In this context, Schmemann described how life viewed through the lens of the Eucharist looks:

> Grace is perfecting nature everywhere we look. Now nothing in the world looks the same. To the naked, secular eye nothing looks different, but to the sanctified, consecrated eye every object and moment has a new potentiality. Once we have seen God invite himself into the house of Zacchaeus for supper, or stop for dinner in Emmaus after a long day's walk, there is no meal which is purely secular. Once we have seen Christ on the green hills of Galilee and the crowded streets of Jerusalem, we privilege neither the pastoral nor the political. Once we have seen God on the cross there is no corner of suffering or darkness where our spiritual eyes do not see him moving. Once we have seen God in Hades, we know there is no length to which he will not go to find us.[33]

In this way, Schmemann provided a way for political theology to participate in the liturgical. "Recovery of this dangerous memory,"

---

[30] Morrill, *Anamnesis*, p. 145; quoting Metz, *Faith in History*, pp. 76–7.

[31] Morrill, *Anamnesis*, p. 143.

[32] Morrill, *Anamnesis*, p. 143.

[33] David W. Fagerberg, *Liturgy Outside Liturgy: The Liturgical Theology of Fr. Alexander Schmemann* (Hong Kong: Chorabooks, 2018), p. 204.

comments David W. Fagerberg, "would be beneficial to any who isolate the liturgical life from politics, and the political life from liturgy."[34]

León van Ommen, in recognizing that liturgy forms a space in which the worshipping community practices reconciliation, is concerned lest this may sound as if "the real thing" is reconciliation in the political realm. But he is, in fact, pointing to the reconciliation which is at the heart of the gospel. This gospel reconciliation is rehearsed in and through the liturgy. The liturgy, for van Ommen, fosters a spirituality of reconciliation. By participating in the liturgy, we let ourselves be shaped into a liturgical spirituality of reconciliation.[35]

The Buried Giant, liturgy, and Christian destiny

King Arthur's intention in making the community forget, we realize, is the same tactic employed by national leaders and governments that use propaganda, denial and censorship to bury, reshape and distort the deeds of the present as much as the past. The fact is that memory is not the culprit; the fault lies in the reshaping of memory, the telling of history, the story of the community. *The Buried Giant* embodies a poignant truth. When national armies invade the sovereign territory of their neighbour, when soldiers are ordered to commit atrocities, their leaders and commanders are not only inspired by greed, lust for power or ideology. They also want to punish their enemies for wrongs they have done—and to achieve the destiny they think their history has bestowed on them. "Who knows what will come," asks Axl, "when quick-tongued men make ancient grievances rhyme with fresh desire for land and conquest?"[36]

In this way, *The Buried Giant* leads us to question whether remembering is preferable to forgetting. But he also shows how our

---

[34]   David W. Fagerberg, "Review of Bruce T. Morrill, *Anamnesis as Dangerous Memory*", *Theology Today* 58:1, pp. 128–9, here at p. 129.

[35]   van Ommen, *Suffering in Worship*; van Ommen, "Worship with care", Scottish Episcopal Institute Journal 3:4 (2019), pp. 101–16.

[36]   Ishiguro, *The Buried Giant*, p. 323.

human destiny is, indeed, to remember. Memory ultimately cannot be evaded, and therefore has important work to do if it is to be a blessing and not a curse. Memory must retrieve, restore and release the people, the events and the concepts that most significantly shape the course of human lives.

If our human destiny, then, is to remember, the Christian destiny is to "do this in remembrance of me". The liturgy does not offer immediate answers and instant healing. And liturgy can be abused and even become sacrilegious—an abomination—when it is appropriated for the idolatrous worship of nation or denomination.[37] But the liturgy—the Eucharist—is the place where truth is rooted, where healing is nurtured and where the reconciliation of the world begins.

---

[37]   Matthew 24:15–16; Luke 21:20–1.

List of David Jasper's Publications

Authored books

Coleridge as Poet and Religious Thinker: Inspiration and Revelation
(London: Macmillan, 1985; Allison Park, PA: Pickwick
Publications, 1985).

The New Testament and the Literary Imagination (London:
Macmillan, 1987; Atlantic Highlands, NJ: Humanities Press, 1987;
reprinted, Eugene, OR: Wipf and Stock, 2009).

The Study of Literature and Religion: An Introduction (London:
Macmillan, 1989; Minneapolis: Fortress Press, 1989). (Translated
into Korean, 1999). Second edn 1992. Reprinted, Eugene, OR:
Wipf and Stock, 2009.

Rhetoric, Power and Community: An Exercise in Reserve (London:
Macmillan, 1993; Louisville, KY: Westminster/John Knox Press,
1993). Reprinted, Eugene, OR: Wipf and Stock, 2009.

Readings in the Canon of Scripture: Written for Our Learning (London:
Macmillan, 1995; New York: St Martin's Press, 1995). Reprinted,
Eugene, OR: Wipf and Stock, 2009.

*The Sacred and Secular Canon in Romanticism: Preserving the Sacred
Truths* (London: Macmillan, 1999; New York: St Martin's Press,
1999). Reprinted, Eugene, OR: Wipf and Stock, 2009.

The Sacred Desert: Religion, Literature, Art, and Culture (Oxford:
Blackwell, 2004).

A Short Introduction to Hermeneutics (Louisville, KY: Westminster
John Knox Press, 2004). (Translated into Chinese, Hong Kong,
2008; translated into Hungarian, Budapest, 2021.)

The Sacred Body: Asceticism in Religion, Literature, Art, and Culture
(Waco, TX: Baylor University Press, 2009).

The Sacred Community: Art, Sacrament, and the People of God (Waco, TX: Baylor University Press, 2012).

Literature and Theology as a Grammar of Assent (London: Routledge, 2017).

Heaven in Ordinary: Poetry and Religion in a Secular Age (Cambridge: The Lutterworth Press, 2018).

The Language of Liturgy: A Ritual Poetics (London: SCM Press, 2018).

What a World Thou Art: Reflections on four Poets and Religion: The St Aidan's Lectures, 2018 (Glasgow: Scottish Episcopal Church, Diocese of Glasgow and Galloway, 2018).

Joint author

(With Ronald C. D. Jasper and Peter Coughlan) *Pray Every Day* (London: Collins, 1976; published as *Everyday Prayer*, New York: Pueblo, 1978).

(With Allen Smith) *Between Truth and Fiction: A Reader in Literature and Christian Theology* (London: SCM Press, 2010).

(With Ou Guang-an) *Literature and Religion: A Dialogue Between China and the West* (Eugene, OR: Pickwick Publications, 2020).

Editor

Images of Belief in Literature (London: Macmillan, 1984; New York: St Martin's Press, 1984).

The Interpretation of Belief: Coleridge, Schleiermacher and Romanticism (London: Macmillan, 1986; New York: St Martin's Press, 1986).

(With T. R. Wright) *The Critical Spirit and the Will to Believe: Essays in Nineteenth Century Literature and Religion* (London: Macmillan, 1989; New York: St Martin's Press, 1989).

(With Colin Crowder) *European Literature and Theology in the Twentieth Century: Ends of Time* (London: Macmillan, 1990; New York: St Martin's Press, 1990). Reprinted Eugene, OR: Wipf and Stock, 2009.

(With R. C. D. Jasper) *Language and the Worship of the Church* (London: Macmillan, 1990; New York: St Martin's Press, 1990).

(With A. M. Allchin, J. H. Schjoerring and K. W. Stevenson) *Heritage and Prophecy: Grundtvig and the English-Speaking World* (Aarhus: Aarhus University Press, 1993).

Postmodernism, Literature and the Future of Theology (London: Macmillan; New York: St Martin's Press, 1993). Reprinted, Eugene, OR: Wipf and Stock, 2009.

Translating Religious Texts: Translation, Transgression and Interpretation (London: Macmillan; New York: St Martin's Press, 1993).

(With Mark Ledbetter) *In Good Company: Essays in Honor of Robert Detweiler* (Atlanta, GA: Scholars Press, 1994).

The Arts and the Church: The Cinema (London: Aston Training Scheme, 1995).

(With Stephen Prickett) *The Bible and Literature: A Reader* (Oxford: Blackwell, 1999).

(With Brent Plate) *Imag(in)ing Otherness: Filmic Visions of Living Together* (Atlanta, GA: Scholars Press, 1999).

(With Robert Detweiler) *Religion and Literature: A Reader* (Louisville, KY: Westminster John Knox Press, 2000).

(With Bill Hall) *Art and the Spiritual* (Sunderland: University of Sunderland Press, 2003).

(With George Newlands) *Believing in the Text: Essays from the Centre for the Study of Literature, Theology and the Arts, University of Glasgow* (Bern: Peter Lang, 2004).

(With Andrew W. Hass and Elisabeth Jay) *The Oxford Handbook of English Literature and Theology* (Oxford: Oxford University Press, 2009).

The Selected Works of Margaret Oliphant: Part II, Volume 8. Writings on Biography II (London: Pickering and Chatto, 2012).

(With Dale Wright) *Theological Reflection and the Pursuit of Ideals: Theology, Human Flourishing and Freedom* (Farnham: Ashgate, 2013).

(With Ramona Fotiade and Olivier Salazar-Ferrer) *Embodiment: Phenomenological, Religious and Deconstructive Views on Living and Dying* (Farnham: Ashgate, 2014).

(With Geng Youzhuang and Wang Hai) *A Poetics of Translation: Between Chinese and English Literature* (Waco, TX: Baylor University Press, 2016).

(With Jenny Wright) *Truth and the Church in a Secular Age* (London: SCM Press, 2019).

(With Michael Fuller) *Made in the Image of God: Being Human in the Christian Tradition* (Durham: Sacristy Press, 2021).

Contributions to books

"Pusey's Lectures on Types and Prophecies of the Old Testament", in Butler, Perry (ed.), *Pusey Rediscovered* (London: SPCK, 1983), pp. 51–71.

"The Two Worlds of Coleridge's 'The Rime of the Ancient Mariner'", in Watson, J. R. (ed.), *An Infinite Complexity: Essays in Romanticism* (Edinburgh: Edinburgh University Press [for the University of Durham], 1983), pp. 125–44. [Reprinted in *Nineteenth Century Literature Criticism*, vol. 197 (2008).]

"Gerard Manley Hopkins: Language and Poetry", in Dayras, Solange (ed.), *Le Symbole Religieux et l'imaginaire dans la Litterature Anglaise* (Paris: Université Paris-Nord, 1987), pp. 145–64.

Critical Introduction to Coleridge's *Confessions of an Inquiring Spirit* (Minneapolis, MN: Fortress Press, 1988), pp. 7–16.

"S. T. Coleridge, *Confessions of an Inquiring Spirit*", in Dayras, Solange (ed.), *Parole Biblique et Inspiration Litteraire* (Paris: Université Paris-Nord, 1989) pp. 119–30.

"In the Sermon which I have just completed, wherever I said Aristotle, I meant St. Paul", in Warner, Martin (ed.), *The Bible as Rhetoric: Studies in Biblical Persuasion and Credibility* (London and New York: Warwick Studies in Philosophy and Literature, 1990), pp. 133–53.

"Walter Pater's Remoter and Ever Remoter Possibilities", in Gerhart, Mary and Yu, Anthony C. (eds), *Morphologies of Faith: Essays in Culture and Religion in Honor of Nathan A. Scott. Jr* (Atlanta, GA: Scholars Press, 1990), pp. 278–90.

"Siding with the Swine: A Moral Problem for Narrative", in Detweiler, Robert and Doty, William G. (eds), *The Daemonic Imagination: Biblical Text and Secular Story* (Atlanta, GA: American Academy of Religion, 1990), pp. 65–76.

Article on S. T. Coleridge, in Cooper, David (ed.), *A Companion to Aesthetics* (Blackwell Companions to Philosophy), (Oxford: Blackwell, 1992), pp. 73–5.

Articles on "Coleridge", "The Fantastic", "William Godwin" and "Religious Thought: Wesley, Swedenborg", in Raimond, Jean and Watson, J. R. (eds), *A Handbook to English Romanticism* (London: Macmillan, 1992).

"Literature and Theology", in McGrath, Alister (ed.), *The Blackwell Encyclopedia of Modern Christian Thought* (Oxford: Blackwell, 1993), pp. 335–9.

"N. F. S. Grundtvig and S. T. Coleridge: The Hymnwriter and the Poet", in Allchin, A. M., Jasper, David, Schjoerring, J. H. and Stevenson, Kenneth W. (eds), *Heritage and Prophecy* (Aarhus: Aarhus University Press, 1993), pp. 103–13.

"Response to Robert Scharlemann", in Klemm, David E. and Schweiker, William (eds), *Meanings in Texts and Actions: Questioning Paul Ricoeur* (Charlottesville, VA and London: University Press of Virginia, 1993), pp. 314–17.

"Art and the Biblical Canon", in Griffith, Michael and Keating, Ross (eds), *Religion, Literature and the Arts* (Sydney: Australian Catholic University, 1994), pp. 37–52.

"Teaching Literature and Theology: A Lesson in Two Parts", in Davies, J. M. Q. (ed.), *Bridging the Gap: Literary Theory in the Classroom* (West Cornwall, CT: Locust Hill Press, 1994), pp. 55–70.

"Trespassing in the Wilderness: New Ventures in Canonical Criticism", in Blaicher, Gunther and Glaser, Brigitte (eds), *Anglistentag 1993 Eichstätt* (Tübingen: Max Niemeyer, 1994), pp. 381–91.

"Seeing Pictures: Reading Texts. Violating the Body: Violating the Text", in de Graef, Ortwin et al. (eds), *Sense and Transcendence: Essays in Honour of Hermon Servotte* (Leuven: Leuven University Press, 1995), pp. 209–23.

"Word and Image", in Hamilton, David S. (ed.), *The Reading for Today* (Glasgow: Trinity St Mungo Press, 1995), pp. 1–23.

"The Art of Bill Viola: A Theological Reflection", in Sparrow, Felicity (ed.), *Bill Viola: The Messenger* (Durham: The Chaplaincy to the Arts and Recreation in North East England, 1996), pp. 13–17.

"'Living Powers': Sacred and Secular Language in European Romanticism", in Porter, Stanley E. (ed.), *The Nature of Religious Language* (Sheffield: Sheffield Academic Press, 1996), pp. 214–25.

"On Systematizing the Unsystematic: A Response", in Marsh, Clive and Ortiz, Gaye (eds), *Explorations in Theology and Film* (Oxford: Wiley-Blackwell, 1997), pp. 235–45.

"Reflections on the London Conference on the Rhetorical Analysis of Scripture", in Porter, Stanley E. and Olbricht, Thomas H. (eds), *The Rhetorical Analysis of Scripture* (Sheffield: Sheffield Academic Press, 1997), pp. 476–82.

"Time And Narrative: Reflections from Paul Ricoeur", in Dayras, Solange and Sys, Jacques (eds), *La Conscience Religieuse et le Temps* (Lille: Villeneuve-d'Ascq: Université Charles-de-Gaulle-Lille III, 1997) pp. 39–49.

"J. M. W. Turner: Interpreter of the Bible", in Exum, J. Cheryl and Moore, Stephen D. (eds), *Biblical Studies, Cultural Studies: The Third Sheffield Colloquium* (Sheffield: Sheffield Academic Press, 1998), pp. 299–314.

"Literary Readings of the Bible", in Barton, John (ed.), *The Cambridge Companion to Bible Interpretation* (Cambridge: Cambridge University Press, 1998), pp. 21–34.

"Stately Palace Domes from Myth to Reality—Images of the Raj",
   in Edelson, Maria (ed.), *Images of India in Literature in English*
   (Łódź: Łódź University Press, 1998), pp. 35–41.
"Afterword: Otherness ad infinitum", in Plate, Brent and Jasper, David
   (eds), *Imag(in)ing Otherness* (New York: Oxford University Press,
   1999), pp. 213–19.
"How Can We Read the Bible?", in Gearon, Liam (ed.), *English
   Literature, Theology and the Curriculum* (London and New York:
   Cassell, 1999), pp. 9–26.
"Turner and the Resistance to Interpretation", in Zelechow, Bernard
   and Paycha, Danièle (eds), *Cult and Culture: Studies in Cultural
   Meaning* (Paris: Université de Cergy-Pontoise, 1999), pp. 193–211.
"'What Happened in the Cave?': Communities and Outsiders in
   Films of India", in Plate, Brent and Jasper, David (eds), *Imag(in)ing
   Otherness* (New York: Oxford University Press, 1999), pp.123–33.
"Believing Beyond the Unthinkable: Is there really life after death?"
   Zelechow, Bernard and Paycha, Danièle (eds), *The Holy and the
   Worldly* (Paris: Université de Cergy-Pontoise, 2001), pp. 111–16.
"The Bible in Literature", in Rogerson, John (ed.), *The Oxford
   Illustrated History of the Bible* (Oxford: Oxford University Press,
   2001), pp. 278–91.
"The Death of God: A Live Issue?", in Haney, William S. II and
   Malekin, Peter (eds), *Humanism and The Humanities in the
   Twenty-first Century* (Lewisburg, PA: Bucknell University Press,
   2001), pp. 88–99.
"Light in the Darkness of the Heart: Art and the Spiritual", in Taylor,
   Barbara (curator), *An Exemplary Life*. Exhibition Catalogue
   (Bury St Edmunds Art Gallery, March 2000). Reprinted in
   Contemplations on the Spiritual. Exhibition Catalogue (Glasgow
   School of Art, May 2001), pp. 39–41.
"Literature and the Possibility of Theology", in Hunter, Alastair G. and
   Davies, Philip R. (eds), *Sense and Sensitivity: Essays on Reading the
   Bible in Memory of Robert Carroll* (Sheffield: Sheffield Academic
   Press, 2002), pp. 331–42.

"The Subject on Trial and Baudrillard's Nightmare", in Haney, William
   S. II and Pagan, Nicholas O. (eds), *Ethics and Subjectivity in
   Literary Cultural Studies* (Bern: Peter Lang, 2002), pp. 193–204.
"From Interdiscipline to Multidiscipline: How One Thing Leads to
   Another", in Filipczak, Dorota (ed.), *Dissolving the Boundaries*
   (Łódź: Łódź University Press, 2003), pp. 7–15.
"From Modernism to Postmodernism", in Ridgeon, Lloyd (ed.), *Major
   World Religions: From Their Origins to the Present* (New York:
   RoutledgeCurzon, 2003), pp. 289–323.
"Literature, English", in Houlden, Leslie (ed.), *Jesus in History, Thought,
   and Culture: An Encyclopedia* vol. 2 (Santa Barbara, CA, Denver,
   CO and Oxford: ABC Clio, 2003), pp. 541–51.
"Echoes of God's Laughter: Why Theologians Should Read Novels", in
   Volkova, Elena (ed.), *Life Conquers Death: Religion and Literature*
   (Moscow: MGU, 2004), pp. 40–7.
"In the Wasteland: Apocalypse, Theology and the Poets", in
   McCullough, Lissa and Schroeder, Brian (eds), *Thinking Through
   the Death of God: A Critical Companion to Thomas J. J. Altizer*
   (New York: State University of New York Press, 2004), pp. 185–97.
"Jesus the Actor: Edwin Morgan's *A.D. A Trilogy of Plays on the Life
   of Jesus* (2000)", in Bekkenkamp, Jonneke and Sherwood, Yvonne
   (eds), *Sanctified Aggression: Legacies of Biblical and Post-biblical
   Vocabularies of Violence* (London: Continuum, 2004), pp.132–9.
"Screening Angels: *The Messenger*, Durham Cathedral, 1996", in
   Townsend, Chris (ed.), *The Art of Bill Viola* (London: Thames and
   Hudson, 2004), pp. 180–96.
"Literature: Critical Theory and Religious Studies", in Jones, Lindsay,
   Eliade, Mircea and Adams, Charles J. (eds), *The Encyclopedia of
   Religion*, 2nd edn (Detroit, MI: Macmillan Reference USA, 2004).
"Literature", in Bowden, John (ed.), *Christianity: The Complete Guide*
   (London and New York: Continuum, 2005), pp. 710–14.
"Romanticism in European Literature", in Taylor, Bron R. (ed.),
   The Encyclopedia of Religion and Nature, vol. 2 (New York:
   Continuum, 2005), pp. 1422–4.

"Settling *Hoti's* Business: The Impossible Necessity of Biblical
    Translation", in Long, Lynne (ed.), *Translation and Religion: Holy
    Untranslatable?* (Clevedon and Tonawanda, NY: Multilingual
    Matters Ltd, 2005), pp. 105–14.
"'Down Through all Christian Minstrelsy': Genesis, James Joyce
    and Contemporary Vocabularies of Creation Studies", in Hunter,
    Alastair G. and Van der Stichele, Caroline (eds), *Creation and
    Creativity: From Genesis to Genetics and Back* (Sheffield: Sheffield
    Phoenix Press, 2006), pp. 35–44.
"Literature and Film", in McLeod, Hugh (ed.), *World Christianities,
    c.1914–c.2000, The Cambridge History of Christianity*, vol. 9
    (Cambridge: Cambridge University Press, 2006), pp. 582–92.
"Only Irresponsible People would go into the Desert for Forty Days:
    Jim Crace's *Quarantine* or the Diary of another Madman", in
    Joseph, Clara A. B. and Williams Ortiz, Gaye (eds), *Theology and
    Literature: Rethinking Reader Responsibility* (Basingstoke and New
    York: Palgrave Macmillan, 2006), pp. 35–45.
"'The Wheels of the Chariot': Religious Language in English and
    German Romanticism", in Visser, Irene and Wilcox, Helen (eds),
    *Transforming Holiness: Representations of Holiness in English and
    American Literary Texts* (Leuven: Peeters, 2006), pp. 95–111.
"Asceticism as a Way of Love", in Middleton, Paul (ed.), *The God of
    Love and Human Dignity: Essays in Honour of George M. Newlands*
    (London: T. & T. Clark, 2007), pp. 117–26.
"The Study of Literature and Theology" in Hass, Andrew W., Jasper,
    David and Jay, Elisabeth (eds), *The Oxford Handbook of English
    Literature and Theology* (Oxford: Oxford University Press, 2009),
    pp. 15–35.
"Do Not Hide Your Face from Me: The Sacred and Profane Body
    in Art and Modern Literature", in Llewellyn, Dawn and Sawyer,
    Deborah F. (eds), *Reading Spiritualities: Constructing and
    Representing the Sacred* (Farnham and Burlington, VT: Ashgate,
    2008), pp. 223–37.
"The Eucharistic Body in Art and Literature", in Watson, Natalie K.
    and Burns, Stephen (eds), *Exchanges of Grace: Essays in Honour of
    Ann Loades* (London: SCM Press, 2008), pp. 213–23.

"The Bible", in McLoughlin, Kate (ed.), *The Cambridge Companion to War Writing* (Cambridge: Cambridge University Press, 2009), pp. 61–70.

"Biblical Hermeneutics and Literary Theory" in Lemon, Rebecca, Mason, Emma, Roberts, Jonathan and Rowland, Christopher (eds), *The Blackwell Companion to the Bible in English Literature* (Oxford: Wiley-Blackwell, 2009), pp. 22–37.

"Nathan A. Scott Jr's *The Wild Prayer of Longing*", in Sugirtharajah, R. S. (ed.), *Caught Reading Again: Scholars and Their Books* (London: SCM Press, 2009), pp. 41–53.

"Termes Récurrents dans l'Univers Kantien: 'Sujet' et 'objet' chez S. T. Coleridge", in Gallet, René et Guibert, Pascale (eds), *Le sujet romantique et le monde: la voie anglaise* (Caen: Université de Caen Basse-Normandie, 2009), pp. 209–22.

Articles on Gadamer and Hermeneutics in Patte, Daniel (ed.), *The Cambridge Dictionary of Christianity* (Cambridge: Cambridge University Press, 2010), pp. 443–4, 508–9.

"Konstnären och religionen i samtiden", in Ekstrand, Thomas, Essunger, Maria, Martinson, Mattias and Westerlund, Katarina (eds), *Mening och mönster: Festkrift till Carl Reinhold Bråkenhielm* (Uppsala: Uppsala Universitet, 2010), pp. 184–95.

"*The Pilgrim's Regress* and *Surprised by Joy*", in MacSwain, Robert and Ward, Michael (eds), *The Cambridge Companion to C. S. Lewis* (Cambridge: Cambridge University Press, 2010), pp. 223–36.

"Pre-Raphaelite Biblical Art in Wales", in O'Kane, Martin and Morgan-Guy, John (eds), *Biblical Art from Wales* (Sheffield: Sheffield Phoenix Press, 2010), pp. 139–53.

"'Something Understood': From Poetry to Theology in the Writings of George Herbert", in Hodgkins, Christopher (ed.), *George Herbert's Pastoral: New Essays on the Poet and Priest of Bemerton* (Newark, NJ: University of Delaware Press, 2010), pp. 271–87.

"The Desert in Biblical Art: William Holman Hunt's *The Scapegoat*, in the Manchester Art Gallery", in O'Kane, Martin (ed.), *Bible, Art, Gallery* (Sheffield: Sheffield Phoenix Press, 2011), pp. 54–66.

"The Desert Landscape: A Sunlit Landscape Amid a Night of
Nonbeing", in Guibert, Pascale (ed.), *Reflective Landscapes of the
Anglophone Countries* (Amsterdam: Rodopi, 2011), pp. 243–53.
"Interdisciplinarity in Impossible Times: Studying Religion through
Literature and the Arts", in Walton, Heather (ed.), *Literature and
Theology: New Interdisciplinary Spaces* (London: Ashgate, 2011),
pp. 5–18.
"The New Theological Humanism and the Political Future", in Brittain,
Christopher Craig and Murphy, Francesca Aran (eds), *Theology,
University, Humanities: Initium Sapientiae Timor Domini* (Eugene,
OR: Cascade Books, 2011), pp. 64–74.
Articles on "Desert", "Desert: Literature", "Desert: Visual Arts",
"Desert: Music", "Desert: Film", in *Encyclopedia of the Bible and its
Reception* (New York and Berlin: Walter de Gruyter, 2012).
"Communities of Oppression and the Recovery of the Sacred
Community", in Stoker, Wessel and van der Merwe, W. L. (eds),
*Looking Beyond? Shifting Views of Transcendence in Philosophy,
Theology, Art, and Politics* (Amsterdam and New York: Rodopi,
2012), pp. 401–12.
"Religion", in Thormählen, Marianne (ed.), *The Brontës in Context*
(Cambridge: Cambridge University Press, 2012), pp. 217–23.
"Art and Religion in the Contemporary World", in Noake, Richard and
Buxton, Nicholas (eds), *Religion, Society and God: Public Theology
in Action* (London: SCM Press, 2013), pp. 66–80.
"The Artist and the Mind of God", in Jasper, David and Wright, Dale
(eds), *Theological Reflection and the Pursuit of Ideals* (Farnham:
Ashgate, 2013), pp. 157–72.
"Knowing for the First Time", in Boscaljon, Daniel (ed.), *Resisting the
Place of Belonging: Uncanny Homecomings in Religion, Narrative
and the Arts* (Farnham: Ashgate Publishing, 2013), pp. 9–20.
"Metaphysical Philosophy, Scriptural Revelation and Poetry", in
MacSwain, Robert (ed.), *Scripture, Metaphysics and Poetry*
(Farnham: Ashgate, 2013), pp. 123–32.
"The Spiritual in Contemporary Art", in Arya, Rina (ed.),
Contemplations of the Spiritual in Art (Oxford: Peter Lang, 2013),
pp. 231–45.

"The Eucharistic Body", in Fotiade, Ramona, Jasper, David and
Salazar-Ferrer, Olivier (eds), *Embodiment: Phenomenological,
Religious and Deconstructive Views on Living and Dying* (Farnham:
Ashgate, 2014), pp. 131–42.
"Narrative Ways of Being Religious", in Brown, Frank Burch (ed.),
The Oxford Handbook of Religion and the Arts (New York: Oxford
University Press, 2014), pp. 130–45.
"Om å komme hjem: Et tema I det tjuende århundrets litteratur og
kultur", in Gulliksen, Øyvind og Justnes, Årstein (eds), *Fra Svar Til
Undring: Kristendom I Norske Samtidstekster* (Norway: Verbum
Akademisk, 2014), pp. 217–32.
"Finding the Otherness of God in Literature", in Schmiedel, Ulrich and
Matarazzo, James M. Jr (eds), *Dynamics of Difference: Christianity
and Alterity: A Festschrift for Werner G. Jeanrond* (London:
Bloomsbury, 2015), pp. 293–300.
"Returning to the Spiritual in Art: From Kandinsky to Rothko", in Kim,
Sebastian, Kollontai, Pauline and Yore, Sue (eds), *Mediating Peace:
Reconciliation Through Visual Art, Music and Film* (Newcastle-
upon-Tyne: Cambridge Scholars Publishing, 2015), pp. 29–37.
Article on S. T. Coleridge in Parizet, Sylvie (ed.), *La Bible dans les
littératures du monde,* vol. 1 (Paris: Cerf, 2016), pp. 572–3 (in
French).
"Between Worlds: Ding Fang and Landscape" (published in Chinese
by Renmin University of China, 2016), pp. 303–10.
"Literary Approaches to the Study and Reception of the Hebrew Bible",
in Barton, John (ed.), *The Hebrew Bible: A Critical Companion*
(Princeton: Princeton University Press, 2016), pp. 455–79.
"Liturgy and Language", in Runcie, Catherine A. (ed.), *The Free Mind:
Essays and Poems in Honour of Barry Spurr* (Sydney: Edwin Lowe,
2016), pp. 212–20.
"Two Nineteenth Century English Translations of *The Travels of
Fa-hsien (399–414* AD)*:* An Episode in the Translation of China in
England", in Jasper, David, Geng Youzhang and Wang Hai (eds),
A Poetics of Translation: Between Chinese and English Literature
(Waco TX: Baylor University Press, 2016), pp. 159–73.

"The Space of Liturgical Being", in Økland, Jorunn, de Vos, J. Cornelis and Wenell, Karen (eds), *Constructions of Space III: Biblical Spatiality and the Sacred* (London: Bloomsbury, 2016), pp. 217–26.

"Amour et relations humaines: Une lecture de Jeremy Taylor et des théologiens carolins", in Bethmont, Rémy et Gross, Martine (eds) *Homosexualité et traditions monotheistes* (Geneva: Labor et Fides, 2017), pp. 279–96.

"From Romantic China to Victorian Sinology", in Huang, Paulos Z. (ed.), *Yearbook of Chinese Theology, 2017* (Leiden: Brill, 2017), pp. 155–65.

"Beauty and the Eucharistic Body of Christ", in Brewer, Christopher R. (ed.), *Christian Theology and the Transformation of Natural Religion: From Incarnation to Sacramentality: Essays in Honour of David Brown* (Leuven: Peeters, 2018), pp. 129–44.

"Jim Crace: Inventor of Worlds", in Shaw, Katy and Aughterson, Kate (eds), *Jim Crace: Into the Wilderness* (London: Palgrave Macmillan, 2018), pp. 165–80.

"Liturgy as Spiritual Performance in the Early Christian Church", in Eddy, Robert and Malekin, Theo (eds), *Time, Consciousness and Writing: Peter Malekin Illuminating the Divine Darkness* (Leiden: Brill, 2018), pp. 123–38.

"The Origins of Truth in Philosophy, Theology and Theory", in Jasper, David and Wright, Jenny (eds), *Truth and the Church in a Secular Age* (London: SCM Press, 2019), pp. 17–32.

"Teaching the Bible and Literature", in Boscaljon, Daniel and Levinovitz, Alan (eds), *Teaching Religion and Literature* (London: Routledge, 2019), pp. 24–33.

"Osłabianie teologii przez literature. David Jasper odpowiada na pytania Tomasza Garbola I Lukasza Tischnera", in Garbol, Tomasz and Tischner, Lukasz (eds), *Literatura a religia wyzwania epoki swieckiej* (Krakow: Uniwersytetu Jagiellonskiego, 2020), pp. 787–815 (in Polish).

"Being Human in the European Tradition and the Post-Enlightenment Response", in Fuller, Michael and Jasper, David (eds), *Made in the Image of God* (Durham: Sacristy Press, 2021), pp. 134–54.

"Saving the Soul", in *Sacred and the Everyday: Comparative Approaches to Literature, Religious and Secular. Orienta Aura, Book Series No. 2* (Macau: University of Saint Joseph, 2021), pp. 35–42.

"Legge in Oxford", in Chow, Alexander (ed.), *Scottish Missions to China: Commemorating the Legacy of James Legge (1815–1897)* (Leiden: Brill, 2022), pp. 66–80.

Refereed articles in journals

"Supporting the Radicals: A Poetic Contribution", *The Heythrop Journal* 12 (1981), pp. 407–16.

"On Reading the Scriptures as Literature", *History of European Ideas* 3/8 (1982), pp. 311–34.

"Philosophy and Revealed Religion: S. T. Coleridge—The Later Years", *Durham University Journal.* LXXVI (N S XLV) (1983), pp. 51–8.

"S. T. Coleridge. The Poet as Theologian. Two Late Poems", *The Modern Churchman* 26:1 (1983), pp. 35–43.

"God's Better Beauty: Language and the Poetry of Gerard Manley Hopkins", *Christianity and Literature* 34:3 (1985), pp. 9–22.

"The New Testament and Literary Interpretation", *Religion and Literature* 17:3 (1985), pp. 1–10.

"Re-review: Stopford A. Brooke's *Theology in the English Poets* (1874)", *The Modern Churchman* 27:4 (1985), pp. 47–52.

"'And After Art . . . Nothing', Iris Murdoch and the Possibility of a Metaphysic", *University Quarterly* 40 (1986), pp. 137–46.

"The Poetry of the Resurrection", *Theology* 84 (1986), pp. 96–102.

"The Limits of Formalism and the Theology of Hope: Ricoeur, Moltmann and Dostoyevsky", *Literature and Theology* 1 (1987), pp. 1–10.

"Some Romantic Theories on Religious Symbolic Language", *The Heythrop Journal* 281 (1987), pp. 31–9.

"Criticism and the New Testament", *PN Review* 15:2 (1988), pp. 37–41.

Review Article on Alter, Robert and Kermode, Frank (eds), "The Literary Guide to the Bible", *Religion and Literature* 20:2 (1988), pp. 75–80.

"Two or Three Gathered in His Name: Reflections on the English Pastoral Tradition in Religious Poetry", *Christianity and Literature* 38:1 (1988), pp. 19–32.

"A Hermeneutika harom utja", *Lelkipasztor* 64:4 (1989), pp. 194–9 (in Hungarian).

"Language and Liturgy", *The Modern Churchman* 31:1 (1989), pp. 1–6.

"Preserving Freedom and Her Friends: A Reading of Coleridge's *Watchman* (1796)", *The Yearbook of English Studies* 19 (1989), pp. 208–18.

"St. Mark's Gospel and the Interpretive Community", *Religion and Intellectual Life* 6:3–4 (1989), pp. 173–81.

"Between Literature and Liturgy: A Pragmatics of Worship", *Anglican Theological Review* 74:4 (1991), pp. 375–87.

"N. F. S. Grundtvig, S. T. Coleridge—The Hymnwriter and the Poet", *Grundtvig Studier* (1991), pp. 56–68.

"Den engelsk-amerikanske tradisjon", *Kirke og Kultur* 97:1 (1992), pp. 15–27 (in Norwegian).

"Study of Literature and Theology: Five Years On", *Literature and Theology* 6:1 (1992), pp. 1–10.

"Interpreting the Classics: A Problem for Literature and Theology", *Graphé* 2 (1993), pp. 58–66.

"Interpretations of the Old Testament in Modern Fiction", *Scandinavian Journal of the Old Testament* 7:1 (1993), pp. 7–16.

"The Old Man Would Not So, but Slew His Son", *Religion and Literature* 25:2 (1993), pp. 120–29.

"Time and Narrative: Reflections from Paul Ricoeur", *The Heythrop Journal* 34:3 (1993) pp. 302–5.

"Living in the Reel World: The Bible in Film", *Modern Believing* 35 ns (1994), pp. 29–37.

"Apocalypse Then and Now: From Revelation to *The Atrocity Exhibition* via Warsaw", *Graphé* 3 (1994), pp. 173–82.

"The Old Testament in Modern Fiction", *Theology* 97:778 (1994), pp. 276–83.

"The Bible in Arts and Literature: Source of Inspiration for Poets and Painters: Mary Magdalen", *Concilium* 1 (1995), pp. 47–60.

"From Theology to Theological Thinking: The Development of Critical Thought and its Consequences for Theology", *Literature and Theology* 9:3 (1995), pp. 293–306.

"Untitled: Theology and American Abstract Expressionism", *Religious Studies and Theology* 13/14 (1995), pp. 21–35 (reprinted in *ARTS: The Arts in Religious and Theological Studies* 7:3 (1995), pp. 17–24).

"Violence and Postmodernism", *History of European Ideas* 20:4–6 (1995), pp. 801–6.

"The Death and Rebirth of Religious Language", *Religion and Literature* 28/1 (1996), pp. 5–19.

"De la theologie à la pensée theologique: l'évolution de la pensée critique et ses consequences pour la theologie", *Graphé* 5 (1996), pp. 177–94 (in French).

"Religion and Literature: Critical Reflections on Reading the Bible; Literature, theology and culture to 2000", *Koers* 61 (1996), pp. 21–36.

"Bible v umeni a literature: priklad Marie Magdaleny", *Theologicky Sbornfk: Zebro Adamovo* 2 (1997), pp. 45–54 (in Czech).

"Theology and Postmodernity: Poetry, Apocalypse and the Future of God", *Svensk Teologisk Kvartalskrift* 73 (1997), pp. 1–7.

"The Death of God: A Live Issue?", *Biblicon* 3 (1998), pp. 19–26.

"From Romanticism to Postmodernism: A Literary or a Theological Inheritance?", *Norsk Teologisk Tidsskrift* 99 (1998), pp. 67–74.

"In the Beginning was the Word: Review Article of Steinberg, Leo, *The Sexuality of Christ*. 2nd Edition", *Biblical Interpretation* 6:3–4 (1998), pp. 426–36.

"The Twenty-Third Psalm in English Literature", *Religion and Literature* 30:1 (1998), pp. 1–12.

"The Gaps in the Story: The Implied Reader in Mark 5:1–20", *Svensk Exegetisk Årsbok* 64 (1999), pp. 79–88.

"Can we Speak of Christian Poetics?", *Literature and Religion: The Journal of the Korean Society of Literature and Religion* 5:1 (2000), pp. 139–54.

"The Paradox of a St Francis of Aberdeen", *The Chesterton Review* 27:1–2 (2001), pp. 47–54.

"Echoes of God's Laughter: Why Theologians Should Read Novels",
Theology 106:834 (2003), pp. 414–20.

"Cultural Studies and the Nineteenth Century: Theology and
Literature", *Nineteenth Century Studies* 17 (2003/4), pp. 47–51.

"Wanderings in the Desert: From the Exodus to *The English Patient*",
Literature and Theology 18:2 (2004), pp. 139–54.

"The Erotic and the Mystical in Postmodernity", *Theology and
Sexuality* 11:2 (2005), pp. 71–6.

"Literature, the Logic of Suffering and the Love of God: The Poet
Speaks the Unspeakable", *Literature and Religion: The Journal of
the Korean Society of Literature and Religion* 10 (2005), pp. 1–26.

"Review Essay: Slavoj Žižek, *On Belief* and *The Puppet and the Dwarf:
The Perverse Core of Christianity*", *Iowa Journal of Cultural Studies*
7 (2005), pp. 118–20.

"Down through all Christian minstrelsy: Genesis, James Joyce and
Contemporary Vocabularies of Creation", *Diskurs, Literatur &
Religion* (2006) (www.literatur-religion.net), pp. 1–7.

"Artistic Ways of Being Religious: Narrative", *Journal for the Study of
Christian Culture* (Beijing), 18 (2007), pp. 194–210 (in Mandarin).

"*Confessions of an Inquiring Spirit* (1840) de S. T. Coleridge: sa
place dans l'histoire de la critique biblique", *La Revue LISA/LISA
e-journal* 5/4 (2007), pp. 2–12 (in French).

"Contemporary Christian Theology through the Arts and Culture",
Journal for the Study of Christian Culture (Beijing), 18 (2007), pp.
179–193 (in Mandarin).

"Christian Hermeneutics after 9/11: Nihilism and the Hermeneutics of
Attention", *Sino-Christian Studies* 6 (2008), pp. 7 27.

"Contemporary Christian Theology through Literature: An Interview
with David Jasper (Hu Hong)", *Foreign Literature Studies* (Wuhan,
China) 30:4 (2008), pp. 1–5.

"Reading Theological Texts", *Journal for the Study of Christian Culture*
(Beijing) 20 (2008), pp. 3–24 (in Mandarin).

"The Two Worlds of Coleridge's 'The Rime of the Ancient Mariner'"
(Reprinted from 1983), *Nineteenth Century Literature Criticism*
197 (July 2008). [See first entry under Contributions to Books.]

"L'oeuvre d'art comme acte religieux. *La Madeleine repentante* de
     Georges de la Tour", *La revue LISA/LISA e-journal* 7/3 (2009),
     Festschrift Honouring René Gallet, pp. 2–8.
"Reading Texts Theologically", *The Yearbook of English Studies* 39
     (2009), pp. 7–19.
"A Study of Literature and Religion: A British Perspective", *Religion and
     Literature* 41:2 (2009), pp. 119–24.
"The Politics of Friendship in the Post-Christian West", *Journal for
     the Study of Christian Culture* (Beijing) 24 (2010), pp. 20–33 (in
     Mandarin).
"The Artist and Religion in the Contemporary World", *Text Matters:
     A Journal of Literature, Theory and Culture* (Łódź) 1 (2011), pp.
     216–27.
"The Arts and Modern Christian Architecture", *Theology* 114/5 (2011),
     pp. 353–62.
"The Spiritual in Contemporary Art", *Art and Christianity* 65 (2011),
     pp. 2–6.
"Academic Adventures in China", *World Sinology* (Centre for Sinology
     Studies, Renmin University of China) 10 (2012), pp. 228–33.
"Humanism and Belief in Literature: Seeking a Grammar of Assent",
     Literature and Theology 26/3 (2012), pp. 252–64.
"The Poetry of the Oxford Movement: Theology in Literature",
     International Journal for the Study of the Christian Church 12/3–4
     (2012), pp. 1–14.
"Academic Adventures in China", *Christianity and Literature* 62:4
     (2013), pp. 582–92.
"Returning to Thinking Theologically: Breaking Down the Borders
     Between East and West—An Interdisciplinary Exercise", *Limes:
     Borderland Studies* 6:2 (2013), pp. 149–58.
"New Directions in Ecumenical Liturgy: Vatican II and the
     Constitution on the Sacred Liturgy", *Theology* 117:2 (2014), pp.
     107–15.
"The Return to the Visual in Theological Thinking", *Creativity Studies*
     7:2 (2014), pp. 108–17.
"Returning to Thinking Theologically", *Journal for the Study of
     Christian Culture* (Beijing) 31 (2014), pp. 67–81 (in Chinese).

"The Translation of China in England: Two 19th Century English Translations of the Travels of Fa-Hsien (399–414 A.D.)", *Literature and Theology* 28:2 (2014), pp. 186–200.

"Aspects of John Henry Newman", *The Newman: The Journal of the Newman Association* 96 (2015), pp. 10–16.

"Retrieving a Theological Sense of Being Human", *Literature and Theology* 29:2 (2015), pp. 125–37.

"The Role of Sinology in the Twenty-first Century: A Western Theologian Reflects on the Development of Sino-Christian Theology", *International Journal for the Study of the Christian Church* 15:4 (2015), pp. 320–30.

"Love and Human Relationships: Readings from Jeremy Taylor", *Theology* 119:2 (2016), pp. 99–107.

Review Article "In the Image and Likeness of God: A Hope-filled Anthropology: The Buffalo Statement Agreed by the International Commission for Anglican–Orthodox Theological Dialogue", *International Journal for the Study of the Christian Church* 16:3 (2016), pp. 245–8.

"A Critical Spirit and the Will to Believe: Habits of Mind in Literature and Theology", *Scottish Episcopal Institute Journal* 1:1 (2017) (online), pp. 6–9.

"The First Night out of Eden: David Malouf's *Remembering Babylon*", *Literature and Theology* 31:2 (2017), pp. 215–30.

"'Heaven in Ordinary, Man Well Dressed'. Prayer and the Language of Prayer and Worship", *Ignaziana rivista di ricerca teologica* (Special Issue: *The Drama of the Spirit*, in memory of Michael Paul Gallagher SJ) (2017), pp. 1–11.

"Jim Crace: Inventor of Worlds", *Theology* 120:3 (2017), pp. 181–9.

"The Role of the Arts in the Church of Tomorrow", *Scottish Episcopal Institute Journal* 1:4 (2017), pp. 3–19.

"Literary Approaches to the Bible", *Journal for the Study of Biblical Literature* (Henan University), 17 (2018), pp. 24–65 (in Chinese).

"Literary Similarities and Cultural Differences: A Comparative Study on Zhuangzi and the Book of Job (with Ou Guang-An), *Scottish Episcopal Institute Journal* 2:1 (2018), pp. 22–37.

"The Question of Episcopal Authority in the Scottish Episcopal Church", *Scottish Episcopal Institute Journal* 2:4 (2018), pp. 4–10.

"Reflections on the Maturity of Religion and Theology in Literature: A Cultural Dialogue", *Christianity and Literature* 68:1 (2018), pp. 131–40.

"Remembering Charlie Moule", *Scottish Episcopal Institute Journal* 2:2 (2018), pp. 3–6.

Review article of Judith LeGrove *Geoffrey Clarke: A Sculptor's Materials*, *Art and Christianity* 96 (2018), pp. 10–11.

"The Weakening of Theology by Literature is Not a Bad Thing" (Interview with Tomasz Garbol and Łukasz Tischner), *Konteksty Kultury* 15:3 (2018), pp. 271–90.

"Finding Theology in Contemporary Chinese Fiction", *International Journal for the Study of the Christian Church* 19:2–3 (2019), pp. 160–74.

"Issues in Sino-Christian Theology", *International Journal for the Study of the Christian Church* 19:2–3 (2019), pp. 120–32.

(With Jeremy Smith), "*The Lay Folks' Mass Book* and Thomas Frederick Simmons: Medievalism and the Tractarians", *Journal of Ecclesiastical History* 70:4 (2019), pp. 1–20.

"Poetry and the Language of Prayer and Worship", *The Glass* 31 (2019), pp. 28–34.

"Seeking Christian Theology in Modern Chinese Fiction: An Exercise for Sino-Christian Theology", *Religions* 10:8 (2019), <https://www.mdpi.com/2077-1444/10/7/422/htm>, accessed 1 September 2022.

"Church and State in the Nineteenth Century and the revival of Thomas Becket", *International Journal for the Study of the Christian Church* 20:3–4 (2020), pp. 251–63.

"Duty, Destiny and the Way of the Good Man", *Journal for the Study of Christian Culture* 44 (2020), pp. 52–64 (in Chinese).

"Samuel Taylor Coleridge, *Confessions of an Inquiring Spirit*", *The Glass* 33 (2020), pp. 26–32.

"The Case of Bishop George Bell", *Scottish Episcopal Institute Journal* 5:1 (2021), pp. 31–7.

"Disciplined Interdisciplinarity", *Text Matters* (2021), pp. 1–16.

"Evelyn Underhill—*The Grey World*", *Scottish Episcopal Institute Journal* 5:4 (2021), pp. 21–6.
(with Oliver O'Donovan and Trevor Hart) "Learning from the Pandemic", *International Journal for the Study of the Christian Church* 21:2 (2021), pp. 138–47.
"The Priest in the Novels of Graham Greene", *Theology* 124:2 (2021), pp. 84–92.
"Thomas Frederick Simmons: A Forgotten Victorian Clergyman", *Scottish Episcopal Institute Journal* 5:3 (2021), pp. 133–46.

Scottish Episcopal Church Contributions

David Jasper's service to the Scottish Episcopal Church includes participation in the work of its Doctrine Commission, on which he has sat as commission member, consultant and convenor. The Commission has produced a number of publications: he contributed to the following endeavours, and edited *Theology and the Power of the Image*.

Sketches towards a Theology of Science Grosvenor Essays no. 1 (Edinburgh: Scottish Episcopal Church, 2004).
Theology and the Power of the Image Grosvenor Essays no. 2 (Edinburgh: Scottish Episcopal Church, 2005).
The Inter-Faith Encounter Grosvenor Essays no. 3 (Edinburgh: Scottish Episcopal Church, 2006).
The Shape of our Church Grosvenor Essays no. 4 (Edinburgh: Scottish Episcopal Church, 2007).
On Salvation Grosvenor Essays no. 5 (Edinburgh: Scottish Episcopal Church, 2008).
Death and Resurrection Grosvenor Essays no. 6 (Edinburgh: Scottish Episcopal Church, 2010).
Thinking the Nicene Creed—Incarnation Grosvenor Essays no. 7 (Edinburgh: Scottish Episcopal Church, 2011).
Marriage and Human Intimacy Grosvenor Essays no. 8 (Edinburgh: Scottish Episcopal Church, 2012).

Prayer and Spirituality Grosvenor Essays no. 12 (Edinburgh: Scottish Episcopal Church, 2016).

Theology of Authority in the Ministry of the Church Grosvenor Essays no. 13 (Edinburgh: Scottish Episcopal Church, 2020).

The Doctrine Committee under David's second Convenorship also produced two books:

David Jasper and Jenny Wright (eds), *Truth and the Church in a Secular Age* (London: SCM Press, 2019).

David Jasper and Michael Fuller (eds), *Made in the Image of God* (Durham: Sacristy Press, 2021).

EU GPSR Authorized Representative:

LOGOS EUROPE, 9 rue Nicolas Poussin, 17000 La Rochelle, France

contact@logoseurope.eu